HARD
LESSONS

HARD LESSONS

*Understanding
and addressing
the dangerous
challenges
facing today's
youth*

Dr. Lauren J. Woodhouse

Macmillan Canada
Toronto

First published in Canada in 2000 by
Macmillan Canada, an imprint of CDG Books Canada

Canadian Cataloguing in Publication Data

Woodhouse, Lauren J.
Hard lessons : understanding and addressing the dangerous challenges facing today's youth

Includes bibliographical references and index.
ISBN 0-7715-7682-X

Youth 2. Youth – Counseling of. I. Title.

HQ796.W662 2000   305.235   C00-930252-2

This book is available at special discounts for bulk purchases by your group or organization for sales promotions, premiums, fundraising and seminars. For details, contact: CDG Books Canada Inc., 99 Yorkville Avenue, Suite 400, Toronto, ON, M5R 3K5.

1 2 3 4 5 PC 04 03 02 01 00

Cover and text design: Counterpunch / Peter Ross
Cover photo: Archives of Ontario, Herb Nott collection, AO 4667, C 109-4-2-52.1

Macmillan Canada
An imprint of CDG Books Canada Inc.
Toronto

Printed in Canada

TABLE OF CONTENTS

This book is dedicated to Ron DeAngelis, and the administrative staff, teachers, students, parents, counsellors and police, paramedic and medical personnel in Littleton, Colorado; to Carla Hochhalter, the mother of a Littleton casualty who became another one during the last stages of this book; to Rev. Dale Lang and his family and congregation in Taber, Alberta; to all adolescents, and particularly those in my life who have taught, tried, trusted, and shared with me; and to all adults who rededicate themselves, in new and courageous ways, to parenting all our children. This is my gift of active love.

ACKNOWLEDGEMENTS

The following people have contributed to or supported the considerable mental and emotional work that made the completion of this project a reality.

I thank, as always, Kristan and Wesley for being part of my life; my beloved cousin Frank for his exceptional sensitivity, his love, and his bravery; Tracy for being someone I hope to call a friend; Luke and Kyle for existing; Paul for being courageous in the face of new realities, and for learning that there are things he neither understands nor can fix; Michael Carenza for passing on his sense of humour, heart, and will to love; Helen for reminding me that I am a lotus; Rory, Sky, and Michael for barely tolerating me while I wrote this book; Ron DiAngelis for his courage as he continues to tend to fearful hearts and minds; John-John for staying tangibly connected even when I seem not to be, but am; Liam who had to look at me after weeks of "night-writes" and only laughed once; CarolAnn Reynolds and Ted Regan for caring about me, rekindling my dreams during tough times, and being enthusiastic about this book and my other endeavours; Mike Duffy for always making me feel loved and lovely; James Broadhurst for his contagious enthusiasm about getting this book into readers' hands; Anna Stancer for wrestling with a very rough first draft. Liba Berry for her copyediting; and Robert Harris at CDG Books who, in spite of his position and influence, remains a kind and open man archaically reachable by telephone, and always welcoming and willing to talk. I also want to thank Michele Worton for reminding us of the blessing that is each day, and V. Lindstrom for touching my life and challenging my personal adherence to high and solid fences between neighbours.

I am inexpressibly grateful to the many parents, students, and teachers who shared their personal experiences and concerns, and many of whom allowed me to use their stories in this book. You have humbled and honoured me with your trust. You will always be in my heart.

To those of you whose stories were not used in full as case studies, know that you are between these pages. I have learned, and continue to learn, from being with and listening to you, my youthful, always challenging, and infinitely rewarding teachers.

AUTHOR'S NOTE

The case studies in this book are not fictitious. They focus on the commonly faced issues and concerns of adolescents, their parents, and their teachers. The increasing caseload of more harrowing stories are the substance of a book of another kind and with another objective. Here, I have positioned theory and experience to explain the difficulties faced by our children, and the challenges we are confronted with as parents and teachers in managing what is, arguably, the most critical time in the lives of young people.

As a psychotherapist, I have had the privilege of working with the children discussed in this book, and I have been privy to their fears, confusions, and struggles. Each of them reminds me that it *is* more difficult to grow up now than it was 20, even 10, years ago. Each of them has also proved that the most insular and unreachable children can be reached with an open heart and mind, and insightful patience.

The children whose stories provide human testimony to the problems discussed in *Hard Lessons* are both brave and generous. Even though their names were changed to protect their privacy, they were adamant about sharing their experiences. Their hope is that their stories will bring understanding and assurance to other troubled adolescents. Most of their parents also felt a positive obligation to assist other frightened, overwhelmed, and well-meaning parents.

In addition to other extensive research done for the purposes of this book, I have used several studies conducted by the International Institute for Child Security (IICS), an organization comprising academics, social scientists, mental health professionals, and physicians.

I feel it is important to note here that while many common, contemporary adolescent and parental challenges have been covered in this book, I have had to limit myself to covering those problems or issues that best represent current dangers facing our youth. Had I had unlimited space and pages to work with, I would have touched on innumerable additional challenges faced by boys and girls in the process of growing up.

Lastly, the use of the pronouns "he" and "she" when discussing adolescents in general will be used interchangeably throughout this book unless I am specifically referring to a boy or a girl.

Uninvited Stranger

They can't see me anymore,
they even seem or pretend to
not know me.

Like a stranger arriving
uninvited for dinner, when
they have to, they treat me
with nervous politeness, eyeing
each other for some hint
as to who I am, and
what to say.

I'm not sure either, and
I wonder if I've changed on
the outside too, and have a
different voice, or face, or if
I smell like the scary, dead
things I see in my sleep.

I once felt they'd
feel my holding back tears,
my fears, and my need for them
to find me, and
take me back.

But I don't hope anymore,
about anything,
and I leave every place
I pretend to be
knowing I'll never be more
than an uninvited stranger.

—*Kevin B., 15 years old, three weeks*
prior to a suicide attempt

FOREWORD

Despite assurances from sociologists that over a longer period of time
the numbers have actually diminished, statistics show that between 1988
and 1998 there has been a 77 per cent increase in violent crime committed
by youth.

Not surprisingly, this increase has caused tremendous concern. The public has accused lawmakers of coddling delinquent youth and is demanding
tough action, insisting that youth must be made more accountable, and that
this must be done through legislation that puts more youths in adult court
and all youths facing stiffer penalties. But these are only band-aid solutions.

While there is no doubt that we must hold our youth responsible and
that the punishment must fit the crime, there is no real evidence that
incarceration or stiffer penalties have any positive effect on the behaviour of
youth. In fact, there is some concern that more severe sentences (including
more prison and for longer periods) may actually increase the likelihood
that young offenders will become hardened, anti-social, and predisposed to
commit even more violent crime when they are released.

One thing is certain. Police services across the country have recognized
that these problems cannot be solved by any one segment of society. The
efforts of law enforcement alone are clearly not sufficient to curb the effects
of this very complex problem. Even if the solution were that simple, the
costs (both financial and emotional) would have a stifling effect on the
ability of the police to control crime and to react to it.

What is necessary is that we acknowledge that youth violence is a
symptom of a much larger problem. And once we find appropriate alternative strategies to deal with the causes of the negative behaviour that leads
to violence, we will, as a community, finally see a change in the numbers,
downward.

Those strategies are the focus of *Hard Lessons*. I believe that this book provides important insights and alternatives in the form of emotional and psychological support through family stability. I would highly recommend and encourage the type of interaction and communication that Dr. Woodhouse describes, advocates, and practises. I hope that the book will provide the reader with an understanding of the pressures our children feel, and make clearer the possibilities within all of us to make a positive difference in their lives.

Terry Dreaddy, chief, Taber Police Service
Taber, Alberta
March 2000

Introduction

DO YOU KNOW THIS BOY?

There is a teenage boy heading out to school after a weekend spent mostly alone, bored, on the Internet for a few hours Saturday night when his parents were out, and hanging out "wherever" with some "guys he met" on Sunday. His homework isn't done, or completely done, but almost, but that doesn't matter. The teen knows he's going to hear the same old thing again about irresponsibility and penalties and be asked why, why, why, just like last week and the week before, and years before that.

But he's in a hurry and can't think too much about it because he's rustling around in his torn jean pockets for his magnetic I.D. card just to get into the school to get into more trouble. If he can't find it, the guard on duty will have to go through the fingerprint file on the computer, compare his with his picture, and then he'll definitely be late. The guard's darn computer takes what seems like six hours to boot up in the morning—at least when he's going to be late, which is just about every morning. And being late for homeroom only adds another repetitive, predictable lecture to another boring day, and sometimes a form letter sent home called "The Truancy Issue and Your Child," addressed, of course, to his parents. No way. He needs them to take as few glances at his "scholastic progress" as possible. If they only knew it was a joke. But they don't.

He finds his prison-like I.D., runs to grab a bus, and then sprints through the back of a mall to get in before the last bell. He swears, remembering that he didn't turn off his TV. He has one in his room and it's always on. He likes it—no, he needs it on all the time, but lately his dad has been telling him to turn it off when he's not watching it. His dad doesn't get that he is always watching it in a way. He likes it on when he's trying to get some boring homework done just to keep a teacher off his case the next day. He has it on while he plays video games, even when he falls asleep and when he wakes up. He has no intention of turning it off when he's home, but his mom checks every once in a while, and she's supposed to tell his dad. Luckily she hasn't yet.

As he rapidly descends upon the school, he sees the new security guard on the main door. There are guards on all the doors, but they keep changing the one on the main door because, well, he has to be more professional, more like a cop, ready and willing to pull his gun on a student or a student imitator.

The teen reaches the door and the man doesn't remember him from yesterday. Who would? After all, there are 3,800 students in the school. So, the teen rustles through his jacket and pants again as the man watches him. The guard seems to be "checking him out" as if he's about to draw a gun or something. Finally, the boy finds his I.D. and, even though the magnetic strip that slides through the metal box attached to the steel doors identifies him, the man looks at the picture and then at the boy, then at the picture again, until he's certain they are representations of one and the same "okay" kid. The guard finally buzzes him in, but now the teen is really late and he sprints through three sets of halls, takes two sets of stairs four steps at a time, and launches into homeroom in time to get to his chair and desk before the teacher looks up.

The boy and others in the class are in a glazed-eyed-glum

Monday morning mood. School just feels so "out there" and irrelevant. Most of them "want" what they keep hearing they need in the way of "an education," but school? There's got to be a better way!

The young man is feeling particularly frustrated today. His weekend ended with a typical lecture from his father. Seems the only time he sees his father is for the "Sunday night lecture." The boy understands that his father's busy, that he's not off playing golf all the time or anything, but he's always at work, or doing something for work. His dad's a chartered accountant and wants his son to be a lawyer. So does the boy. There's a specific, cool guy on "L.A. Law" who he knows he could end up like, if only . . . He's failed so many subjects that he can't remember, but he's still mostly in the grade he's supposed to be in for his age. The school just keeps pushing him ahead, or he drops English for Geography and then settles on Shop and passes. He got his motorcycle that way—by fixing up an old one in class. He's lucky his dad doesn't understand the system. He thinks his son is passing—with low grades, but passing.

His dad would never know how much the boy had once wanted him to be proud of him, but he doesn't even hope for that anymore. He just tries to keep his father dumb about school things. Plus, his dad worships all these "heroes" the boy can't possibly measure up to. For example, his dad reads all about that investment guy, Michael Milken, and goes to all his public lectures to meet him. His father calls him "Mike," as if he knows him and they're buddies or something. The boy wishes he could be like Michael Milken. He can just imagine his dad's pride if he were! This amazing guy scammed a whole bunch of people with those junk bond things, went to a tennis-camp prison for rich guys for two years, and still has billions to spend! Barring being a rock star, the boy wishes he could be Michael Milken, or famous and scary like Mike Tyson, or a rich, maniac like some of those guys in the movies. Now, *that* he could get off on!

Getting paid millions to Uzi, punch, kick, and blow the guts out of people.

Suddenly this thought, this comforting diversion, makes him sad and anxious. He feels he might cry, and wants to get up and run from the room like a panicked baby. He is a maniac. He's just lucky that his mom hasn't told anyone that he's hit her, that is, his father especially. He can't tell anyone, but he thought about it when he heard that his second cousin got kicked out of the house for breaking his mother's arm. This was after a long time of hitting her and pushing her and calling her incredibly gross names that you wouldn't even dare call a prostitute. A prostitute would hit you back! Moms don't.

It doesn't matter that he's seen his dad hit his mom more than once. It doesn't. He wishes he didn't, or could stop when he feels those feelings coming on. He knows she's a cool lady—smart, has a degree, writes for a newspaper, but he loses it and punches her and she cries and looks at him as if he's a monster that's torn her heart out. He wants to die when he thinks of that look, but he can never go and say he's sorry. Inside, he wants to just sit and be held, and cry with her. He wants to feel her warmth and sort of smell her the way he did when he was little. He wishes he could just lean against her until he falls asleep. But that's sick. He must be sick. Even his little brother doesn't, or his sister. He wonders why, if he's the oldest, he needs her so much. Sometimes he thinks he hates her. He needs her so much, but he's not supposed to need her anymore and she treats him more and more as if he's a grown-up, like his dad tells her to. But he feels he needs her more, not less, than he did even a year ago.

He is almost aware that much of what he feels is shame, or as if he's bad or something almost all the time. People give him dirty looks for no reason, and he gets followed around in department stores as if an all-points bulletin is put out whenever he goes into a mall. It seems as if the security staff is just waiting for him to make a break for it with a wide-screen TV. No matter what, he always expects the loud beeping signal to go off every time he leaves a store, whether he's stolen something or not. Sometimes he has, but he's not stupid: he's careful to remove the metallic identifier or the plastic, red-dye clip hidden in jeans and stuff. If only he just had lots of money—NOW! He'd be like O.J., guilty as sin, most think, but free as a bird because of money. Money! If he was rich, people wouldn't give him dirty looks.

Even his girlfriend, or sort of girlfriend, is backing off because he can't go forward. It takes too much effort, as if someone said, "How are you?" and you actually had to tell them. You'd drop dead from exhaustion and depression after two days! But she bores him too. He doesn't even want to have sex with her anymore. He can have sex whenever he wants, started at 13, but he has this place he goes to on the Net where, well, he has this special page, and a special "girl" who does whatever you want and, darn it, it's his business what he does with her, but it's better than wasting energy messing up, or talking, or trying to leave after. He wonders, though, why it's usually after his Net kicks that he ends up hitting his mother. Not always, but often. He wishes he could stop.

He can see how all these kids each year kill themselves one after another in some kind of pact. Even parents want to kill themselves. He doesn't know one friend with happy parents. They're not all mean or anything, just always stressed-out, scared about money, always lecturing about the "value of a dollar," but pretending they're cool. It makes you want to rob a bank, or hit some rich people's houses, sell some stuff, and bring them money so they'll shut up about it. They're always scared, and it's scary. Who'd want to grow up and be like that if that's what growing up and being an adult is like? He's partly angry because that's what they want for him—"a future." No way. He tries not to think about it.

He doesn't think he wants to end up like one of those kids who say screw it and kill themselves, or blow away anyone in their path for as long as they can shoot. Not yet, anyway. Probably never. But he's scared that he's thought about it, sort of imagined it, especially at night before he goes to sleep. He thinks his friends have too. But when it happens, and it keeps happening, none of them say anything about it. They just look at each other when people talk about kids losing it and killing people, and then shut up. They get really quiet. They all know they take their dad's hunting rifles out now and again, and sneak off and shoot stuff, but they don't talk about it when kids just like them start shooting other kids and teachers. They're afraid they'll get sucked in or something, as if it's contagious.

Plus, he can't forget what happened to a friend of his one summer way up in northern Ontario. The kid was messing with his dad's gun and decided to take potshots at cars on a highway. He hid in the bushes and shot and shot until this car swerved off the road and a whole family crashed and one kid was killed. He ran and hid, got the gun back in its place and lied for three months when the police kept questioning him. But they caught him and sent him to a juvenile farm where he has to work and take special classes and then do something for the family he wrecked. His friend wrote him once, and told him he wishes he hadn't been caught. He didn't mean to kill anyone, he just wanted to shoot at people. It wasn't killing, it was getting to pretend to kill, just to feel better.

Thinking of what his friend and so many other kids have done, and do, he wondered if perhaps if he did it, shot at someone or something, he wouldn't hit his mother anymore. But sometimes he wants to kill his father too. He wouldn't want to be caught though. Life is bad enough. In fact, if these are the "best years," as his uncle, and his father and most adults say, there's no way he wants to get any older. If anything, he wants to be small again, with no I.D.'s, and no more fears of being nothing, of being everything his dad keeps warning him he's going to be. No more hitting his mother for reasons he can't understand, and no more trying to keep going with nowhere really to go.

Luckily he often looks sick, and then says he's sick, and gets to leave school early. Once he waited in sub-zero temperatures for hours on the steps of his house because his dad changed the security-system code and forgot to tell him and he couldn't get in until someone else came home. But usually he can have the house to himself for a few hours and smoke with his window open and go crazy with his video games, mutilating and blowing things up. Even though they're only games, there are usually human forms that you get points for killing and, with the harder games, for figuring out the best and fastest way to do it. There's even a game where you get to smash your teachers and parents, and anyone who gets in your face. If he loves anything, he loves these games. The killing games. He kills and kills, and mangles and mashes and kills again until he's drained and hungry. But he can wait to eat. He can go for hours on empty.

Before anyone gets home, and everything goes tense and silent, he needs to visit his special friend, his "Net girlfriend" who, like the video games, makes him feel great. If the dial-up is quick, he can have her for a good hour—and then maybe, if he's done enough, had enough, he can sleep. He has to sleep now. He can't sleep at night. He thinks too much, about nothing, which scares him. He wishes he remembered dreams, or had a good one, even once. He'd go to sleep just to try to get it back.

A fantasy? No. A rough, dramatic little fictional scenario? No again. This boy's edited thoughts represent both the thinking and the context in which many of today's adolescents exist.

This boy might remind you of your son, and he might not. Your son might be either veritably content and focused, as a minority are, or a stranger putting on a good act for you at home. Many adolescent children do, and many in emotional crisis were deemed to have had problems only after the fact of a tragic form of acting out.

This boy is real, as are his feelings, thoughts, actions, and the social context in which he is trying to understand why he should grow up, and how to manage his daily pain. For a "girl," as I insist on referring to a female child under age 18, the dilemmas and pain are just as great, the supersensitivity regarding self-worth more confusing, and rage turned inward into sadness more likely to lead to clinical depression and related self-destructive behaviours.

It should more than dismay and agitate us that a majority of our adolescent youth live an intense, quiet, yet sometimes deflectingly boisterous day-to-day trial between childhood and adulthood. It should further disturb us to know or admit that they live it without viable, pertinent guidance. Most of us, as parents, teachers and other concerned adults, *do* do our best. However, our "best" has been weakened, diluted in its impact on our children. Factors and influences, of gargantuan proportions, unforseen even five years ago, such as the highly influential effects of made-to-sell violence offered in the media and access to the dark dimensions of the Internet, are working against us. Significantly, a multitude of new, overlapping and highly influential social and cultural factors have the power to, at the very least, nullify the effects of our love.

Given where we have come and *wherever* we are headed as a culture, our adolescent children are both scary and scared. And given the common necessity of latchkey parenting—that is, having our children see themselves off to school from an empty house, and to return to one as well—these children are also lonely. Were we, as a culture, prepared to produce a "psychology of adolescence," we, as adults, would not only have an easier time of it, we would save lives. It is not the purple hair, navel rings, or drooping jeans, that is, the cosmetics, that this current generation of adults is confronted with by their children. It is, rather, that a generation is growing up in pain which, with or without the accessibility of firearms, makes a minority kill, an even greater minority kill themselves, and renders others merely lost, addicted, homeless, or otherwise estranged.

Sometimes, all we feel we can do is distance ourselves, pull back for the sake of maintaining our own sanity. Yet, distancing, for whatever reason, is perhaps the most common mistake made by parents of challenging young adolescents (12 to 15 years of age) and middle adolescents (14 to 15 years of age) as well. If we know we are inclined to deal with interpersonal problems this way, we should either discipline ourselves to ensure that we do not "abandon" our adolescents or seek support in order to avoid doing so. To the average adolescent, backing away can only be interpreted as rejection, as well as confirmation of their already low sense of worth or value in a strange, unsafe world. Our adolescents' almost infantile fear of the world, and the related need for extra support and demonstrative love will be further explained in the following chapter. The still virtually unexplored and misunderstood reality of adolescence will serve as a framework for the remaining chapters and lessons.

In *Hard Lessons*, I hope to clarify much that is still confusing to us about our unpredictable adolescents, including something as fundamental as *how* to approach them to talk. Having had substantial experience counselling both so-called normal and extremely troubled, even criminal, youth, I am confident that I have created a new model for understanding and attending to adolescents in general. The following chapters contain explanations of our adolescent children's stages of development; recommendations regarding how to address the security of our children at school; a definitive look at the effects of the media on our children; and, among other aspects of managing adolescents, how we can parent more effectively while burdened with our own new and burgeoning individual responsibilities. It should be noted that while most of the lessons and influences discussed in this book relate to the socioeconomically advantaged North American adolescent, the emotional vagaries are common to all adolescents in our culture. *Hard Lessons* provides practical applications, not just theoretical insights. We have learned the hard way, by seeing that our children can become sufficiently lost to kill others or themselves without our being aware of their estrangement, to know that the way we deal with adolescents has to change. We need hands-on help to assist and support our youth. That help, I trust, lies for us all in the pages to come.

The Adolescent Maze

I loved to ski with my dad, but I felt as if one day he just out of the blue decided I was a creep. Our neighbour saw my friend and me smoking a joint, but I'd only done it once before. Once, and he didn't believe me. My mom didn't either. That was the start of it all. We never talk, I'm a liar and a "druggie," and every second day I get told I'm going to get kicked out. They say I'm not the son they knew; well, they're not my parents either! At least I *miss* them. They don't care about me anymore—not that I can see.

—*Tyler, 14, an A-plus student now applying to vocational school*

It is little wonder that recent social and technological changes are having such a profound, and not always pretty, effect on today's adolescents. The child is virtually being "re-formed" during adolescence. His infantile "soft spot" has returned, and in his fear and confusion, he is as impressionable as a newborn—without either the protection, the constant support, or the unconditional love that a newborn receives. In fact, at the very time in his life when he regresses to a fear-induced infantile neediness—adolescence— he is being told to grow up, take on more responsibilities, and stay out of his parents' way. Most of us are lucky: they go, but they eventually come back intact.

Case Study

Sandi and Jessica

Sandi is a 40-year-old parent and patient whom I had been seeing for three years, assisting her in dealing with her own personal issues. She has two children, one within a couple of years of adolescence, the other slightly younger. She was married to a placid, quiet man—an accepting, if not active, stepfather to the children—and the home was stable and relatively happy. In fact, Sandi had a particularly close and affectionate relationship with her daughter, the younger of the two children. The girl, Jessica, would, at 11 and 12 years of age, snuggle up with her mother to watch television, or climb into bed with her to chat and share stories about her day. Notably, however, Jessica felt detested by her brother, Larry, who did hold his sister in obvious contempt. Sandi did her best to keep them apart, to discipline Larry for his cruel behaviour and to reward him for acceptable behaviour.

Things moved along with this quasi-manageable sibling tension for the first years of the therapy.

Sandi experienced crisis when the children became adolescents, and when, within months, Jessica's behaviour went from sweet and lovingly attached, to angry, rude, dishonest, and estranged. Upon turning 13, the child went from being an A student to failing at school and then dropping out. She bloomed physically to become strikingly beautiful, and began using makeup that made her look considerably older and more sexual. To her mother's dismay, she also began to take birth control pills. The young girl would go out and be dropped off at all hours by young men. Most nights Sandi had no idea where daughter was.

Sandi is relatively progressive as a parent. However, the daily verbal fights and disobedience, combined with what was for Sandi an almost demonic change in her child, began to take its toll. Unable to cope with any more stress, Sandi treated the fact that her 15-year-old son was neither going to school nor working, and was clearly taking delight in the fights between his mother and his still-detested sister, as a mere side issue. At least he stayed in, she would tell me in sessions. She could deal with him later. Meanwhile, she began to have daily, and increasingly severe, migraines as a result of her uninterrupted anxiety and fear regarding what she felt was the certain illfate of her daughter. In fact, in spite of firm, therapeutic direction away from her obsessive "what iffing," Sandi became so ill she had to leave her job, thus adding financial pressure to the mix.

Most of us experience a distancing from our adolescents. However, to best understand the fundamental challenges faced by our teenagers, we must have a basic understanding of how they arrived at a critical, *re-formative stage*; that is, a developmental stage during which they are re-forming their childhood activities as they are confronted with the challenge of somehow becoming adults. We must also consider both the inner and outer worlds of the child, a factor we often find difficult to remember and apply when we are dealing with confused, depressed or endangered teenagers.

When I do Victim-Witness Counselling after a tragic, scarring event involving disturbed and violent youth, my patience is repeatedly tested by the easy assumptions at the root of both reporter's questions and made-for-TV pop analysis. Many of us still look *only* for external causes of delinquent or violent behaviour. In sound-bite interviews related to extreme and highly public events, I am often asked if I think it is a divorce, an alcoholic mother, televison or video games that caused a child to, for example, kill his brother and set himself on fire. I am not even given the option of all of the above, let alone an opportunity to speak to this highly impressionable developmental stage. And while external factors are clearly significant, we have to understand the point or stage at which they have their most powerful and potentially dangerous effect on youth. Otherwise, we will continue to perform more psychological autopsies, giving us little opportunity for prevention.

PRE-ADOLESCENCE

By the third year of life, a child begins to distinguish between what is real in the outer world and what exists as images and activity in her inner world. In fact, it is in this third year of life when external stimuli are critical to the formation of personality as the child picks and chooses from among external influences, and gives them meaning in her inner world. It is the period during which the still highly impressionable child starts to formulate and weed through external reality in order to put images, impressions and reponses together to form a personality.

However, compared to adolescence, what the three-year-old is exposed to during this primary period of personality formation is strictly limited. The limitations by virtue of age, linguistic ability, physical agility, restricted environmental exposure, limited social contacts, lack of exposure to reading and writing, and intense parental protection make this early developmental stage safe, and largely conducive to the early formation of a healthy personality.

It is also during this guarded or healthily restricted period when a child begins to make choices as to what she will or will not absorb in the way of information or influence. Partly influenced by parental reactions, prefer- ences, and conditioning, a child will take in and form lasting impressions— imprints—which will stay with her into adulthood. A child will, for exam- ple, out of nowhere, utter something at five or six years of age at the dinner table that will astound her parents. They struggle to figure out where such a thought or impression came from, unaware that the child has already taken on a degree of psychic autonomy from the parents. Indeed, the child is already separating from the parent, developing her own thoughts, postures and, sooner than we ever expect, opinions.

Importantly, concurrent with the development of an autonomous child, between the ages of three and four, she is also learning new and more com- plex lessons in adaptation. As the child is exposed to more and more of the outside world, and as parents become less intensely attentive, she develops adaptive patterns unique to her own genetic makeup, combined with pat- terns adopted in and endorsed by her environment. By selecting what she will take in during the third and fourth year, the child is preparing herself for survival in the still-unknown, wider, outer world.

It is important to note that the expressive and defensive patterns adopt- ed in these early years are primary and deep-seeded. They may be moder- ately adjusted as the child grows older; however, they are pretty well what the child has in the way of modes of expression, expectations, protections, and categories of comprehension by the time she reaches puberty and ado- lescence. For example, the classic first-day-of-school trauma is very real for a child because it is entirely foreign, new, frightening, and uncategorizable. What were preset, protective patterns that provided a degree of security for the child (even in difficult homes) are inadequate when it comes to such a new sensory and physical experience. In essence, the first day of school is a very real trauma, a profound threat to most children, and a life and death terror to some. In fact, for the latter group, if the terror is not recognized and dealt with sensitively, it can result in lifelong problems with relation- ships with new people and environments, and with change in general.

As children mature in the outer world, they continue, quite remarkably, to use early, formative patterns to unconsciously decide what they will take in, as well as what they will learn and how they will compute knowledge.

We see in the period between 7 and 11 years of age hints of what is to come in the way of independence and potential obstinance. In fact, it is in this "pushy" stage in a child's development during which one frequently hears a parent, usually a mother, exasperated and exhausted, uttering the phrase *"My God, what are you going to be like when you're a teenager!? Give me strength!"* The child has reached an explorative period of "individuation," or separation from others, and a stubborn attempt to self-define. She has developed a precarious self she holds on to with persistent tenacity. Still in need of the protection of mother, the child will, with this safeguard in mind, push to assert herself against parental influence as she experiments with the possibilities and limits of separateness. The child does this at a stage when she unconsciously suspects that the mother is no longer just the nurturer, but also the parent who can take away and withhold, and who therefore still has great power over the child.

In a way, now that the child has had a peek at the outside world, she is testing the still-memorable dependence she had on her mother. This is one of the first indications of the mixed feelings children have particularly for their mothers with regard to their need for her versus their *fear* of their need for her. This issue comes up again, very disturbingly for children, in early adolescence. This period is referred to as the "latency stage." Simply put, the child's defenses are "latent," poised just beneath the surface for when she might have to deal with her growing fantasies and suspicions about the outside world. She is not yet overwhelmed or frightened, just wary. Nor does she know that she will be intensely rechallenged upon entering the *real* years of adolescent turmoil.

One last important point must be made about *all* the stages from infancy to adolescence. In spite of the fact that psychology and psychiatry now have a better understanding of how a child can actually affect his own development, there is no question that intensive, parental nurturing is still critical to healthy development at all stages. What the pioneering psychoanalyst Dr. Donald Winnicott called the "facilitating environment," the "safe, secure and love-filled environment," must remain so, regardless of whether the child is a toddler or a preteen.

As a child is learning who he is, he needs, in spite of protestations to the

contrary, the steady, consistent and effectively communicated love of the parent. This is a given, and a challenging one at that. Not only are we prone to assume that our child needs us less as he repeatedly tells us to back off, some of us also relish the opportunity to ease up on the quantity and quality of our active parenting. We feel that we can leave the child more to his own devices, that we should give our 11-year-old more privacy, and that we can finally have a break now and then by becoming less involved and active. This normal, virtually universal, assumption among parents is made more difficult to change when there is less time than ever before for parenting given the lifestyle and responsibilities of the hyper-busy modern adult. This challenge will be further addressed in chapter 7, which discusses the how of postmodern parenting.

ADOLESCENCE

Defined by *Webster's Collegiate Dictionary* in 1975 as *"the period between childhood and the age of majority,"* and by the same dictionary in 1995 as *"between being a child and manhood,"* it is clear that adolescence is a "time of life" historically and, until very recently, treated lightly in both social discussion and serious psychological and psychiatric literature. Most parents eagerly talk about and share information regarding the progress of their infants and toddlers. Adolescence, however, has not evoked the same kind of enthusiastic interest. Even social scientists have been, and are still, slow to study, analyze, and prescribe new, effective ways of parenting and educating adolescents. It is as if, as a culture, we have always perceived this period in a child's life as static, a kind of developmental holding pattern in which a child stays for a while on a tenuous automatic pilot; or remains acceptably *un*piloted and without flying skills, and then is expected to emerge to make a smooth landing into adulthood. Consequently, we have inadvertently left our adolescent children to deal with this critical developmental period on their own.

We have also, in spite of the odd check-in here and there, led them to believe that they are meant to just do it on their own, adding to their anxiety, and exacerbating their feelings of inadequacy. We *and* our children have shared the tacit notion that it is up to them, after the age of 11 or so, to arrive at adulthood, equipped, revving to go, and in one relatively undamaged emotional and psychological piece.

However, to understand adolescence, it is critical that we take into consideration the progression from the stages described above. That is, we must look at a child's arrival at adolescence as a point of confrontation with new and bewildering realities, new sensations and emotions, and biological changes for which he is entirely unprepared. These changes and challenges, combined with a usually marked decrease in the attention the child receives from busy parents, are ingredients for profound disruption and disturbance.

COPING WITH ADOLESCENCE

Re-formation

By the time a child reaches 11 or 12, pubescence, he has formed what are referred to as "constructs." Constructs are merely categories and structures which, while not entirely tight and certain, allow the child to function with a manageable amount of fear and an adequate sense of security in his, *not our*, world. The child steadies himself in the years just before adolescence as an increasing amount of information and a constant barrage of overwhelming stimuli both accompany him and force him to adapt, mature, and grow. He is also, unconsciously, of course, re-experiencing his own mind, making constant adjustments to previous constructs and assumptions, and experiencing the unpredictability and uncontrollability of his acceptance and rejection in the wider outer world. To this extent, and this way, we have to allow him to experiment and take chances. We cannot tell him to *"Grow up!"* and to *"Stay where I can see you at all times!,"* without exacerbating his confusion and anxiety.

Sexuality

It is amid the immeasurably challenging period of early adolescence that children secretly discover their sexuality. And, while sexual self-discovery is crucial in their development and determines some of their behaviours, it does not explain everything or even most of what goes on in their young bodies or heads. However, the effects of becoming sexual are important to an understanding of some of the confusion and fears faced by young adolescents.

Significantly, due to the struggle to find a place in, and to determine their value in the external world, their sexuality and aesthetic marketability become important issues, and worthy of at least behavioural, if not necessarily actual, sexual experimentation. By exploring their potential for mere sexual desirability, they are also coping with and, in a way, competing with their discomfiting awareness of their parents' sexuality and imagined sexual activity.

As a child discovers and is baffled, frightened, and often guilt-ridden by his sexual self, he also becomes increasingly aware of and disturbed by the sexuality of his parents. Further, as he keeps his discoveries secret, he feels that he, himself, has been kept in the dark about the sexual activities of his parents. As a newly discovered and additional element of separateness, this factor and its emotional offshoots are usually intensely disturbing. If he has retained even a moderate connection with his parents, this feeling of separateness, and distrust, can be traumatic.

Moreover, at the same time as the child is recognizing and hiding his own sexual feelings, needs, and attractions, and reluctantly coping with the sexuality of his parents, he is also attaching the elements of sexuality to others in his world, whether they be teachers, friends, television personalities, or movie heroes. With sexuality preoccupying a child at this stage, he is more likely to physically retreat than to act.

Relatedly, the discovery of a sexual self, and the sexuality of those around him, is further disturbing and confusing, especially for a boy, because it happens at the same time that the child discovers his physical strength and his potential for hurting others. Until this point, he has been innocuous and observant, with little reason to measure his potential for aggression. Other than the odd schoolyard jostle, the child has been managing in the world primarily by looking outward and taking cues from circumstances and people around him. He has been on an intense learning curve, alertly taking in and computing his surroundings in order to formulate a way of being and coping in the world.

However, this stage of discovery and formation is prematurely interrupted by the adolescent's traumatic discovery of previously unacknowledged physical and sexual factors that shake his still-precarious emotional foundation. For the first time in the child's life, he is crushed by the realization that he cannot, and feels that he *may* not, remain attached to the protectiveness and unconditional love of mother forever. For one thing, he has discovered that he is a sexual entity, as are the mother and the father. Confused by his sexuality and unnerved by that of his parents, the child cannot trust himself to differentiate between his love and need for parental affection and his sexual desires.

If parents were aware of the number of tortured, self-punitive hours spent by children in their early- to mid-adolescent years attempting to cope with what they feel is a sexual need for a parent, every caring parent would take a course in sex education, and then repeatedly talk about this issue to their children. Our culture is sufficiently closed and our institutions, including the family, unresponsively remiss in this area to cause and intensify an already nightmarish period in a young adolescent's daily, even hourly, life. Indeed, as the confusion, guilt, and self-loathing persist and usually increase, the further the child pushes off from the family—that is, from the only place where he has experienced a sense of security, acceptance, and protection, not to mention, the deepest of loves.

Isolation

The child does not make a conscious choice to thrust himself into the world and away from his family. If he did make a conscious choice, he would probably figure out a way to stay. Commonly referred to as the

Oedipal stage in adolescent development (spanning approximately from 12 years to 17 years, but very intense in the early teenage years of 13 to 14), this period of physical and sexual recognition spawns so many new and disturbing feelings that the child irrationally feels as if he must dissociate himself from his family for both his and the family's protection. The child feels that he is a threat to one or both parents, as well as, to a lesser degree, to his siblings.

Critically, something else takes place in the early adolescent psyche concurrent with and biologically related to the discovery of the physically strong, sexual stranger he feels and sees in the mirror. In addition to suddenly sensing himself as a foreign self, the child gains access to a new range of imaginative images. Partly as a psychic and biological defence mechanism, a new world of unlimited fantasy opens up to the child and becomes the place in which he most often resides. However, in spite of the fact that the imaginative space is accessed in self-defence, it is not always either a pleasant or a safe place for the child to be or, especially, to stay.

Anger and Fear

As the adolescent child deals with a multitude of new feelings, sensations, and worries, as well as with an ongoing barrage of challenges from his increasingly complex outer world, his fantasy world can be both (or either, in some cases) a place of creative working through, critical to his ability to manage the chaotic and painful outer world, or it can be a place of distorted and distorting danger. Depending on a multitude of unpredictable factors (except for the obvious ones such as early bonding, family or parental love, poverty, the presence of abuse, the absence or presence of criminal influences, and so on), his fantasy world can lead him to places and experiences of a much more daunting nature.

By necessity, adolescent children recede into their inner worlds both for comfort and for relief from the complexity and overstimulation of their social reality. We tend to forget how impossibly difficult it was if we fell outside the tightly defined realm of the popular adolescent or student. In fact, the very factors, most of which were and still are social—such as gender behaviours, style of dress, sexual desirability, the "life-and-death" issue of looks in general—are now *more* narrowly defined and cruelly enforced than ever. All adolescents, back then and now, used and use their fantasy worlds to try to make sense of the imperatives for acceptability and to escape the pain associated with not meeting them.

The mix of factors both confronting and being taken in by adolescents can result in their retreating into a hell of a place to hide. The simultaneous coming together of first, uncomfortable discoveries related to sexuality and separateness, especially with respect to parents and the child himself, second, unequivocal messages regarding what is interpreted as "forced maturation," and third, having these factors compounded by intensified social pressures, virtually pull the adolescent child back from, and out of, the external reality. The highly impressionable and fertile fantasy world of the adolescent mind is both powerful and potentially distorting of the adolescent's general perspective on life and on his development as a whole.

It is due to his return to and increased reliance on the inner world that the adolescent is able to redefine, create, and re-create a manageable reality. And while what is manageable for the child can be a nightmare for those around him, it is his primary way of coping during this period of cata-clysmic upheaval from approximately 12 to 14 years of age.

This is the period during which a child, for example, tells lies with appar-ent pathological ease and virtual self-credulity. It is also a time when a child can project his fear of and anger at himself onto those around and closest to him. The mother, in reality coveted and needed more than ever, can become a focal point for anger, even for verbal and physical abuse. She becomes the symbol of all things changed and gone wrong in that she can no longer protect the child from the outer world. This focal period, with this specific, trigger point for anger, is the worst and most precarious period in the storm of adolescence. The child thrives and drives on fantasy, and it affects his behaviour at home, school, and with his peers.

Not only can this adolescent stage be the most frustrating and worri-some period for parents, it is, as implied, the most critical period for the child. Reaching its peak in the mid-adolescent years, it is the time when parents endure the most trying and potentially destructive forms of acting out. It is also the mean age for both child suicide and child homicide.

Understandably, if unfortunately, this stage is also the period during which we are most likely to distance from our child. We have our own insecurities, responsibilities, and decreasing level of emotional and mental endurance, but we still have to fulfill our responsibility to lead. Distancing puts us in a "supporting actor" role in the child's fantasy that we have to back off because he is dangerous or because he has sexual thoughts or other self-condemning illusions. At the very least, our letting go has one common result. It enables our child to use our distancing as confirmation that he really is alone, rejected, even, in teen speak, "hated" by the primary people in his life.

The *"You hate me!"* we all get from adolescents is just one common expression symbolic of the child's acting out and trying to push away, *and* to (be allowed to) hold on at the same time. As the adolescent flails in his new, transitional, and ever-changing reality, he can seem, as one frantic parent described to me over the telephone, "berserk!"

Experimentation

For this reason, it is important, if not always easy, that we allow for harmless experimental behaviours which we might find annoying. Purple hair, chain belts, baggy pants with the waist at the thighs, taking a puff of a cigarette, and, among many other individually creative forms of expression and individuation, a general air of apathy and insolence, are merely par for the course. We must be able to use our own judgment to differentiate between what is annoyingly normal and necessary for the child, and what is indicative of a potentially serious problem. We should also not be afraid to ask. The lady with the "berserk" son called when her son swore at her, threw an apple at a picture on the living-room wall and then left the house. The poor woman was in shock and was ready to call the police in case her son had headed out on a murderous rampage.

The woman was right to ask if she was unsure, and, indeed, in this case, the behaviour, as long as it was not occurring every hour on the hour, was relatively common. In fact, the less frightened and condemning we are with respect to behaviour that does not harm others, harm the child, show a profound and profane disrespect for us as parents and other adults, continuously disrupt the family, and that does not either result in the destruction or disappearance of property, the more likely we are to remain connected to the child. If we overreact and overcondemn, we provide confirmation of the child's sense of otherness and separateness.

Moreover, an adolescent is subjected to what are at first incomprehensible hints that adults in general are suspicious or fearful of him. He is watched more alertly by security and other personnel in stores, and many middle-aged and elderly people hold their purses a little tighter or secure their wallets when passing a teenager on the street. We should be attempting to affirm moments, even split seconds of thoughtfulness, helpfulness or, in some exceptionally trying cases, mere passive neutrality. Most importantly, we must not make the mistake of on the one hand, ignoring our child, and on the other hand, looking only at our child through the prism of delinquency. To do so, and many parents fall into this self or energy-conserving trap, is to risk pushing or allowing our child to float to the nearest behavioural edge.

THE END OF ADOLESCENCE

It is important that we not become overly fearful by concentrating only on the bad news we hear about lost, desperate, and violent adolescents. Nor is adolescence itself a stage that we should dread. It is equally as important that we realize why, how, and what inner strengths accrue to our children during adolescence as it is to be aware of their vulnerability and potential for losing touch, and being lost to us.

Much has been said about the disruption that comes after the latency period, when the child is still holding tentatively to beliefs about the world acquired in earlier years. This disruption, however, has a purpose and is vital to the further maturation of the child toward adulthood. For example, by having retreated to his inner world, and to have wrestled with versions of reality and illusions, eventually, in the normatively healthy child, a fundamental aspect of personhood is developed. We all need to be able to "go within," and the adolescent learns much about his inner world by having found both refuge and relief there. The fact that the child also comes face-to-face with his adolescent demons is, though unpleasant and precarious, a potentially positive experience that affects his development, as well as his accumulation of self-knowledge.

Sandi and Jessica Revisited

Sandi ended up spending her days in a dark room, with sunglasses on, due to her constant migraine, awaiting word of her daughter's whereabouts and condition, while all the time, she realized later, she was fine. Meanwhile, her teenage son, now living contentedly in the finished basement, spent his days sleeping, drawing violent pictures related to death and killing, and watching and rewatching violent videos from his private collection. He was also playing video games for hours at a time. His mother knew, but needed a break before she attacked the other half of the overlapping problem.

At the mother's request (the stepfather was quietly and calmly uninvolved), I saw each of her children at my office. I saw Sandi's daughter first and was surprised and fascinated to discover a bright, precocious, lovely, and savvy young girl. She was significantly more knowledgeable about the ways of the world than her mother realized, and was going through an agonizing period of self-discovery and detachment.

Jessica knew that she would have to attend school to finish at some point, but had found a part-time job in the meantime. I believed her when she told me she was not taking drugs and was impressed with her concerns about both birth control and sexual protection. Still, her behaviour at home was rude, angry, and profane. In relation to this, she made one of many references to having to grow tougher after being so "battered down" by the verbal abuse from her brother. In fact, true or not, Jessica pointed to his cruelty as one reason for her erratic appearances and behaviour at home. No one would or could stop her brother's abject abuse.

Now, Jessica did not come into the office, shake my hand, take a chair, and openly talk about her life. It took some pulling, nudging, and establishing trust, and an ultimate belief in my promise of confidentiality. After all, I was her mother's therapist, something that had concerned me when Sandi requested that I see her children. It was another (potential) form of control, and I couldn't imagine that they would or should be expected to come, and was prepared to provide referrals. I was, therefore, immediately impressed that Jessica came at all, let alone that she did so with virtually no protest. Also surprising was the degree to which she was aware of her nasty and disrespectful behaviour toward her mother, as well as her irresponsibility in staying out late and not phoning her mother to check in. At the same time, Jessica wasn't about to make any changes, including, among other things, giving up her boyfriends or meeting a requested 10:00 p.m. curfew.

She did, however, express concern about her mother, which I deemed to be sincere. She "wished" that her mother would "stop freaking out" over her hair, makeup, nails, multiply pierced ears, choice of footwear and jewelry. Jessica pointed to her mother's constant criticism, and her "scary ranting about getting killed and stuff" as part of the reason that she'd "die" at home if she had to be there all the time. She also said that she avoided telephoning because she would hear the same kind of dire warnings about the pervasively violent and "doom and gloom" world in which Jessica was now trying to make friends.

This young girl did have problems, and it is rational to have serious concerns about her education and sexual activity, not to mention her active night life and the suddenness of her change in behaviour. Though common, such a precipitous change would startle most parents. However, her mother's staying up, sometimes all night, to confront and condemn her, along with the constant, repetitive, and graphic criticisms of Jessica's looks and lifestyle, were counterproductive. Jessica was extremely, even unusually, confidently stubborn, and would merely leave amid the tirades, stay away for longer periods and return looking and behaving more dramatically.

Jessica gave many "I don't know(s)" in answer to questions about her actions, perceptions, and feelings, but she did have a solid sense of the problematic way in which she was behaving, and of the risk she was taking in putting off her education and spending time with questionable older men. Her hours away, she said, were important to her, and she described a variety of strategies she had developed to ensure her safety, all of which were clearly well thought out. In other words, Jessica was acting out in disruptive ways, but was relatively well grounded in reality, and understood the unpleasant consequences of her actions.

The adolescent's greatest source of anxiety and anger was the reactivity, anguish, deterioration, and nonspecific, fearful wrath of her mother. She was able to say that she loved her mother, but also admitted to having to ignore her. The more isolated and anxious her mother became as she awaited the next episode with Jessica, the more Jessica stayed away.

She needed some firm discipline, a retraction of privileges (for example, the removal of the telephone and TV set in her bedroom and the cessation of regular drives to wherever she wanted to go on weekends), as well as some household responsibilities to impose more structure on her life.

She would also have benefitted earlier by a clearer understanding of her mother's expectations.

Rather than becoming sick and periodically hysterical with fear (related more to an incident in the mother's background than to the actions of her child) and nagging her daughter, Sandi would have served them both well by taking charge and renegotiating their relationship. Within two to three weeks into the change in her daughter's behaviour, Sandi could have adjusted the style, areas, and degree of her authority. Her style or tone could have gradually become more conversational, communicating a renewed respect for the young girl. Sandi could also have lightened up in certain areas, such as telephone usage and the number of chores the girl was responsible for. Moreover, Sandi could have relaxed her rigid posture toward Jessica, and allowed her daughter more requests related to going out, having a friend in, or playing her stereo a little too loudly after dinner.

Gradually decreasing the tension that comes with adolescent-parent conflict allows the child room for nondefensive self-discovery and thought. Shifting from strict and unrelenting, to moderately open and fair, gives the child room for both studying the new guidelines and for making sense of the incident or mistake. It also implies that the parent's love has been reinstated. Had Sandi been able to remain balanced through Jessica's acting out, she would have enabled the teenager to stay closer to home and not lose either face or opportunities to test herself in a wider social context.

Given that Jessica was significantly more resilient than her mother, a new "balance of imbalance" had to be struck. Sandi suffered considerably by not realizing that she had no choice but to allow for some new behaviours and freedoms. She also would have served the whole family well, including the silent but observant son, by first, managing her own reactions, and second, taking the time to clarify the areas in which she could fairly exert a restrictive influence. In that Sandi had had complete control over Jessica for well over a decade, she did not, without a great deal of counselling, see that there were disciplinary positions between complete control over her daughter, and no control whatsoever. By mismanaging her own fears related to losing her daughter, as well as those related to her own fundamental fear of life, she merely triggered her daughter to express more dramatic modes of defiance. By not recognizing and calmly addressing the fearful and confusing nature of Jessica's sudden attempts at detachment, Sandi increased her daughter's sense of isolation and pushed her further from a home the teenager had not expressed a wish to leave. She could have used the opportunity to formulate stipulations for the "lost" boy in the basement.

Were Sandi to have observed and then responded in this way, she would have stayed well, instead of collapsing in fear and anxiety, which frightens and alienates any adolescent. Moreover, Sandi could have made specific requests of Jessica which would have provided her daughter with a modicum of structure. The firm establishment of limits such as adjusted, flexible curfews, attendance at a certain number of meals a week, and rules regarding acceptable behaviours at home, presented by an apparently resilient parent, can also help the parent to keep tabs on, and maintain a supportive relationship with, the adolescent during the experimental phase of her re-formation.

Sandi also had to accept that both her children had entered a stage when the absence of and abandonment by their biological father had become a consciously painful factor in their development. She had difficulty accepting this because *she* wanted her children to remain oblivious to and indifferent about his existence and seminal role in their lives. A typical example of parental self-mismanagement.

Sandi added to her children's pain and confusion by imposing *her* fear, needs, and anger on them, thus impeding their ability to work through their own developmental and parental anger. While Jessica was throwing herself into the world to test her viability and desirability, her brother was hiding in the basement, refusing to risk rejection in the world. For each child, there needed to be some discussion and exploration around, among other things, the issue of the missing dad. Nothing speaks louder than the unspoken word—especially with adolescents.

With one child in a hyperactive state of "pushing off" and the other in a state of retracted torpor, Sandi was unprepared to deal with the new demands made by her children's adolescent acting out.

She had to get counselling herself to address both her inclination to be overly protective with her daughter, and to be voluntarily blind to her son's unhealthy inactivity and viewing habits.

In counselling, Sandi found that her abusive relationship with her first, alcoholic husband had made her paranoid about her daughter's safety and relationships with men. With respect to her son, she admitted knowing all along that he was the child most affected by her taking the children and leaving their father. She feared what she suspected was his silent anger, and felt guilty as well. She recognized that enabling his habitual hiding out and asking nothing of him was not serving either of them. In fact, she realized, if she did not give him a deadline by which he must be looking for a job, she was actually increasing the risk of his becoming both alcoholic and angrily abusive, just like the father he missed.

SUMMING UP

Much that appears to be and feels "crazy" about adolescence is—but, crazy in a normal and common way.

Adolescence is an explosive stage following a period of latent or unexpressed confusion in the preadolescent. During the adolescent years, the child angrily reviews and revisits what he was taught and what was modeled for him in the home. As he necessarily, albeit often reluctantly, makes adjustments to "push off" from the family to function in new environments, he is usually anxious, always frightened, and quick to lay blame for a variety of real and imaginary ills on the parents. The laying of blame and other forms of criticism of the adults in the child's life are usually infantile expressions of need, disturbance over the issue of sexuality, and the fear of being alone in the external world. He is irrational, feeling misled and tricked, and this must be addressed by parents in as many heart-to-heart talks as possible. Moreover, the child should be showered with active expressions of love on a daily basis, whether he appears to resist the love or not.

What the adolescent is really struggling to achieve amid his own private storm is to find a way "home." Regressed and extremely needy, the best he can do, with mature guidance and support, is, metaphorically, to find himself a new one.

WHAT TO DO

1. Remember, adolescents are still children. Stay with them.
2. Adolescence is a period of "growth and shrinkage," "progression and regression." Pay special attention to those moments when a child is expressing her needs. For example, if she wants to go to a special rock concert with friends, do not reflexively say no. Ascertain who she is going with, check it out, offer to drive her, or ensure that another parent is. Work it out.

   However, do not be surprised or disturbed if just the next week, she shrinks away from another similar opportunity. With our M.O. intact, we are prone to ask her why, after we have just allowed her to go and have a good time, she now wants to stay home and watch TV. Don't assume that something happened, especially if she was fine for days after the night out. More than likely, she is going through a short regressive stage and wants to stay both closer to home, and to you.
3. Listen and look for the need amid the acting out, or the "meaning in the machination." Our children can be screaming words at us which are actually symbols. For example, when a child in my life once screamed with profanity that I hated him, had it in for him, and wanted him out of my life, he really meant, with rage coating his despair, that I didn't love him, found him to be too much, and wanted him gone. So, instead of slamming a door to cut them off, calming children down and trying to interpret the real meaning and pain in their message can be an opening and bonding experience.
4. Don't overreact to adolescent rejection. It is experimental, temporary, and is most probably their reaction to feeling rejected themselves.

5. Don't overreact to innocuous, "weird" behaviours. They, too, will pass.

6. Affirm (congratulate, extol) the adolescent for *anything* done right or well. Also, continue to hug your child for no reason when he is just sitting at a table or passing through a room. The affection computes.

7. Hold your adolescent when he breaks down—or at least try to. He may have forgotten the feeling of parental comfort, and may be unsure as to whether it is still there for him.

8. Talk, ask, talk, ask . . . *and* provide silence so that the child *can* dare to utter her fears.

9. Don't criticize adolescent children for the way they dress or for what they do with their make-up or hair. Short of fashion statements that involve self-mutilation, public nudity, rancidity, gang uniforms, or the breaking of a school dress code, it doesn't matter in the adolescent scheme of things.

10. Try to remember the intensity of your teen years. Then multiply it by 10,000 and *re*-imagine. Empathy for and patience with your adolescent can be emotional escapes from the retrospective.

Girls and the Mandate of Womanhood

2

All of a sudden I don't get to wrestle with my brother, who's my twin, and my dad doesn't hug me and give me beard-burn anymore. What did I do except turn 12?

—*Haley*

Before we look at the specific social and cultural factors that contribute to the current crisis among our youth, it is important that we understand the challenges faced by girls and boys in common, and those confronted and experienced differently by each gender. With this additional layer of understanding, we can better examine the potentially and often disruptive role of an adolescent in the modern family, and we can look with more clarity at the adolescent's susceptibility to search out or passively give in to influences and intoxicants of a distinctly modern kind.

As mentioned in the previous chapter, the early adolescent years represent a period when a child is attempting to establish a separate and autonomous identity—independent of mother, father, and the miserable or manageable comfort of the family. Moreover, for the most part, the period represents a subconsciously reluctant "push-off" from the familiar to the untested and new, as well as toward the dubiously perceived state of adulthood. In the case that follows, the adolescent girl's resistance and confusion is related to the sudden and unavoidable mandate of being female.

Case Study

Allia

Allia had become sufficiently depressed by the age of 13 that her family physician had both medicated her and suggested that she seek therapy for her "endogenous depression." The word "endogenous" refers to "inside," and an endogenous depression is, therefore, seen as one related to some internal factor, even a biochemical or genetic factor, rather than external circumstances or events, such as the death of a relative. Externally caused depression is called "exogenous depression," and is perceived much differently by physicians, parents, teachers, and other adults than its endogenous counterpart—as much in adulthood as in adolescence, and especially where girls are concerned.

Bright, athletic, tall, and appearing much more mature than her years, Allia was quiet and "pleasing" in the therapy sessions with me, but did not display any of the symptoms of an organic or endogenous depression. As I continued to work with her, attempting to look for characteristics related to what she and her parents referred to as the "diagnosis," and remain open to other possibilities, I began to discern the results of an old story.

Allia started menstruating early, at 9 years of age, and while her starting her period was dealt with discreetly by both her parents, they well-meaningly adopted a celebrative, transitional posture toward the event. She was lovingly congratulated and given more supportive attention around and during menstruation, even though, as Allia told me, she took great pains to hide any hint of the onset of what she referred to as her "bloody time." She felt, and episodes and circumstances she shared with me supported her perception, that as soon as she started to menstruate, more was expected of her.

As the middle child in a family of two boys and one girl, Allia began to be treated as the eldest or most mature, and was suddenly, if tacitly, expected to take on more responsibility. By the age of 11, for example, she was deemed the "babysitter" for her two brothers, one of whom was older than her by two years. She would be told, or "booked" in advance so that she would not make any plans to be with friends or attend a school activity or sport event on the day or evening in question.

Further, up until her "bloody time," she had been in her element, playing road hockey in the streets with the boys, climbing trees, clinging to and swinging with the precision of an acrobat from branches leading to the backyard tree house, and playing evening softball on summer nights with neighbourhood children and adults. Then, in subtle and not-so-subtle ways, she was discouraged from continuing her participation in these healthy, childhood activities.

One evening, when she was ten years old, during late-summer, as darkness fell earlier over the streets and lawns of the middle-class suburb where she lived, she was the only girl playing road hockey with seven boys. As she played, she noticed that her father had come to the end of their driveway and was watching. She sensed something new and different in his observation. He wasn't watching with pride or interest in the game. He looked angry and concerned, the way he looked when one of the children had done something wrong and was about to be punished. As he stood there, slowly and slightly rocking back and forth in his huge shoes and jingling the change in his pockets, Allia became increasingly unnerved, and decreasingly involved in the game. The boys, oblivious to the reason for her inattentiveness, teased her about her lack of resilience. As Allia joked back in self-defence, she remained instinctively cautious and self-conscious under the strangely scrutinous eye of her father. She soon left the game.

Allia walked toward her home and her father with a sense of shame that she could not understand, but that remained memorable for years to come. When she reached her father, he nodded sternly and turned to walk with her to the house. It was during a therapy session that she remembered that he said something like, *"Atta, girl. Especially at this time of the month."* And he followed her inside the door and locked it behind them.

It took Allia three years to realize that her father's actions, and others that came later, had something to do with sex, and her, and fear. But even then, she stopped playing road hockey with the boys and sat with the mother and daughter spectators during softball games. The boys didn't seem to notice—they were having too good a time—and when her mother and father were around, they looked at her fondly as she sat amid the girls and women supporting their male family members.

During that same year, Allia described going out for Halloween in some fun costume she couldn't remember. What she did remember was that she was only out for about 20 minutes before she went home, suppressing tears and feeling the same stinging, free-floating shame that she had felt that late-summer night playing road hockey.

At the third house she went to, Allia told me, the door was answered by an older couple who, while they were tittering with the smaller (shorter) children, were eyeing Allia with disgust. Allia described feeling as if they thought she had stolen something or that they were mistaking her for someone who had thrown eggs at their house the night before, when tricks preclude the offering of treats. Then, with a condemning look, combined with something she'd seen in her father's eyes the night he stood at the end of the driveway, the man said, *"Aren't you a little old to be out streetwalking? This is for children!"* She was stunned, and speechless. She felt as if a bolt of sharp and splitting light had sliced through her skull to her heart, leaving her entire body trembling with humiliation. Shy at the easiest of times, she merely lowered her head, as if in admission of some horrible crime, folded her treat bag against her belly, and retreated to the street and toward her home.

Allia's 11-, 12- and 13-year-old friends, along with other neighbourhood children kept on trick-or-treating as she willed herself to invisibility. When she reached her home, she attempted to avoid her parents. Passing them on the way to her room, she muttered something about a stomachache in response to her parents' dreaded query, and as soon as she could, she broke down and wept.

Allia learned quickly. She knew it all had something to do with being a girl. There were episodes at school when, for example, she would offer to help the teacher move a table, and the teacher would look at her with curious disapproval, then ask a boy to help. Both the teacher and the boy would look back at her mid-task as if to emphasize some kind of protocol around which she had been almost perversely remiss. But, she started to "get it," and at around 11 years of age she began to think before she acted. She learned to strategize as to how to bring her will to help, her physical agility, her multiple skills, and her intelligence to episodes in her daily life without, as she said, *"being hated."*

By about the age of ten onward, Allia was confronting the not-so-subtle issue of social gender distinction, including the fact that there were limits and areas to which she must submit and adhere with respect to her actions and expressiveness. However, in sessions with me, she admitted to a "secret knowing" earlier on, even in early elementary school. In retrospect, she realized that she needed to be, or felt she was supposed to be, in a state of knowing denial about something that had troubled her early in her development. She felt, to use her words, "often squished and squashed" in her actions and expression, whereas, she observed early, her brothers were both encouraged and lauded for acting or expressing in similar ways. Moreover, even when she was very young, she noticed that these tacit regulations had nothing to do with strength or anatomy. They just were. What her parents referred to as her "early stubbornness and determination" were actually, she discerned later, her repeated, spontaneous attempts to express herself in ways that she would soon realize were anathema to most adults in her limited social sphere.

Allia remembered many such incidents as if they were moments in which she was burned, as if she could still pinpoint and share patches on her body where the skin was thin and discoloured. She remembered, for example, that all three children were taught etiquette. At times when the family was together, there would be discussions about table manners, proper telephone salutations, and one-on-one greetings. Once when Allia's father brought a colleague home for dinner, her parents beamed at her brothers as they shook the man's hand upon being introduced. However, when she stepped forward to shake the gentleman's hand, Allia sensed her parents' tension and embarrassment, including "that creepy, dark look" on her father's face, and noticed the man's amusement.

Later, in spite of the fact that she had politely waited as long as possible before leaving the room in embarrassment, she was admonished for exiting too soon after a guest's arrival and not offering up the tray of hor d'oeuvres. She felt she couldn't win, and after each such episode, she felt further degraded and further discouraged with respect to this mysterious array of unregulated regulations. They hadn't existed, or she hadn't noticed them from the playpen—or she might have prepared herself earlier and avoided the humiliation.

Allia realized that much of what she had been picking up had been a kind of shared secret. Her parents never told her to be different or to hold back at a sport so as not to defeat a boy, nor did her teachers lecture on boys being allowed certain actions and behaviours and girls not being allowed the same latitude. This was the nineties after all! *No one said these things aloud*, and, if they did, they were ridiculed or admonished. "It just was," everyone seemed to know, and no one talked about it.

Allia learned not only to tacitly share the secret, but also to ascribe to a new, covert code of conduct to which she was expected to adhere at the risk of social and familial rejection. By the age of eight, she would discern in therapy, she had become vigilant, even furtive in her attempts to catch each and every signal related to the acceptability of her behaviour. She recalled feeling even then, or especially then, that it was a life-or-death mandate. She felt that if she did not manage the ongoing puzzle successfully, she would not be loved, and that she would, in a very real way, be rejected by her family. She soon learned the basics about when to be demure, inactive, deferential, pleasingly passive and, to various degrees, "sweetly feminine" in various ways and in a variety of social contexts. At the same time, she tried to grow up and to aspire. This last dimension of her early thinking, as was the case with her learning the "un-rules" that felt critical to her survival, she kept to herself.

COPING WITH WOMANHOOD

The "Split"

Two important but unusual factors allowed for the uncovering of Allia's inner pain. First, she was articulate. At 13, Allia was still sufficiently, if initially unconsciously, in touch with the anger related to what she later referred to as "lying and unfairness" to be able to articulate what we came to call the "split." She discovered that she was enraged that she had had to fake who she was in order to avoid, as she saw it, being rejected or exiled from the family, from her school, and from childhood ties with neighbours. The fact that Allia could and did come to see that she had split herself into two selves—a hidden, real self, and a performing false self—gave her some relief. Moreover, that she could still express the anger beneath her despair was her saving grace. She wasn't depressed per se, she was healthily, maladaptively angry.

Secondly, by articulating how and when she felt she had to perform in an acceptably feminine way, my young patient was able to assist me to discover her individually frustrating experience of *reluctant fraudulence*. That is, she was stubborn and active and athletic, but she had had to fake certain behaviours, even weaknesses, when she sensed or was confronted with the obvious displeasure her strengths brought out in her parents and other adults. I had seen it many times before in female youth who were much more damaged, and who were compensating in much more extreme ways than Allia. Some young girls, less trusting of their instinctive discomfort, decide that they must be crazy and getting their signals crossed. They remain split well into womanhood, but suffer particularly during this critical period when they sense something is neither right nor real.

In our first sessions, even Allia came across as a fine actress, not as a real person or troubled adolescent. Used to seeing the "It's a Take!", or "Best Actress," syndrome in adult women, I witnessed it in a rough, ill-fitting form in a brilliant young girl. In short, Allia enabled me to see beneath and beyond the layers of both her strained social act, one she clearly felt was also appropriate in therapy, and, as a result, to connect with and feel her anger. We were then able to chip away at the layers of her apparent depression to get to the roots of what was really camouflaged anger and a sense of deceitfulness.

Confusion and Conforming

The early to mid-late years of adolescence are often, at least for a time, character-debilitating. At a point in the child's development when she has not yet developed character that is a strong and full sense of herself in the world, she finds that where her most important, new relationships are concerned, her gender plays a predominant and limiting role. Having already been exposed to much that defines them as male or female, adolescents are put to the cruellest and most confining of tests, regardless of how enlightened or "non-sexist" the teachings have been in the home.

Still, and more so than ever, the postmodern adolescent has to conform, or appear to conform, to the intensified social and cultural definitions of *real* girls and *real* boys. This two-pronged process of developing a real self and a sexual or gender-specific self is a significant factor when it comes to understanding the current generation of confused and troubled youth. The same process and factors are at play with children who become inauthentic, tightly conformist, and intolerant young adults.

While children of both genders are subjected to unrelentingly impressive imagery regarding their emergent roles as adult males and females, girls have, in one fundamental way, a different and more permanently contorting experience than boys. As the comparisons in the next chapter further explain, boys "push off" *toward self* in early adolescence on a journey during which images and models of male aggression play a fundamental and determining role. Girls, on the other hand, are prodded by imagery and a variety of social pressures to "become female" earlier than boys are pushed to "become men"—the term "man," in our culture, implying personhood, as opposed to the terms "woman" or "female," which imply *merely* woman or female and all the expectations and limitations that the gender descriptions themselves imply. The standards or models to which girls and boys are still directed are of critical importance to the ultimate interplay between men and women, as well as to the perpetuation of a still male-directed culture. Girls "push off" *out of self,* toward an acceptable model of femaleness. Boys, at least in theory and opportunity, "push off" *toward* self and personhood.

At adolescence, both girls and boys enter a world in which they look for and absorb added cues regarding the nature and consequences of certain behaviours. Both also look for acceptable ways to express who they think they are, and to further find ways to display a degree of independence from the family. At the same time, and while coping with their own feelings related to sexual self-discovery, boys and girls are swamped with messages and directives related to their gender and gender efficacy, that is, their gender-related value and acceptability in their various environments. In fact, both girls and boys learn early that gender or sex overrides the muffled messages related to personal growth, moral independence, intelligence, individuality, even talent. And the messages are destructive to the emergence of an autonomous and expressive adult self, especially with respect to the developing female.

The Imposter Syndrome

There are two fundamental aspects of the relearning and re-formational process for girls that are profoundly destructive. They are also, invariably, the two driving and determining factors for a female adolescent's finding herself in trouble or unable to cope.

First, there is the conscious or unconscious acceptance of fraudulence— of the faking and performing of a false self to be acceptable to others. Second, there is the consequence of the first factor—the toxic effect of feeling deceitful and in collusion with others about the still-confusing secret regarding the necessity of presenting a fraudulent or false self.

The false self is the fraudulent or impostering self, and the Imposter Syndrome, still a significant strain in most women and mothers (who model it for their daughters), is a vague feeling of dishonesty or fakery which affects the girl's (and the woman's) sense of legitimate competency, success, intelligence, and self-esteem. In short, the syndrome leaves the adolescent girl unsure of what about her is real, and what is the social act. And the syndrome persists into adulthood.

So, at the same time as the female child is reluctantly letting go of mother during the necessary and usually premature period of detachment, she is also testing her acceptability and value in the world. Girls and boys alike face a similar period of self-experimentation, and through cause and effect adopt the "right" behaviours. However, in the case of the female child, she is also picking up on more of the subtle and not-so-subtle messages she experienced but could not discern as a little girl. While the dictates for femaleness, and ultimate inauthenticity, might have been moderate and manageable in the limited environment of the home, at or just before adolescence the rules related to female "okayness" and "not okayness" intensify and come from a variety of new, external sources. The strengths for which she might have been applauded earlier in her life no longer hold the same value or elicit the same kind of praise. In fact, they may be frowned on. As a result, the girl is caught, without clear instructions, between who she was, and was overtly taught to be in the way of bright, athletic, competitive, and so on, and what she now, apparently, must adopt in the way of unspoken but mandatory self-distorting, even self-limiting behaviours.

For the now quietly confused and angry adolescent girl, this unspoken "secret" related to the social necessity of mixing some real with many acted-out, distinctly female behaviours, is experienced as a frightening and disillusioning conspiracy. She feels that everyone she ever trusted had been both withholding something from her about herself, and accepting of what she would have to do to herself to have a place in the world. In the girl's mind, those closest to her knew all along that, unlike her brothers, she would have to endure a ritualistic contortion of who she was once she became a "young woman." And the fact that the fuzzy cues and wafts of displeasure were never fully explained, even discussed in politically correct homes, the child experiences them as evidence of deceit and betrayal on the part of her parents and other adults. Further, as she learns that she must adopt fraudulent or impostering behaviours, and that this is to be part of her placing herself in the world, she loses much of her earlier formed self-esteem.

At this painful point, the adolescent girl also suffers the first of what will be increasing or intensifying behaviours related to an absence of self-trust and self-respect. The child ultimately internalizes and blames herself for the incomprehensible nature of her arrival at this age and place of fakery. And she suffers the first stabs of self-contempt that come with being fraudulent and with living a lie. Virtually overnight, the confident, explorative child becomes a confused, self-questioning adolescent *female*. Her early adolescent years are spent managing a real and a fake self, usually learning to hide the former and to highlight the latter, and being rewarded for doing so. As a survival instinct, the child learns to cultivate more that is acceptable, and to suppress what is real and perhaps less pleasing to others.

As was the case with Allia, the female child responds to encouragement, and attempts to adopt and emulate the styles and modes of presentation that are encouraged, and to stifle and hide those activities, expressions, and postures that are not. Sadly and perilously, this struggle to conform and need to survive reaches its peak during the stage preceding adolescence, when the child is still latently accepting and non-rebellious. Therefore, while the child is picking up signals related to the necessity of increased independence and is discovering her own sexuality and that of others, she is also wrestling with the secret, strict, and limiting mandates related to gender behaviour. She is female, the messages tell her, and she can be whatever she wants. However, she is also admonished regarding certain expectations, constraints, and models related to her femaleness which are in direct contradiction to accomplishment, intelligence, and independence. Amid this process the female child is compelled to split into at least two formative identities—one in which she attempts to be independent, smart, and strong, and one in which she struggles to apply the lie, the fraudulence, in order to acquire validity and acceptance in a "boy-girl" world.

Experimentation

In addition to her inner struggle to manage and apply the split in new environments, the young female adolescent also starts to compare her behaviours to those of boys of the same age. She further monitors and adjusts her behaviour by observing the behavioural nuances of other, usually older, girls, women, and, notably, models and television and movie stars.

She practises, and picks and chooses from among the perfect stereotypes in order to manufacture the best possible version of an inauthentic, distinctly female self.

Young adolescent girls practise flirting, experiment with ways and styles of expressing and camouflaging their intelligence and athletic skills, and turn to makeup, body piercing, tight clothing, and other aspects of standard, adolescent and adult female cosmeticism to continuously renew, redefine, and act out the stereotypical tenets of girls living and functioning in relation to boys. And when they do it well, they are quickly catapulted into early womanhood—frequently at a mere 12 or 13 years of age—and always with a semiconscious awareness of the manicured manifestations of "the lie."

Further still, in that they feel like imposters, like versions of acceptable femaleness, they naturally adopt other dishonest behaviours. The incorporation of a sense of sanctioned dishonesty into the child's psyche is the mere starting point for the child's manipulative race against other women in the historic competition for the best man. It is also the beginning of the "pleasing" and "me last" behaviour deemed attractive in both girls and women. It is also the beginning of the end of legitimate selfhood and of the child's sense of deservedness in relationships and in life in general.

Fear and Anger

As girls frantically try to conform and to mix split selves in order to function and be accepted in the world, most of them are unaware of the source of their anger. However, if you talk to them, they are aware of their secret fear. They are fearful of growing up, and they are even more fearful of the secret mandate to nurture, and to adopt and hone other behaviours to ensure that their femaleness predominates over their character. As a result, the female adolescent, and eventually, in a different way, the female adult, functions with varying degrees of repressed rage. However, expressing anger is considered a male characteristic and behaviour, and, as such, is even deemed to be healthy for a boy.

The same healthy venting of anger is still seen as inappropriate in female behaviour. Consequently, young female adolescents are much more prone to depression, a result of the suppression of anger, and much more likely to end up in therapy. When a girl child does not act out in anger per se, but is, rather, distinctly quiet and moody, for example, she is automatically deemed to be merely, youthfully depressed.

Rebellion

Given the restrictive nature of the female mandate, the girl child is also without a channel or form of expression for her confusing and alienating anger directed solely at parents, teachers, and adults. Once entirely acceptable to us, she clung to our love as she struggled to discover her effectiveness in the world. She was further praised as she learned and showed off new skills and talents. But when childhood is, for no apparent reason, suddenly replaced by the urgent message to hide who she really is, the child, though mandated not to, has the urge to find some way to rebel or punish us for bringing her to this place of toxic uncertainty. As she finds it increasingly difficult to manage the splitting transition, both her anger at and her alienation from us can understandably take her to damaging and dangerous places.

For young girls, rebellion is often the only way that they can find some kind of temporary self-definition or identity, as well as a new way and place in which to belong. Parents are well advised to ensure that the child remembers where she belongs, and that home be a place where this mix of real and fake personas is discussed as early as the child starts to pick up on cues, either at home, at school, or in the playground. A young girl will characteristically come out and ask, in vague terms, of course, and it is important that we answer her directly and fully. If she does not ask directly, but becomes unusually quiet or moody at about 10 or 11 years of age, the chances are that this issue is bothering her.

Addressing the issue of boys' behaviours and girls' behaviours, and how society makes mistakes in how it likes boys to act and girls to act, is healthy. The issue of socially enforced gender behaviours can be discussed even earlier (in addition to when the child seems bothered by the discovery) in the context of life not always being fair, but that the child's value is irreducible.

Girls self-direct their anger; boys are more likely to smash windows or get in a fight. Unfortunately, self-directed anger blurs and distorts everything else in the child's world, and her perceptions culminate in what can become a daily attack on herself. While a female adolescent might be driving her parents or teachers to distraction with obnoxious behaviour, her real fight is with herself. Therefore, while she is angry, but cannot, by a certain age, direct, or even consciously discern, her anger anywhere but at, and in, herself, she isolates herself by alienating the once-anchoring people in her life. In a strange way she is protecting those about whom she is emotionally ambivalent, protecting herself from her need to be "taken back" and praised and loved, and positioning herself for a new way to find acceptance or to belong. This is by far the most vulnerable and dangerous point in her development.

The girl's solitary floundering in the void between childhood and the adoption of an acceptable female self, along with feelings of distrust, alienation, and self-directed anger, contribute significantly to the high suicide rate among adolescent girls. Other forms of self-destructive rebellion include sudden and intense drug use, gang affiliation and, ironically, a usually temporary descent into promiscuity. The child who was one day struggling to understand her role as a female, to learn and to mimic the confusingly limited symbols of female desirability and sexual distinctiveness, frequently takes a dive into the Madonna Syndrome—the overacting out of exaggerated sexual gestures, clothing, and behaviours. Frightening and appalling to parents who never encouraged the flaunting (merely the exhibiting) of female sexuality, the child is both carrying out her mandate and overdoing it in a usually unconscious expression of anger.

Again, as parents, we can nip some of this overacting in the bud by addressing the behavioural stereotypes earlier, when the child is ready. However, if we see signs or obvious visual indications that our daughters are acting out in exaggerated, seductive ways, we need to address this immediately. A sit-down with mother and father, brought together from separate living spaces if necessary, is urgent, but the child must feel loved and attended to, not attacked. She is getting enough contempt from herself. In the context of what she knows is a serious chat, joking with the child about her makeup, fishnet stockings, or short skirt, is a good way to start. We cannot look alarmed or rejecting, but, rather, concerned and loving. We then have to communicate an understanding of why she has adopted a new dress or behavioural code, and encourage her to talk about her feelings regarding her appearance and behaviour. We also, of course, have to set limits and dictates, but keep on talking, at least weekly, to see her through this extremely vulnerable period. Not easy, but not as difficult as bringing her back if we lose her to conditions and circumstances beyond mere theatrics.

Belonging: Gangs

By observing the female adolescent at least as closely as we have tended to observe and watch for "naughtiness" in boys, we increase our chances of catching the child before she falls into another form of adolescent rebellion typical to girls. As mentioned, the female adolescent is poised to find a new way and place to belong, and her sexual acting out, whether it be with imagery or active sexual involvement, often leads her to new and dangerous places. By being overtly sexual, she is both rebelling against the mandate and meeting her need to "go home," to be re-accepted and cared for. Sex and drugs are, therefore, attractive escapes for girls who, on the one hand are deliberately acting out, and on the other hand, need sedation or an escape from their shame and anger.

Also, for a price, one of which is obedience and loyalty, the young adolescent girl can find a renewed sense of belonging by committing to a subculture or to an actively or inactively deviant group or gang to which she pledges allegiance in exchange for protection and identity. The need to rebelong is so overwhelming for a girl that, especially if she is experiencing the extremes of early adolescent confusion, she will do almost anything to be accepted into some social group, even and especially if it is a questionable one. One can see why middle-class suburban girls tend more toward gang affiliation than do boys.

In early adolescence, boys tend more toward solitude and isolation, while girls attempt to resocialize, to re-create a sense of family and familial protection. Having been treated with more delicacy and been fed direct and indirect messages regarding her lesser strength, her fragility, and her need for protection, the early and mid-period of extended detachment and isolation is extremely frightening for a girl. It should not be surprising, therefore, that girls generally join small gangs led by an older boy, and, secondarily, by an apparently strong but obedient female. In fact, while acts of solitary violence and child homicide by female teenagers is still virtually unheard of, girls have and do participate in gang-related beatings and murders, both in the United States and Canada.

During the early adolescent years, a young female adolescent can find and gain acceptance in a new, surrogate family unit, and if the unit comprises equally, if differently, angry adolescents, it can serve not only as a new home, but also as a vehicle and channel for her anger. The child's gratitude for being accepted, her resulting loyalty, and her blurred identification with the gang enable her to participate in otherwise impossibly violent behaviours, and, relatedly, to also both share and turn her anger away from herself and project it onto someone or something else.

In fact, there is no underestimating the degree of relief brought to a young girl by her finding a way to re-direct her self-hatred and self-directed anger. However, as I have seen several times as a therapist, if and when a girl is suddenly exiled from this "new family," the rejection and renewed experience of isolation can be so devastating that it can be life-threatening. Exile by order of one's first critical set of adolescent peers (as well as by one's first boyfriend) is frequently the reason given by young adolescent girls for attempted suicide.

With this in mind, it is logical that an ill-thought-out attempt to punish a child away from such an affiliation can be futile. Her new place of belonging, her "soothing space," is with the gang. It has, in a way, become her drug of choice and she will fight to the end to maintain her connection. To pull too hard at a female child who has found a way to put off her confrontation with her maturing, female self, and to re-belong and to feel safe is usually to lose her to one degree or another. It is best that we overtly or covertly check up on the group, watch and listen intensely (unless the child is involved in criminal behaviour or in obvious danger, in which case we act quickly and dramatically), and step up our time with and active affection for our daughter when she is at home. The objective is to lure her back to a memorable, still safer place of belonging.

Allia Revisited

Allia's therapy left her less saddened and more determined to assert herself in the direction of her goal to attend medical school.

As is the case with all therapeutic processes, though, she was not left without ongoing, even new challenges. She felt better to the extent that she understood that she had repressed a self-gnawing anger, and that her unconsciously doing so had resulted in apparent depression, and very real, debilitating sadness and self-contempt. However, she felt that her need to assert and to be herself to get good marks and to compete with boys for positions at universities was not going to be easy. Even her parents, otherwise intelligent and progressive people, worried about her being hurt along the way if she did not give in or ascribe just a little to the ways and powers of feminine wiles. In fact, Allia realized that what she had discovered about the effects of the mixed messages and secret agendas regarding her gender still required her to be less than honest with her parents, teachers, and even some of her friends.

Allia was not, as yet, interested in boys, but pretended to be after a remark she overheard from her brother, and merely frowned upon, not objected to, by her mother. Her brother said, "*Shh, she's probably a 'Leso.'*" The fact that Allia wasn't dating at 14 had been an issue with some girls at school, and she had been mocked, but she had never been taunted, nor had she ever thought that anyone would think of her in the way reflected by her brother's comment. She had not considered the extreme perceptual consequences of not dating or of appearing to be disinterested in boys.

In fact, as Allia shared in a few urgently scheduled sessions, she did have embarrassing sexual feelings for boys, and she also felt ashamed that she masturbated. The remark she'd overheard, and what she now irrationally imagined to be others' suspicions as well, devastated her. Totally out of character, she didn't want to go to school, nor did she want to stay at home where, again, in a different way, she felt like an unwelcome stranger subject to perverse suspicions. She felt as if she couldn't win.

Allia became more silent than ever at home, and left each day pretending to go to school. In fact, she was going to the university library to attempt to keep up with her schoolwork. Nevertheless, she was missed at school and her parents were contacted regarding her apparent truancy. Her troubles compounded.

A confrontation took place one evening when she was sneaking in to sleep in her room. Her mother, and then her father, confronted her with her suddenly delinquent behaviour. Her mother asked her where she was going during the day, and implied that she was spending time with questionable company. Her parents made repeated references to the advantages she had in terms of their upper-middle-class status, related opportunities for education, and the potential for a "good marriage." The lecture and admonishments intensified, their voices continued to rise, and her mother and father eventually ended up arguing with each other about Allia's apparent problem.

Allia was unresponsive. She just answered yes and no to interrogations related to drugs, sex, and her apparent "street wandering," and left her parents with no relief from what they were imagining were Allia's disobedient ways. Allia felt re-exiled and confused. She felt sufficiently guilty about avoiding school, even though she was preparing for exams at the library every day. But she felt even more guilty and shamed as a result of the kind of questions her parents were asking, and the assumptions they had to have made in order to ask them. She could not even bring herself to respond to clarify. She couldn't and didn't know where to start. They were asking and pushing for confessions from a place totally foreign to their daughter. However, in her own confusion, and due to her insecurity, some of the implicit condemnation seeped into her heart and added a new layer of doubt to her already shaky sense of self.

She wept as quietly as possible that night as she tried to block out the sounds of her parents arguing in the room down the hall. It had been so simple. She had had a plan to limit and survive her humiliation. However, somehow, her strategy had made her into something even more foreign and frightening to her "stranger parents." Thankfully, this bright and fundamentally responsible girl called the next day and reached out.

After seeing Allia twice in this latest course of therapy, she agreed to let me ask her parents to come in with her for an appointment. She was frightened, but even she knew how dangerously close she was to giving up. As a therapist, I felt that Allia was a potential suicide—as are many young girls who muddle through but refer to their close call later in their lives. I attempted to assist Allia to explain exactly what she had been trying to do, and why, but she had great difficulty talking about her sexual feelings and related humiliation. Further, her parents kept saying that all she had to do was "come to them" and "tell them" what was going on. And they meant it. They clearly loved their daughter but, as is the case with so many of us, they had no idea how much their daughter had been suffering. They didn't understand the "depression" for which she was originally referred to me, nor this latest stage in which she felt exiled and profoundly misunderstood. They also, it was evident from their protestations, didn't understand why their child felt that she could no longer trust them. When most, if not all, was out in the open, they appeared to be perplexed by how apparently simple and manageable it all was. They left, still confused by Allia's retreat into a private place and process to cope.

Allia's mother made an appointment with the school and explained, both defensively and proudly, that Allia had been studying elsewhere. She also criticized the school for not noticing that her daughter had apparently been persecuted on school grounds. Each parent started to try to give Allia more space, and more obvious and frequent signs of love. Allia returned to her studies at school, and, with her head down, continued to strive to meet her goal. Though she didn't discuss this with her parents, she tried, when she could, to display more attentiveness to boys. Though shy, she stole herself to make the odd attempt to flirt and flatter, thus eliminating, for the most part, the wrath and mockery of her seemingly better-adjusted female peers.

SUMMING UP

The development of the female child *is* distinctly different from that of boys. She realizes, in the precarious early stage of adolescence, that she cannot just be herself in the world, but rather that she has to fit herself into the limiting role and representation of femaleness. This sudden mandate, is perceived as "too little to late," that is, as being asked to restrict herself to the confines of stereotypical female behaviour after years of encouragement and praise for a variety of accomplishments. To the female child, this feels like a deliberate betrayal, based on a long-withheld and untold lie. Consequently, her self-esteem plummets and she is initially pitted against her parents in anger. She then both resists the mandate and acts it out in either normally tentative ways or in rebelliously exaggerated ways that reflect an anger eventually turned against herself. Once she is at least managing the social mandate to be female first, and who she is, if and when possible, the girl proceeds with a predominating inauthentic self and carries anger related to this lie well into adolescence and beyond.

As a result of the adolescent's sense of unacceptability and betrayal, she is prone to look for new, safe, and often unacceptable affiliations in which she can claim and experience a sense of belonging similar to that experienced in her early years of development. Further, a large minority of young female teens act out and exaggerate the sexual mandate imposed upon them, often in the comforting context of a gang.

The majority of adolescent girls, however, merely manage in pain and confusion to meet the increasingly extreme mandates related to femaleness in a male-directed culture. As such, they are extremely vulnerable, estranged, and necessarily deceptive in their awkward, deliberately "sexy" strides toward accomplishment and personhood.

WHAT TO DO

1. Take note, as early as possible, of the gender-specific messages that you directly or indirectly send to your female child. Don't underestimate the efficiency of her "memory bank" where negative information is concerned, or the inefficiency with which she will compute positive information, especially as she grows toward, enters, and passes through puberty.

2. Watch for hints and moments—such as extreme quietude, nonspecific anger, general anger directed at a male sibling, sudden sadness, even a sudden avoidance of school—when your child displays an awareness, worry, or mere recognition of her gender mandate.

3. Be open with your daughter about gender differences—in all ways. Introduce her, in the two or three years prior to adolescence, to the kind of messages she will increasingly be receiving regarding her "objectified womanhood." Help her to understand the messages in a way so as to spare her the feeling that she has been lied to or tricked with respect to the seemingly secret mandate. Show your support for her uniqueness and personal development.

   Take your daughter aside even before she shows signs of being disturbed by the restrictions on her self-representation and talk about general unfairness. Tell her that both boys and girls are encouraged to behave in certain ways by society and by many specific people as well, but that she can handle this the way she finds easiest or best. Also tell her to come to you when she knows what you mean, is experiencing it, or before, during and after. Remind her that you need her to be "her" at home. Importantly, be aware of how we treat our girls versus our boys.

4. Watch for changes in early elementary school which indicate that your daughter is picking up on limiting gender distinctions. Find a way to bring up the subject of cultural gender stereotypes and to assist the child to find and sustain ways in which she can remain true to her character and abilities.

The signs will be similar to those mentioned in recommendation 2. She might, also, however, hear from a boy that "she is only a girl" and ask you to explain the remark. Do so in the way already explained, and remind her that "he is only a boy."

Your child is starting to sense that her bare strengths do not work socially for her when she stops registering for co-ed sports, ceases to participate in neighbourhood athletic activities, gets lower marks at school, and, for example, at 11 or 12, suddenly becomes desperate to wear an unneeded bra, excessively frilly underwear, short skirts, and footwear inappropriate for a girl.

5. Listen to how your children use language in arguments and discussions. When the language implies inferiority or objectification related to gender, address the remarks in a firm, calm manner. Overreacting merely reinforces the existence of a distinction of which the (female) child should be fearful.

6. Watch what you say around your children. We all make the odd remark which, if overheard by our daughters, can cause problems in the future and pain in the moment. Don't underestimate your child's intelligence and attunement to what you think and feel.

7. Watch for preadolescent signs of anger, especially as it is addressed at you—a parent or teacher, or at a brother or male peer.

8. When and if your daughter suddenly becomes obsessively modest, even protective of her body, take note and address the issue in general terms at a later date. Ask her how she feels about her body, but only after you

have engaged her in as much casual discussion as possible about her life at home, at school, with friends and teachers. Her modesty regarding her body is the clearest indication that she is catching on to the mandate and the meaning of her gender.

9. Allow your early adolescent daughter some latitude with makeup and other non-destructive feminine accessories. She is merely experimenting with the mandate. Overreaction will push her further away from home, and further into the culture of female objectification.

10. If your child seems ready, even as early as 10 years of age, have a discussion with her and her siblings, especially with and including a brother or brothers. Ask your children what they think of advertisements they see, things they hear, and models they view inside and outside the home. Further discuss the unavoidable imperatives in cultural sexual stereotyping, and discuss ways that one can get around them without compromising one's character and self-respect. This is the most honest and difficult way of managing the inevitable.

11. Do not push or be overly reactive or demanding as your daughter acts out in annoying ways during early to mid-adolescence. You want to keep her home, and have home remain her place of belonging and refuge. Keep talking, asking, and gently intruding into her world. Connection and communication are the threads that will enable her to make her way through adolescence.

12. Do everything you can, with impassioned reason and understanding, to enable your child to continue to trust in your ability to protect her in a world in which she will periodically feel vulnerable and inferior, and in which she must be dishonest to be permitted to succeed. Help her work through this last one with the "life isn't fair" approach, as well as by telling her that her family is behind her if she wants to do it the hard and honest way. Encourage daughters toward elegant personhood.

Boys and the Mandate of Manhood

3

The thing I hate most about masks is that they never last—you just make an impression with them, and they fall apart. And all that's left is...a face I don't even know.

—*Craig, 14*

For boys, the passage into and through adolescence is typified by three dimensions: the *premature kick-off* from childhood to manhood; *forced independence*; and the expectation and allowance of *premature freedom and self-reliance*. Compounding these three major challenges is that boys also come face-to-face with sexuality, their's and other's, at the same time as they are trying to stretch up and out of childhood.

Case Study

Greg

Greg was brought to me by his parents when he was 13 years old. He, like many preteens spilling over into adolescence, had gone from being relatively playful and mischievous, especially with his mother, to quiet and sullen. His parents decided to bring him to counselling after he displayed what were to them "frightening tantrums."

During the most dramatic episode, Greg's mother locked herself in the master bedroom and telephoned her husband for help. The scene had escalated as the boy at first begged, then raged at his mother, to re-emerge. When she told Greg that she would not come out until she felt safe, his rage roared out of control, and he started to destroy objects in the house while hurling profanities at his bewildered and frightened mother.

Notably, it was around Christmas, and the boy threatened to rip down the Christmas tree as he both implored and ordered his mother to come out and face him. His mother didn't know that he was crying throughout his tirade, and therefore she continued to tell him to stop behaving like a monster, to calm down, or, not only would she not unlock her door, she would call the police. Greg returned to pounding on his parents' bedroom door, and as he did, he heard his mother phoning his father for the second time, as well as a friend. He heard her tone, calm and objective, strange and estranged, as if, Greg described later, she were courageously reporting the presence of a serial killer. As he listened, he felt "crazier," reacting to the contrast between her calmness with a stranger and her terror of him.

He yanked down the Christmas tree, crushed ornaments, and smashed three family pictures (all including him) which had sat on a shelf in the living room. To make matters worse, his ten-year-old sister arrived home during the rampage. She had come home for lunch, as had their mother from work, part of a routine established for the children until they reached a certain age. Greg was supposed to be at school, and one of the precipitating factors for this latest tantrum was that he had stayed home. Upon seeing the wreckage of the tree she had excitedly helped to decorate, his sister started to cry. Greg just stared at her, unable to feel anything, until he "lost it'" and started to scream and yell at her as well. His feelings intensified when he saw his mother appear on the stairwell, call to his sister, and signal his sibling to follow her to the safety of the bedroom. Greg put his fist through a glass china cabinet and left the house. He was cut, covered with blood, and in need of a place to hide.

Greg walked along the railway tracks about three-quarters of a mile from his home. He knew of an abandoned railroad house where kids sometimes hung out on weekends to drink and smoke. He spent the rest of the day there.

He hoped that no one would come into the darkness. He knelt by a small window in which there were just shards of glass left after years of neglect, and he wept. For a time, he rocked back and forth, watching the blood oozing from his hand and arm. He used his uninjured hand to play with it, and realized that he had never before examined his own blood. He had always reacted to it, stopped it, or had it stopped or attended to by someone older—usually his mom. His blood felt cold, not warm, and, after a while, he deliberately scraped his hand along the filth of the urine-stenched floor. He cried again, deeper, choking as he realized that no one would clean his wound or frown in worry over his injury.

Hours later, when he was half-asleep, and a dark figure descended over him in the corner where he huddled, he instinctively whispered the word *"Mom?"* He toughened up and tried to think clearly and to talk fast when he realized it was a patrol officer checking the building. Reluctant to fight with the police, Greg identified himself and was driven home.

The opening of the front door, the sight of his mother and sister still traumatized by his rampage, the look on their faces when they saw him standing with a police officer, and the look on the officer's face as he surveyed the mess that his mother and sister were trying to clean up, made him wish he could fade away. He met no one's eyes and went to his room. As he was heading up the stairs, he overheard his mother tell the officer that they would be fine. Her husband would be home soon and he would handle things. Then she thanked the officer effusively, as if he had just saved her life.

Greg stayed in his room exploring the dried blood on his arm and clothing. He noticed that one spot was still trickling out of a large gash that even he knew would leave a scar.

Greg's father was furious. His mother had described the scene as calmly as possible, even omitting certain details that would really set her husband off. But he had received two desperate messages at work, and he could see the destruction all around him. His daughter ran to him and cried and stammered dramatically about how frightened she had been—how she and mommy had had to lock themselves away or Greg would have killed them. The more the child cried, the more intensely her parents tried to calm her, and the more hysterical she became as she picked up on and reacted to their anger.

It wasn't long into the scene when Greg's father mounted the stairs, striding toward Greg's room like a sheriff heading to a shootout. While mother and daughter retreated to the sitting area off the kitchen, Greg listened as his father's footsteps grew louder and then stopped at his door. His father pushed his door open in a way that made Greg feel as if he expected him to be in there with a weapon. Their eyes met, and then Greg looked away and waited. He was, in the end, surprised by how little was actually said.

He was grounded, which he found ironic. He thought that his mother would have told his father to send him to some after-school program for juvenile delinquents, rather than allow him to be in the house when his father wasn't there.

Soon, his mother didn't seem to feel the need to lock herself in her room when Greg was home, or she just stopped doing it because she had too much to do to sit around in her bedroom fearing her son. She was wary, even a little nervous around him, but wanted and willed him to be okay. After a few days, even his sister acted as if nothing had happened, except when her parents were around. Then she would cower in feigned fear as a result of a remark or a movement her brother made.

COPING WITH MANHOOD

The "Kick-off"

This common case, in which Greg acted out and exhibited what is usually viewed as just early adolescent turmoil, is actually rooted in an earlier, traumatic period during which the boy toddler was first expected to separate from mother. At puberty and early adolescence, a boy is again confused and frightened by the second most intense period of separation from mother. At the same time as he is getting messages from family, friends, the educational system, and the media to move away from mother, the boy, though he wants to push off, actually needs to be closer to her than he has been for a number of years.

During this period, when a boy fights with his mother, he actually feels tormented by what he's doing. It is the opposite of what he really wants and needs. Far from hating mother, the boy wants to return to the intensity and unconditionality of infancy, as well as to the unique tie between a mother and a boy infant.

Further, if a boy sees that he can frighten and *is* frightening to his mother, he becomes more frightened than he already is. The greatest fear of the infant is that his love will be too much for his mother, indeed, that he will destroy his mother because of his limitless need.

Harrowingly for the male adolescent, this need, and the fear attached to it, returns. Moreover, he has these feelings at a point in his development when he knows (and the mother knows) that he could, in fact, destroy her were he to express his anger physically.

In Greg's case he had known for a while that he was now expected to change his behaviours. His father had given him more responsibility and freedom, and his mother had started to depend on him for help and support. At school, he was suddenly being treated like a grown-up, which some days he liked, while other days he resented, feeling he needed more guidance and clarification.

The day he stayed home and lashed out at his mother when she caught him there, he was afraid to go to school. He had a few acquaintances, not real friends, and while they talked about some things, none of the boys shared their secret in common. No one dared. Each assumed that the other was faring better, and that he alone was finding the leap from childhood to "almost-manhood" too much to handle. When Greg's mother reacted angrily when she found him at home in the middle of the day, Greg reacted in fear more than anger, but eventually his fear and frustration escalated to rage. This occurred partly because, on some level, Greg felt (correctly) that his mother was afraid of him. He repeatedly begged her to come out of the locked room, and when she refused he felt crazy and couldn't stop his growing anger. In fact, he raged at his mother for no longer permitting him to huddle against her in safety, and for confirming that he could hurt her.

The fact that his mother felt she had to protect herself from him cut straight to his child's heart. He felt separate, as if he were a stranger, and deemed old enough and capable of harming the one he loved most in the world. Therefore, a large part of his rage was actually despair. In addition, he now felt estranged from his sister, and like an enemy to his father. His role in and out of the family had, he felt, irrevocably changed.

When he smashed his hand through a glass pane in the china cabinet, he was both punishing his mother and punishing himself. She was being punished for no longer knowing him, for being afraid of him, instead of being able to read his mind (which a child experiences in infancy), and for not nurturing him in his state of despair. Somehow mixed in with his turmoil, especially with his sense of being perceived as a physical threat, was guilt related to his sexuality, to his knowing and thinking about his mother's sexuality, and to his awareness of the predominant role played by his father—sexual and otherwise. All this had been eating at him and had reached a peak during this episode.

Earlier, as Greg had felt that he was being booted out of boyhood, he had not been "cutting it" on the adolescent scene. His self-confidence seemed to have vanished overnight, and the limited but influential power he had exerted as a child in the home was gone. In effect, he had gone from a child with security and power, to an ostensibly "mature boy-man" with no power at all. He was terrified, and it didn't seem to matter to anyone inside or outside his home. It was strange to him that no one close to him seemed to understand what he was feeling, let alone that he needed them.

Guilt and Isolation

Greg seemed to feel that he was already failing in this new adolescent role. For one thing, he didn't want to be away from home as much as he was expected to be. And though his father wanted what was best for Greg, his insistent enthusiasm about Greg's joining community hockey and school football teams, and making and spending more time with friends in general, made him feel even more freakish and alone. He felt that his father wanted him out of his hair, even though there had never been any hint of this wish or preference.

Unlike his sister who was still being coddled and cuddled, Greg felt unwanted in the family nest. But he wasn't ready for what seemed to be a compulsory mandate to grow up. He suppressed a discomfiting anger at and resentment of his father for pushing him out and for being the protector of his mother, sister, and the home. He also experienced hurt and rage at his mother for no longer needing to have him near her, and fury and contempt for his teachers who were making similar assumptions about his readiness for manhood. The fact that Greg was angry at and fearful of himself was another sign that he was in trouble. At the very least, he was open to anything and anyone who might pop into his mind or world and offer him a way to channel his anger and confusion.

Common to boys of this age, and related to Greg's acting out and alienation, is a sense that he has nowhere to go. This feeling is compounded by a feeling of nonspecific guilt and "badness." Though many women might be surprised by the notion, boys and men are significantly more sensitive about being perceived as "bad" or "good" people than are girls and women. Girls are taught early on that their okayness is related to whether or not they make people happy or please them. A boy, on the other hand, with early messages and admonishments about being a "bad boy" or a "good boy," works with a blunter sense of himself and of what is expected of him.

In most families, a boy toddler is expected to develop physical strength earlier than his sister, and to be more physically agile and tough. Even in the most enlightened homes, boys are pushed harder and get more negative encouragement related to performance or prowess at an early age (as well as in later years) than do girls. As a result, and compounded over a mere handful of years by the ongoing messages related to male strength, independence, self-sufficiency, self-control, and domination over others, especially women, they come to both covet their biological strength, *and* to fear it. Much more familiar with their anger than girls are, because they had more outlets for it as young boys (but fewer for tears), and because it was more acceptable for a boy to be angry than it was for a girl, the boy fears that he might sometime unleash this discovered strength in anger. In short, he fears hurting someone. In fact, his fear of his physical strength increases proportionately with his anger.

Due to an upbringing different from that of girls, most adolescent boys question whether they are or *can* be "good"—and those who act out in extreme ways, and in extremely violent ways, have given up trying. When they displease others, especially those close to them, they experience shame associated with the suppressed, but always present, "bad self." When Greg's mother locked herself away, for example, she confirmed what Greg had, consciously or unconsciously, felt to be true—that he was "bad," or could be if he did not control himself. Moreover, as mentioned, for a boy, the last person he wants to fear him is his mother—and "bad" is the last thing he wants her to see in him.

Boys can become paralyzed at this stage of their development, trapped between what they perceive as expressed manhood and obedient, suppressed boyhood. Alternatively, they let go and act out their "badness" by getting into trouble outside and inside the home and school. This is evident by the increasing number of boys, 13 to 14 years of age, who act out in destructive or violent ways. In fact, on some level, the delinquent boy is both committing to and protesting against the mandate to mature.

A boy will frequently behave destructively or overly aggressively in an attempt to act out the social mandates of manhood and power, and manliness and prowess by force. There is tension in the child's initial understanding of the rewards inherent in being a "good guy" (obedient, adored by mother, suppressing of his "toughness"), or a "bad guy" (independent, powerful, potentially, self-protectively dangerous), a tension that usually follows the boy into adulthood.

As he is pushed away from the home and out into various social settings—especially the secondary school—it is at least a good imitation of the independent, feared, and respected "bad guy" that is both admired and is most laudable. It is little wonder that in the jargon of contemporary male youth, "bad" has come to mean good or "cool," and the word "good" has disappeared from their language.

Pushed to grow up, and no longer getting "parent points" for being repressively "good," boys either start to strut their strength and test their prowess as bullies, or as neutral, (at least) obnoxious bad guys, or they freeze in the headlights of a non-choice. Either way, repressed and "good," they are isolated socially; "bad" and cool, they, in their minds, lose their families. When a boy does act out, often eruptively, he breaks this historic tension between what is perceived as little boy and feminine goodness, and male badness, by throwing himself off the fence, the middle ground or no man's land between being someone's good boy and a viable male outside the home.

Things are so black and white for boys (and then, to a degree, for men), yet complicated. If the boy hovers at home, as Greg wanted to, hoping not to be forced to grow up, he is avoiding facing these two perceived aspects of himself, as well as having to develop a manageable degree of "badness" to be accepted outside the home. If he stays connected to home, he is viewed as weak or feminine by others, but as "good" by his mother. However, he feels despised by the powerful father and other males around him. Even young females view the quiet, studious, punctual boy as too good to be viable date material. A little bit of "bad" goes a long way, especially in adolescent culture, and evidence of being "good" implies sissiness and evokes mockery and more. This is the "nowhere" place where the early adolescent boy ends up—damned if he does, and damned if he doesn't become at least a little "bad," and suppress the obedient, controlled good boy and the apple of his mother's eye.

Significantly, however, the boy (and most men) rarely forgets both his inclination toward and suppression of the "bad" in him, introduced and discouraged during his early years. Most adolescent boys enter adolescence trying to create *and* walk a tightrope between the "cool bad" young man, and the "good boy" who is mother's son. It is little wonder that boys who precipitously act out in violent ways report feeling relief, excitement, and a sense of freedom. There is clarity and catharsis in letting go and being dramatically, destructively bad, even though, when these behaviours are taken to the extreme, boys usually lose both at school and at home.

Father's Role

As is the case during early childhood development, the adolescent clings to the mother and fears or is less open with the father. Even in the contemporary family, it is the father to whom most children feel they have to prove their worth, and the father whose words and deeds are most heeded. However, if there has been a conscious, consistent, and attentive attempt on the part of the father to create and maintain his own sensual bond with the child, the thrust toward maturity is significantly less traumatic. The less the boy fears his father, and the greater the bond between them, the less frightening are the various aspects of growing up.

In fact, as William Pollack writes in *Real Boys*, boy children benefit for the rest of their lives from an early and continued relationship with their fathers based partially on primitive physicality. Boys who, for example, regularly wrestle and roughhouse with their fathers are invariably much more confident and less fearful of the maturation mandate and of themselves than are the majority of those who do not. When a boy-child exerts his body or physical strength against his father, he is taught restraint. He is shown, in firm but nonshaming ways, that he must manage his physicality, not necessarily control or suppress it as a "bad" thing.

As a result of the physical encounters, the boy also learns that he *can* stop when he is worked up and otherwise excited or competitive. Over time, frequent physicality with his father provides the child with important self-knowledge. It helps the boy balance his perceptions and the powerful multitude of messages regarding the danger inherent in his brute strength. He therefore suffers less when he is angry, letting go of mother, struggling with independence, and looking for ways to communicate his feelings. Perhaps most importantly, while he is feeling the multitude of overlapping feelings related to what is still usually a premature kick off into manhood, he is not as fearful of himself.

Displacement and Loss of Identity

Boys have little choice but to attempt to fake or find a way to manage the fear related to their *forced independence*. Invariably, therefore, they assume whatever role it takes in an attempt to feel safe, if not accepted, in unavoidable new environments. Most just manage to muddle through, changing "masks" and adjusting their style all the way to senior high school and beyond, but all boys are at risk during these challenging years. In fact, boys experience the forced independence as a virtual "brush with death."

Until this point in a boy's development, the umbilical cord has remained symbolically uncut. He came and went at his own pace, still feeling the "right to attachment" to mother, and possessing a sense of identity that placed him at or near the center of the family. When any adult male (father, stepfather, boyfriend, uncle) steps in to push the boy toward manhood, he experiences both his own displacement and a critical loss of identity. It is little wonder that at this point, particularly for male children, bedwetting and nightmares become a source of family irritation. It is of greater wonder that these manifestations, and others, are not more easily understood and addressed by the adult parents of frightened boys.

Ironically, bedwetting recurs for a boy when he is supposed to become more like a man. Consequently, we are often not as sensitive, even tender, about the problem. The boy is horrified by an uncontrollable symptom of anxiety, and our job is to assist him, by talking to him about his feelings, visiting him before he goes to sleep, and providing him with affection.

The combination of experiences may also precipitate a period of acting out. Because the boy feels expelled from the family, he adopts transitional identities or masks that help him to cope with the world. He is acting, and he is still as vulnerable and impressionable as a little boy. Consequently, if he adopts, for example, the common mask of the schoolyard power broker to the bully—he has to adopt behaviours that go along with the role, and he might get in trouble for threatening someone, or for acting tough.

Dylan, one of the boys who initiated the massacre in Littleton, Colorado, in 1999, compensated for being rejected and mocked by his peers by becoming a tough guy. Then he cathartically played with the idea of making a bomb. Along the way, building on the theme of avenger, and teaming up with a friend, he then decided to use the bomb—and more. Dylan, like most other boys who go to less of an extreme, was vulnerable to his own imagery and storyline. Adolescents do this all the time, especially male adolescents, and a transitional identity can be acted out to the point where it becomes real, with innocuous or serious consequences.

The fact that boys adopt these images, masks, or ways of coping secretly is also significant. The intensity of the secrecy and the compensating sense of independence that comes with secrecy, can itself be the precipitating force behind a seemingly uncharacteristic form of acting out. In their own made-for-coping movie, most boys go through the period of forced independence by being annoying or strange or rude. But their coping mechanism, whatever it is, brings with it a theme and related behaviours to which the hiding boy is vulnerable. It is his pretending and coping that can actually push him into related actions and behaviours for which he then has to take real responsibility.

It is dangerous for parents to expect their boys to suddenly stop acting like boys and grow toward manhood, and then turn their backs. While I have said that certain surface behaviours should be left alone, certain other indications of a boy's coping with the use of imagery should not be ignored. A Canadian boy I have treated suddenly took to walking around with a large, real-looking .38-calibre revolver (a pellet gun) in his pants. I have heard of a similar case in Nebraska of a boy doing the same with an apparently unloaded gun.

In the Canadian case, the 14-year-old boy's sister mocked him, and when his parents noticed, they half whined, half irritably asked him what the heck he was trying to pull off. They viewed "packing the piece" to be somewhat like a belated, daily Halloween act, and told him he was being ridiculous. He didn't care. In fact, he just smirked, packed it a little tighter and left the room. His sister and parents rolled their eyes and called out something about his being Dirty Harry. But it wasn't funny.

A teenage boy who starts to carry any kind of weapon, and commonly sleeps with it, is making a strong statement about how angry he is. The fact that he is not embarrassed is also significant. He wants to hurt someone. He probably won't, but he wants to, and is suffering from a kind of frustration commonly iced with anger in boys and men. The Canadian boy ended up shooting pellets in his backyard when his working parents were not home and accidentally shot out one eye of a 3-year-old next-door neighbour, and decreased the sight in the child's other eye as well. The boy's family is being sued for everything it has.

Any abjectly strange or symbolically dangerous behaviour adopted by boys should be addressed directly. *"What is that and why?"* is a perfectly reasonable question to ask a boy who even carries around a huge, heavy police flashlight. With anger their salient and compensating emotion at this stage of development, if we take a walk with them, do something alone with them and talk, we can ask them about their thoughts and feelings. It is usually the grieving boy who is angry who will find dramatic ways to act out his anger. In fact, whether we talk and listen to our suddenly gun-toting son or our bedwetting son, we will hear much that is the same. The latter hasn't, as yet, found a way to channel his anxiety and anger into some form of new identity. We can communicate our understanding of the boy's dilemma and remind him that he is real to us, and that we support him. We can also set limits on how and with what he copes, and make sure that we show no signs of pushing him to manly or aggressive behaviours. This does not include, of course, the natural increase in responsibilities around the house, such as taking out the garbage or washing the car. In fact, in spite of his protestations, if we don't make these demands, we are leaving him both freer and more inclined to search for ways to affect his world.

Most important, we have to remember that while adolescents can be very articulate and convincing about what they think they need, they usually don't have a clue, and our job is nowhere near over. Moreover, in reality, they still want and need us to guide them and to set boundaries.

Forced Independence

Most young teenage boys are too free, too early, partly due to unhealthy social requisites or expectations, and partly due to the fact that their anger wears us down and we let go. Moreover, in the absence of the unique, sexually related fear we have for our female children, we allow our young boys to wander, to make "street decisions," and to cope socially on their own well before they are ready to do so without support and active guidance.

For example, the boy in our case study, Greg, felt compelled to stay at home. Instinctively aware of his own vulnerability, he railed against his parents' assumptions that he was "okay in the world," including at school, where he consistently suffered humiliation, both with his peers and with teachers. Unable to communicate this, let alone admit it, he resisted forced independence and acted out his need at home. Ironically, as a result, he was pushed further from the safe familiarity of his family. Eventually, under the guise of there being something wrong with him, he was brought to see a therapist.

The powerful messages related to the male mandate are, to say the least, overwhelming, and the failure to meet or appear to meet the various dimensions of the mandate are profoundly shaming for the young male. Moreover, modern male role models, extreme and contorted versions of those with whom we or our parents identified, make the mandate virtually impossible and thus further disturbing for the young boy. Boys secretly cower at the otherwise exciting, even arousingly impossible antics and foolhardy bravery of a Bruce Willis in the endless *Die Hard* series. Yet, given the unchallenged consistency of powerful media imagery that initially contrasts with the fragile interpretive inner world of the young boy, he is ultimately left with no alternative but to conform.

At what feels to the boy like the day or moment when he is meant to learn to be self-reliant, there are really no real, viable, or overtly socially acceptable choices. Some boys secretly scrounge for some version of self-reliance between "superman" or "super-stud" at one end of the spectrum, and "wuss" or virtual (and detested) "femininity" on the other. The no-win is intensified for the boy because he is also aware that his mode or style of real or imitated self-reliance implies much about his now-significant sexuality. He feels as if he is no longer permitted to be a boy, and he cannot possibly measure up to what appears to be the only model of manhood.

It is no wonder, then, that when a boy is expected to rely on his own will, wants, and devices, he can either become frightened and paralyzed, and do nothing, or he can manage his way into his own form of re-creation in order to put off or avoid the challenge of self-reliance.

To expect that boys from the ages of 12 to 17 (and often older) will become self-reliant in exactly the way we perceive self-reliance to take effect, is to make an impossible and dangerous assumption. Dylan, in Littleton, Colorado, was assumed to be self-reliant by parents who were good and intelligent people. His interest and diligent work with whatever mechanical entities he spent his spare time fiddling with was probably a source of pride and relief to his parents. He was out of their hair, and he was apparently learning something. They just didn't think to check on just *what* he was learning, *what* he was creating, and in *what ways* he was defining himself in the world. Polite, and in every way normal (other than spending hours of self-directed learning in the family garage and having an affinity for black T-shirts), who among us could say, if he were our son, we would definitely have investigated the nature of what he was *really* doing?

Dylan came to rely on what he could, on an image, an amalgam of many of the same type portrayed in the media, and supported and literally armed by easily accessible homicidal how-to's on the Internet. And then, after a period of faking and harassing, as part of an otherwise acceptable, socially endorsed macho image, he went beyond threatening and talking tough, and committed mass murder in a wider theatre.

Retrospectively, in the managably sickening process of the psychological autopsy, we can understand how and what happened to this boy. However, although there will be other boys similarly disturbed to the extreme during their struggle to find a way to be self-reliant, independent, and distinctly male, we now know both the why and the how of the extreme behaviour *and* the prevention.

As mentioned above, we must be direct in our inquiries about and with our boys, and we must encourage, even gently pressure them if necessary until they respond. They need a firm, influential hand to provide alternatives, or at least guidance, during a period which should start later and be accompanied by alternative messages related to character, the nature of real strength and personhood. This is by far one of the predominant challenges of modern parenting.

Mother's Role

Given that many dangerously despairing boys are emerging primarily from the middle to upper-middle class, it is fair to assume that most of them were exposed to some form of feminism growing up. However, the early lessons have taken a back seat in the adolescent boy's psyche and can now actually increase their confusion, shame, even anger. The loving messages about the virtue of manly softness and sensitivity, unless continued and supported by others and in other environments right up to adolescence, might as well have been missed. Mother's loving encouragement is drowned out by other, more urgent behavioural dictates as boys deal with both biological and social imperatives to exhibit self-reliant, independent manliness.

However, on some level, boys still remember their mother's hopes and needs as they relate to the boys' thinking and behaviours. In a culture in which a popular teen clothing company sells jeans by virtually promoting sadomasochism and other models of male domination, it is impossible for a boy to adhere to an early directive from his beloved mother. Thus, boys struggle, unknowingly, with the feeling that they have somehow betrayed their mothers, and as a result, adopt another layer of shame.

This discomfort is further compounded by the young boy's new awareness of the sexual dimension of those who were recently just moms, dads, and sisters. This extra shame can make both the *premature kick-off* and the premature expectation of self-reliance a period of excruciating confusion. The levels and origins of shame and insecurity are so nonspecific to the boy to be almost mentally crippling. As one boy told me, he felt as if he was *"out of his mind."* He then smirked and said that he wished he could be. I understood.

Greg Revisited

It is both good and unfortunate that Greg ended up in therapy. The reader will recall that Greg had become fearful of school and, without the understanding and support of his parents, especially his mother, he acted out in a way that both frightened his mother and further pushed her away. Frightened by what he saw as a mandate he could not yet fulfill in terms of independence, self-reliance, and imitative, masculine self-confidence, he retreated to the home. However, his retreat was interpreted as recalcitrance, and he was angrily interrogated about his irresponsibility and apparent resistance to education.

However, Greg's fears were rooted in his social confusion and inability to find a transitional identity through the early to mid-years of forced adolescent independence. He did not discover a hobby, he was uncomfortable with sports, and he had not, at the time of his first session, found an interest, healthy or unhealthy, with which he could carry or camouflage himself to his mid-teens.

Moreover, in that he was self-aware, if initially inarticulate, he was frightened by his own anger, particularly the anger associated with his need for his mother. He also felt *"like a freak,"* he said, because he still wanted to be *"just part of the family"* and needed the familiarity and comfortable confinement of home.

When Greg's mother locked herself away from him, she was confirming Greg's worst fears. By barricading herself, and then his sister in the master bedroom, she inadvertently sent him a powerful message regarding his new, if as yet undefined, role, or, perhaps more accurately, about the loss of his old one. Her fear and her calling to her husband and the boy's father for help further confused him regarding what it was he had become or was supposed to have become in the way of an aggressive male. His own mother feared that he would hurt her, when, in fact, worse in Greg's mind, he actually wanted to be near her and be taken back by her. It was the mean demands of a male-dominant and boy-destroying world from which he wanted *her* to protect *him*, not the other way around.

Before what seemed like Greg's sudden fear of leaving the house and going to school, he had been extremely quiet and withdrawn. In fact, his mother had remarked to friends that her playful, mischievous handful of a boy had suddenly taken on the serious silence of a young man. She noted, jokingly, that it was nice to have some peace and quiet in the home now that he was "growing up." Indeed, prior to several lesser, aggressive episodes, Greg had been unusually quiet.

He had spent a great deal of time in his room, and, unbeknownst to his parents, had been watching television, playing video games, and surfing the Net well into the night. He became exhausted and listless and eventually was both disciplined and mocked for falling asleep during classes. His marks plummeted from very high to very low, and this factor, too, convinced him that he was failing in another critical aspect of what was expected of him.

Greg didn't dare tell anyone—until he was "put" in therapy—that he wasn't ready, that he needed more time as a boy, and that he felt lost and out of place in his new environments and up against new social expectations, particularly as they related to his or *the* model of maleness. He did not and could not have known that other boys his age were experiencing similar anxieties rooted in the same mandate for male independence and self-reliance.

Greg, like so many other boys his age, felt both ostracized from his home, and exiled from the new world of men into which he had been casually thrust. He wasn't yet concerned with his sexuality per se, or his ability to perform as a male. This was still far off for Greg. His paralyzing fear centered around whether he could cut it, whether he could learn to imitate what he was suddenly supposed to be as a man. He was unprepared for the huge challenge of imitative self-re-creation.

Greg could very well have ended up in serious trouble. Before his outbursts, he had exhibited all the characteristics of the presuicidal adolescent. His withdrawal, viewed by his parents as pensiveness and, at worst, sullenness, was actually a major and common symptom of depression. Submerging himself in television and other passive media served to both anaesthetize him and powerfully seduce him with easier realities. As we have seen, and studies show, a retreat into television, and unlimited access and involvement with the Internet, can prepare, program, and equip a child for destructive behaviours.

In Greg's case, he was close to applying what he had unconsciously searched for and found in the way of a compensatory mask. He had been considering suicide. However, when Greg was sneaking home from school, he was unknowingly trying to provoke his parents and precipitate events that would actually keep him alive. He knew he would get in trouble and that his parents would be forced to involve themselves, if angrily and only for a while, in his life again. What he did not foresee was a scene in which his fear would be reflected back to him by his uncomprehending and frightened mother. If Greg had not been placed in therapy, even if at first for the wrong reasons, the chances are that he would have seriously hurt himself.

Greg's mother joined him in his fifth session, and his father in his seventh. Prior to his parents' participation, Greg was beginning to see and to accept his fear as normal. He had carried an enormous amount of guilt related to not wanting to grow up, as well as to what he felt was his perverse need for his mother's love.

Greg's parents were stunned by what had been bothering their son and by how serious his condition was. They came to realize that his suddenly resorting to episodes of rage was the only way he felt that he could get their attention and support. They also realized how close they had come to losing their son.

In spite of the fact that Greg's parents were very busy and had serious anxieties of their own (which, they learned, were also affecting their son, thus further increasing his resistance to growing up and going away), the family sat down and set times for various shared activities. One evening a week, and once on a weekend, they planned and started to do something together outside the home, whether it be attending a sporting event, mountain biking, or going to a movie. They also committed to eating three dinners together as a family each week, and at least one on the weekend. The meals were to be accompanied by conversation related to each individual's day or week, as well as to their worries or concerns.

Initially, both children, Greg especially, did better than the parents. However, eventually, each adult opened up about their concerns at work, fear of a boss, insecurity regarding a new project and so on. The children were fascinated to hear about their parents' lives and thoughts, and the husband and wife learned things about their children and each other that continued to surprise them. An agreed-upon pattern of checking in or intruding upon long periods of silence with their children became not only easier, but mutually relaxing and emotionally beneficial.

At the time of this writing, the family is managing at least two meals a week together and one on the weekend. Holidays and ski weekends, which the parents used to take on their own, now include the children. Greg's short bout of truancy stopped, as did his tantrums. An abundantly insecure boy, he is still periodically frightened and suffers from feelings of inadequacy and inferiority, but he is getting better at talking about his feelings. He has also made one good friend who shares his fear of growing up male. In addition, Greg told me, his friend *"is also a nerd and almost as uncool as I am."*

Greg remained in therapy for a while to further sort out what were reasonable expectations for and of himself. Having teetered on the black side of the thin line, Greg is now a boy who, one can predict, will find his way into adulthood with more than an average degree of insight into his position and power as a man.

SUMMING UP

Just as boys are coming to terms with the necessity of a final detachment from their mother, they are thrust into an unguided scramble toward manhood. They are expected to become self-reliant and independent virtually overnight and to cope with, weed through, and find a way to emulate the unrelenting cultural images related to manhood.

Further, as they are experiencing the usually premature kick-off out of boyhood and toward the roles and expectations imposed on boys and men, they are also disturbed by and struggling to come to terms with sexuality in general as it relates to their new roles with their mothers, sisters, fathers, brothers, and teachers.

One way in which boys attempt to cope with the mandate is to re-create themselves by changing surface behaviours. Boys camouflage their fear and fragility by applying the least ill-fitting mask or style of the month. However, in spite of these stop-gap compensations, boys remain anxious well into their teens and beyond.

Boys also retreat to the home in defiance of the tacit and overt directive of parents and teachers. This is merely a clearer sign that a boy needs both more time and adult support in meeting the mandate to leave boyhood and move on to what all boys secretly perceive as the impossible mandate to grow into what our culture has portrayed as a "real man."

WHAT TO DO

1. Repeated, extended periods of quiet on the part of a child are not normal. Intrude upon him and ask questions related to his feelings and inner and outer worlds.

   A common symptom of early adolescent depression and anger in a boy is his spending interminable hours alone, usually in his room. Until recently, this has rarely been intruded upon by parents, who felt they were giving the boy his privacy. Know that if he is spending this much time alone, he has something on his mind and needs to talk.

2. Do not overreact if your son starts to act out angrily. It will further frighten him. Calmly tell your child that you love him, recognize that something is hurting or frightening him, and that you want to understand. Remember, the early adolescent boy really wants to reconnect with mom.

3. Don't push or tease your 13-year-old boy into full adolescence until he signals that he is ready. He will let you know by joining a community sports group on his own, voluntarily taking on more responsibility at home, getting a part-time job to fund a special interest, asking out a girl, and so on. The right moment is different for each boy and there is no such thing as a late bloomer.

4. Recognize the emotional and character differences among "boy children"

or young, male teens. We tend to group them together, especially socially and in schools, as if they were a homogenized group.

5. Find the time to do things with your son—preferably as a family. This
   can be done while still allowing him the space and the "face" to build an
   identity outside the home.

6. Remember how you felt when you were young, and thought about
   someday having to leave home. Remind your adolescent, in loving ways,
   where home is and that it is still his.

7. Do not threaten a recalcitrant child under 16 with being "out on the
   streets" if he doesn't behave. This threat is never forgotten and creates
   an irrevocable gap between you and him.

8. Fathers—play with your son as much as possible. Shoot hoops, jog,
   play one-on-one hockey, wrestle. Do as much physical activity together
   as possible. It is steadying, bonding, and gives a boy insights into his
   physical strength and aggression. Single mothers can try to bring a
   brother, a boyfriend, or a male friend into this role. A maritally
   separated nurse I know schedules the male orderlies and doctors she
   works with into weekly outings with her only son. Each has come to
   enjoy his time with the boy. The organization Big Brothers is also a
   good option.

9. Again, fathers, recognize that your son can become afraid of you in
   pre-adolescence. Spend more time with him in the ways mentioned in
   recommendation 8 to either maintain or to re-create a bond.

10. Eat with your children at least 3 nights a week. Make it "talk time,"
    when all members of the family share their thoughts and feelings.

11. If all other behaviours seem "normal" and the boy is still communicat-
    ing with the family, allow some slack for purple hair and an earring.
    Regarding the latter, ask about it (or other significant body decorations)
    in an interested and curious way. The less negative reaction, the less
    over-reaction (alienation and acting out) from the boy.

12. Listen to the words your son uses. His choice of words, utterances, and
    phraseology will tell you a lot about what he is feeling and thinking. For
    example, a boy who uses the word "kill" in every sentence is, obviously,
    angry. Even the over-use of the F-word is more an indication of anger

than rebellion. Ask your son why he is using a specific word, how he feels when he uses it, and go from there.

13. Suggest therapy to a child only if he seems to want to talk but cannot share something with you. However, first suggest he talk to a relative or older friend. Boys need to remain connected to family and to feel as "normal" as possible.

14. Watch for any signs that you or another adult is playing the "shame game." Being 13 means feeling almost constant shame. Don't exacerbate or confirm the shame our young boys feel in relation to their resistance to growing up. For example, mocking a boy for not playing football is shaming him in an area that touches on his manhood. The same goes for allowing a sibling, or an adult, to tease a boy for not having a girlfriend. Another common example pertains to his looks. If he is scrawny or heavy or has problems with his complexion, ensure that he is not teased in these areas.

Teenagers and Today's Family

4

I didn't want to bother them. They were so busy. Everyone was so busy. Even a teacher I went to asked if I could come back another time 'cause he had to pick up his kid. No one ever stopped, and I needed someone to stop. Just stop. I thought I was going crazy and that I might, you know, do...like...you know.

—*Luke, 13, a boy with a gun he didn't want to use*

The average middle-class two-parent family in North America consists of a working father and a working mother, and approximately two children. The majority of children necessarily go through early developmental stages while in various forms of nonparental care, thus complicating issues of separation and trust later on.

Through elementary school the family is lucky if it can be together for some time in the evening. Indeed, this has become increasingly rare. Parents are exhausted and driven by lifestyle and income demands and anxieties, and children, especially adolescents, are inadvertently left to navigate through much of the complexities of adolescence on their own.

It is little wonder that while there is some anxiety related to the safety of their children, most parents claim to feel anxious about the state of the world but relatively certain that their children will not be victims of a violent tragedy. Going to secondary school is still perceived as an expected, relatively uneventful stepping stone toward adulthood.

The contemporary family constellation is generally loose, fragmented by disparate schedules, focuses, and concerns, as well as by the estrangement that comes with the combination of individual needs, parental absence, and a lack of intimacy. Children feel guilty and angry because their parents work so hard (and continue to tell them so), and many "good" parents appear to resent their children for not understanding what they perceive as their impossible and unending responsibilities.

Baby boomers in general are more likely to see their own lives speed by and to resent aging than they are to notice the subtle and not-so-subtle changes that take place during the development and maturation of their children. Moreover, today's parents, as well-meaning as they are, are also less likely to notice, or to have the time to acknowledge, what can be significant and serious changes in their children's behaviours.

Case Study

Janice, Mark, Sandi, and Steven

Janice and Mark are hard-working parents to Sandi and Steven, their daughter and son. Janice works long hours in retail and Mark is an assistant manager of a bank. Neither parent went to university prior to working, but they were both determined to ensure a better and more prosperous life for their children. To this end, they made sure that Sandi was able to pursue her dream of becoming a competitive figure skater, and that Steven was able to play hockey in a good junior league.

By the time the children were preteens, the family lived in a lovely home with a huge mortgage, were paying off two cars loans, and had several other large outstanding debts. As a result, both parents worked overtime to fund the children's talents and endeavours. Yet, Janice, in particular, took as much time from her work as she could to meet the organizational and transportation needs of the children. She virtually blueprinted Sandi's and Steven's schedules so that one of the parents got the children to their early practices and related evening and weekend events. When one of them could not do so, Janice arranged for other parents of similarly involved children to taxi the children to and from their activities.

Sandi

Both parents were particularly proud of Sandi. She was a beautiful young "woman" at 12 years of age, and became even more so as she entered adolescence. Moreover, she appeared to be excelling in her figure skating. As expensive as it was, each parent was pleased to see Sandi receive accolades for her grace and skill on the ice. She continued to win competitions, and a new and talented coach eventually took Sandi on as a protegé. Everyone saw her promise, and no one could fathom that she might have problems, especially not her parents.

Thinness is a virtual requisite for competitive figure skating, so Sandi worked at keeping her weight down. She became particularly concerned as she began to develop hips and breasts, and took to beating her thighs (*"to disturb the adipose tissue,"* she said later), as well as to binding her chest so as to continue to look sleek and lithe in her beautiful ice-dancing attire. Pleased to be missing meals due to her school and skating schedules, Sandi began to eat less and less, even at the rare meal shared with others. Eventually she felt best about herself and about life when she went days at a time without ingesting anything at all of any substance.

Unbeknownst to her parents, Sandi was also using one of her mother's credit cards to order food replacements and stimulants that would help her to continue to lose weight. She started to drink large amounts of coffee and to take caffeine-filled, over-the-counter diet and energy-inducing pills to both stay awake when she (often) went without sleep, and to give herself frequent and much-needed boosts. Sandi practised early each morning and well into the evening most nights, and would not have been able to continue had she not pumped herself up with whatever stimulant she had on hand. By the time she was competing at one of the highest levels for her age group, Sandi was jittery, intense, and as skinny as a starving doe. Eventually, she became ill—first fainting during an event, and then at least once a day in a variety of situations and environments. It became increasingly difficult for her to skate, and impossible to hide that she was dangerously thin.

In spite of what Sandi had initially seen as an added effort to be a better figure skater (that is, more likely to win), Sandi's coach had to tell her that she could not coach her anymore. She went further to notify the National Figure Skating Association that Sandi should not be competing. Sandi came undone.

One evening, around the time when Sandi would be getting a ride home, her father received a call from the police. The girl's mother was late doing inventory at the store, and Mark had just gotten in. It hadn't yet occurred to him that his daughter should be home. It still seemed relatively early in the evening. He was, therefore, shocked to hear that his daughter had been found wandering along a four-lane highway, weaving off the shoulder onto the pavement, weeping and screaming into the darkening sky. Mark called Janice immediately.

Sandi was home and had gone to her room by the time Janice had rushed through the rest of her work and arrived home. Mark was in the den, and when he saw Janice he launched into an account of what the police had said, and then stopped and just signalled that their daughter was upstairs. Janice made herself a cup of tea and, exhausted, hungry, and irritable herself, mounted the stairs to talk with her daughter.

Sandi would not talk. Or, more accurately, she talked, but told her mother what she felt her parents would easily accept. School was bothering her, she said, and she had been feeling that she was not skating as well as she could. So, after practice, she went for a walk and ended up semi-lost, along the freeway. Janice nodded as her daughter spoke, and cajoled her about her schoolwork and skating. She was relieved. She hadn't known what to think when she'd heard from her husband. She'd just assumed her daughter had been mugged or worse, and had already been furious and resentful that this could happen to "them" after all she and Mark had done to provide for their children. She offered her daughter some tea, which was declined, and clomped heavily back downstairs to tell Mark that all was well. He had gone to bed.

No one from her school had telephoned or written Janice and Mark about Sandi's dramatic weight loss and altered appearance. The teachers who noticed and were concerned were very busy. In fact, they were overwhelmed by both their teaching duties and more serious problems with student behaviour.

Janice, who had a long-standing weight problem of her own, felt that she understood her daughter's devotion to staying thin and, at one point, relatively recently, had even commended her daughter for her self-discipline and model's figure. Rarely seeing her daughter out of her pajamas or clothing, she had not noticed that Sandi had thinned well past the point of good or even moderate health. Even Sandi was surprised that her mother hadn't brought it up.

By this time, Sandi's friends had noticed her weight loss and had asked if she was sick. One friend had blurted out that Sandi was anorexic, just like a cousin of hers. She'd told her that she had better stop starving herself or she'd end up in a hospital, and possibly even dead. Sandi had just ignored the remark, and decided to avoid the girl and anyone else who mentioned her weight.

The morning after the wandering incident, everyone raced around in their usual fashion. Mark, more silent and serious-looking than usual, was out the door first, and then Janice, to check the work she had rushed through the night before. Steven was being lazy, eating toast and watching a few last minutes of television, and Sandi was in her room, presumably putting the final touches on her hair and makeup.

Steven heard a thud coming from upstairs, and turned down the TV to listen. When the sound didn't reoccur, he resumed watching his show and soon went upstairs to perform his eight-minute prep for school. As he passed his sister's room, he noticed that her door was open, but he thought very little of it until he saw her hand and wrist. They were lying limp at the end of her bed as if they were detached from her body—and they were streaked with blood.

It was at least an hour later when Janice received a call at work from the emergency ward at the hospital. Her mind surged with all the worst possibilities. Mark had been in a car accident! Steven's bus had crashed! Mark had had a heart attack! Interrupting her thoughts, the experienced monotone of an emergency nurse told her that her daughter had been brought in by ambulance, had been treated and was fine, but that Janice should come to get her and to speak to one of the doctors.

Janice was confused. Sandi hadn't had practice that morning. How could she have hurt herself? The nurse must have it wrong. When she asked what was wrong with Sandi, what she had broken, the nurse just urged Janice once more to come in, still assuring her that her daughter was fine. Janice hung up the telephone baffled and annoyed by what seemed like the hospital's apparent lack of cooperation. Why so little information? And why Sandi again? Two days in a row! She muttered something explanatory to her supervisor and strode briskly, more irritated than worried, to her parking space. She wondered whether she would get back in time so as to not have to use a sick day or vacation time.

Janice couldn't believe it. Standing beside her daughter in the lime-green cubicle at the hospital, she argued with the doctor that there was no way her daughter had even thought of slitting her wrists. The doctor admitted that the wounds were superficial and that Sandi clearly hadn't planned to succeed at killing herself by cutting her wrists horizontally, barely beneath the flesh, but he was concerned about the girl. She had deliberately mutilated herself and she was clearly starving herself. He further annoyed Janice when he asked her how she hadn't noticed that her 14-year-old daughter weighed only as much as an 11-year-old.

Flustered and still earnestly argumentative, Janice looked at her daughter, then at the doctor, and at her daughter again, as if it was just now sinking in that her daughter was shrinking away and had tried to commit suicide.

Out of the corner of her eye, she saw Steven huddled in the waiting room. A paramedic was talking to him, and he was shivering and as pale as snow. The man was telling him that he had done the right thing by calling 911. But as Steven watched his mother, her mouth working quickly as if she could talk things backwards, her head pitching from side to side as she glared at the doctor and then at his sister, he felt that he might be in trouble. He had the eerie feeling that he had done something wrong by bringing sirens and uniformed men and doctors into their lives, for seeing his sister's blood, and for bringing all this attention to the otherwise intensely private family.

That night after dinner, Janice asked Mark to turn off the television so that they could talk. Sandi had remained in her room after being brought home from the hospital, and Steven, who had finally made it to school, was trying to do his homework. He was having difficulty concentrating. He still felt that something ominous had happened, and that it would only get worse.

Janice told Mark what Sandi had done and hushed him when he swore in anger. After holding his face in his hands for a full minute, he quietly asked how she was. With a hint of moisture in her eyes, Janice said that she wasn't sure. It had been quite a day. She hadn't known that her "champion-to-be" daughter had been discarded by her expensive coach, and she was still struggling with the doctor's suggestion that Sandi was disturbed and needed therapy. She relaxed a little when her husband whispered to no one in particular that the physician had to be overreacting. He then repeated, almost more as a plea than a statement, that there could be nothing wrong with Sandi that wasn't normal for any teenage girl.

Mark grew more agitated when Janice mentioned that she was told that Steven had been in a state of shock over the incident. Mark appeared to scoff at the notion. Steven had done the right thing, he said. He was cool-headed and had done what he thought was right. This was proof that he was fine. And as for Sandi, they'd let her rest tonight and talk to her tomorrow evening and clear this whole damn thing up.

When Janice mentioned that the doctor had recommended Sandi see a specialist in eating disorders, Mark looked tormented again, and slammed the TV remote onto the coffee table, smashing the back and propelling the batteries to a place out of sight under the sofa. Janice was shocked by this uncharacteristic show of aggression.

There was nothing wrong. There can't be, Mark told himself with muted fear. They would talk to the kids. They'd force Sandi to eat, and that would be that. There wasn't time for this, for dealing with it! He had too much happening at the office, and so much going on at home already that he couldn't get any peace and quiet, or real rest, and he couldn't buy into the doctor's sense of crisis!

Janice nodded, and was relieved that she and Mark agreed about the whole matter. She had just needed to hear it from the other adult in the house. She, too, had more than she could handle at work and at home. And they both knew that they couldn't afford a therapist unless he or she was covered by health insurance. Regardless of why, or with what individual, emotional agendas, they appeared to unite in willing everything to be okay. It would be. It was. Soon Sandi would be skating again, and Steven would tease his sister for her "silly" antics. It would be okay, back to normal. Busy, very busy, but back to normal.

BUSY, BOISTEROUS SILENCE

Janice and Mark are not atypical. Still together, but held together most notably by choking financial pressures, and the care, management, dreams, and ambitions for their children, they really could not see, nor want to see, that their daughter had given them a whopping warning sign and a classic cry for help. Nor had either of them seen this coming. Along with approximately 65 per cent of the North American working population, they pushed themselves each day to show up at jobs they disliked, and spent every penny, and borrowed more, to, provide their children with a comfortable lifestyle. They worked to lower their indebtedness, and their devotion to the children they so loved consisted of providing them with opportunities for self-improvement and the development of their talents.

They had given them everything they had not had as children. Janice, in particular, had periodically spoken of this to Sandi and Steven, proud that she and Mark were able to do better than their parents. All in all, they had been doing an above-average parenting job. But they didn't know their children—neither their frightened, insecure daughter, nor their sensitive and perplexed son. Like many of us, they were too busy doing their best to notice and uncover the insidiously secret nature of formative adolescent pain.

Contemporary families are virtually working to rule. Out of 400 parents interviewed by the International Institute for Child Security, over 85 per cent claimed to wish that they had more time to spend with their children, rather than having to spend exhausting, even unhealthily long hours working to spend money on and for their children. More than 90 per cent admitted to working harder, longer hours as their children entered adolescence. They also stated that they had well-meaningly planned it this way, having worked somewhat less when the children were toddlers.

Moreover, they were quick and correct to point out that the promotions and added responsibilities, along with job and personal insecurity, had hit hard just as their children appeared to be able to more or less take care of themselves. These and other parents admit to the insane nature of their lives, yet only about 30 per cent expressed concern about the mental health or development of their adolescents, mostly because their children's adolescence meant more freedom and less guilt for them as parents. Representative of the majority of families with two working parents, good men and women and fathers and mothers, work themselves to the bone, arrive home late, usually check on the whereabouts of their children, and then fall into bed to start the cycle again. Without a call from the school, a visit from a police officer, or someone's reaction to prominent signs of drug use or other kinds of substance abuse, or behavioural problems, children in the postmodern family are, in a way, imprisoned in freedom.

Adolescent children will attempt to muddle through, either unwilling or unable to ask questions or to share their fears with their parents. Children pick up on the fact that we need them to "be okay" when we are overwhelmed, and if you ask adolescents what they take home to their parents in the way of problems or questions, they are quick to admit to sharing very little. Most also casually admit to understanding why it is that, if they are inclined to do so, they don't get a chance to talk things through with their parents. They do, however, watch and sense their parents' moods, styles, and views, and are unconsciously frantic to maintain a connection to the equivalent of moving, invisible targets.

Adolescents are relearning, relistening, and rewatching for cues they can glean from parents who apparently know their way around in an unprecedentedly complex landscape. In spite of appearances, young adolescents will struggle, in whatever way they can, to avoid being alone in the face of what overwhelms them. And until something better or worse comes along, even a fleeting parent can be modelled, imitated, and internalized.

Our children, adolescent or otherwise, miss nothing. In virtually all families, children sense when there is a lack of love between their parents, when their parents are frightened, and when their parents periodically resent them. The child further takes in everything that he gleaned about each parent and the parents' partnership from toddlerhood to adolescence. This is a fundamental dimension of the child's sense of the world—of relationships, the nature of love, problem-solving skills, and their fundamental sense of security or insecurity. As children sit restively on the edge of adolescence, and then fall into the early throes of the period between childhood and adulthood, they continue to take emotional cues from their parents, especially from the most extreme or expressive one. A fearful parent makes for a fearful child, even though the adolescent's fear can manifest as anger, truancy, or missing curfews. Most importantly, a parent's fearfulness can evoke a kind of contempt in an adolescent child because of the feeling of vulnerability and indirect abandonment associated with the realization that his fears can no longer be soothed by a parent now perceived to be weak. Parents who show their emotional cards in this way confirm the greatest fear of the child—that she is on her own in an impossibly insecure and frightening world, as endorsed by the still-salient teacher and model in her life.

In the case of Sandi and Steven, Sandi, emerging as a teenager, had adopted the intensity of commitment and the related "busy-ness" modelled most extremely by her mother and unquestioned by her father. An anxious child, she, like her mother, submerged herself beyond the point of pleasure, in an activity that represented an investment in her future. Later she would admit that she had disliked the routine, the work, and the sheer pain of competitive figure skating for at least three years.

However, she, too, without coaxing, admitted to it being a kind of sedative or, as she put it, a distraction from her fears, worries, and low self-esteem. As her parents were bragging about her, she was joyless. She began to feel dishonest and fraudulent, and then guilty. Finally, and almost fatally, she felt trapped, out of control, and bound to be revealed as a failure.

Fascinating, if not surprising, when the family went into therapy, Janice spoke of feelings identical to those of her daughter. Janice came to see how she had both imposed her own ambitions on her fragile child and transferred much of her anxiety along with them.

For her part, Sandi adopted the classic mindset of the anorexic. With nothing else in her life that she was able to control, or even, she felt, be honest about, she both took control of something as basic as breathing (eating), and unconsciously sent a message to those around her that she was in trouble.

While Sandi, like most anorexics, did have body image issues (like her mother), she was trying to "shrink away," to "die" in a sense so as to not have to face the responsibility and hardship related to becoming a champion figure skater. Nor was she prepared for the frightening and confusing onset of womanhood. Thrust into stardom in her parents' eyes, as well as in the eyes of others, she had reluctantly tried, but felt she could never be the best. And, as was also the case with her mother, she had pushed herself harder and harder with the passive facilitation of her father. Further, she was barely able to suppress, and only for short periods of time, anxiety related to her sexuality and gender. Her attentiveness to her body, her beauty, was one manifestation of the average adolescent girl's gender-related fears.

TODAY'S FATHERS

The majority of contemporary fathers are facing unforseen frustrations of their own. Many are confused, insecure, and unable to plan and move ahead in their careers. Feeling blocked, they are more likely to experience an extreme version of the slow, heartbreaking erosion of youthful dreams and ambitions, also endured by many adults in previous generations. In fact, now most fathers come home at the end of the day wondering if they will have a job, or the same job, up to or just after the next mortgage payment.

Under these circumstances, studies have shown, husbands and fathers tend to self-isolate. They remove themselves from both healthy familial squabbles and from large or small family (or adolescent) problems. It is their very isolation and resultant lack of involvement that has the effect of further propelling the adolescent child into his own place of isolated and insular confusion, or worse.

As was the case with Sandi and Steven's father, Mark, many men become reluctantly passive in the running of the home, in confronting problems inherent in the marital partnership, and with the raising and guiding of older children. They are busy attempting to fulfil the archaic, but ingrained fiscal role of the father, and many have understandably adopted the dictum "Don't Sweat the Small Stuff," the small stuff being that which happens at home and in no way affects the man's income-earning ability.

In spite of the challenges men face, the role of the contemporary father is, more than ever, a critical one. Whether in a "dispersed" home (historically referred to in the negative as a "broken home") or a centralized home, the dad must play a firmly guiding and loving role with both girl and boy adolescents. In fact, he can play a buffering role in relation to the mother and complement her, with the parents agreeing to this division of labour early. Dad can be either the one an adolescent knows he can go to for advice about whether or not to spend one more summer at camp, or work part-time. Alternatively, mom can play this role, and dad can be the one who shows his children that he is open to their grief and confusion and, in this case, empathize with their sadness about never going back to camp.

In general, the father should have a defined role in the emotional life of his children, picked up early on by his children, and deliberately, actively stepped up just before and during adolescence. Again, in pre-agreement with the mother, there is no reason that the father cannot play the role of the initiator of talk about sex and gender with boys and girls. It would both ground and limit the anxiety experienced by boys, and be soothing to have dad answer questions about boys with his daughter.

Fathers must work well ahead of adolescence at preparing themselves for adolescent trauma, as should mothers. Mom might want to be there, but historically she has usually taken on the onus of talk and preparation, and she might not be the best parent to do so. Gay adolescents, for example, 85 per cent of whom are rejected dramatically by the father when they inform parents of their "non-choice," need the father's support in the way of at least initial calmness.

While contemporary fathers do play a greater role in their adolescents' lives than fathers of previous generations, their role should be active all the way along, intensify during adolescence, and be based on what the father does best. Indeed, fathers should teach young children to tie their shoes, not just mothers; and fathers should visit and telephone an adolescent's teacher to check up on their teenager, not just mothers. Supportive presence and effective guidance are the keys to solid fathering. This kind of involvement also tends to demystify the father. A change in perception experienced by a preadolescent child regarding the father's biology, sexuality, and apparent power, can make the father a positive figure in the adolescent's life.

Boys without the participation or presence of a guiding father figure in their lives grow up in fear. While the girl will search for and try to replace the father in her life, with usually disastrous consequences, the boy will most likely try to emulate him. In lieu of emulation, some boys are also vulnerable to unhealthy adult male attentions due to the underside of their tough compensatory exterior. Boys, like girls, want to be held, both literally and figuratively, by the emotionally and biologically stronger adult. The absence of this experience makes more difficult the teenage re-formational period and has profoundly limiting effects on their adult relationships. This is due to the fact that while some contemporary dads have softened to a degree, and are no longer the only disciplinarians, they are perceived as holding power by virtue of their size and strength. The difference for the adolescent with or without the consistent presence and guidance of a father figure is one centered on security, safety and, as a result, confidence. A present and powerful dad is more likely to keep the child from influential, warping influences outside the home.

However, this also means that a father has to manage his emotionality, especially his fear, within reason, around his children and adolescents. Children are attracted to and frightened by fear in each parent, but a fearful father packs a more powerful punch with a child, and the child will carry the same fearfulness into adolescence. Moreover, the teenager will not go to the father as easily, if at all, if she feels he will be frightened or will overreact.

While the need for the loving arms, even a return to the breast of mother, is sorely intense in the preadolescent and early adolescent child, the need for a sense of solid safety, for a line of defence against the world created by the father, is critically important to the maturing child. With this gate between the child and the world missing, adolescents definitely stumble more dramatically—especially boys.

Steven

Steven played hockey almost as well as Sandi figure skated. However, their mother placed most of her own hopes and broken dreams on the shoulders of her daughter. Steven was a quieter, seemingly simpler child. He was insular, obedient, and helpful. Knowing that he played second fiddle to his older sister seemed not to bother him. He loved his hockey, did fairly well in school, and enjoyed reading old history books alone in his room at night. However, he was, in his own way, silently sad.

In fact, Steven had taken on the sadness and apathy he sensed in his father. In addition, he attempted to attend to his mother's frenetic need for order and vicarious success by being as easy, almost as invisible, as possible. He often made his own meals, and twice a month or so did the grocery shopping for his overextended parents. He was a low-maintenance boy. He asked for virtually nothing, except to be able to make his hockey practices and games.

After he found his sister bleeding from her wrists, and before the family had entered therapy, he became even quieter, less intrusive. He twice overheard his mother comment to a close relative about how thankful she was that he was all right. She'd reassert that Sandi was actually fine too, just "going through a phase," but thank God Steven wasn't "acting out" in some silly, dramatic way as well. Steven was pleased that he was pleasing her. However, he had begun to carry a deep soreness in his heart, and it wasn't until much later that he realized that he had taken on the repressed anxiety of the entire family, especially that of his parents, and of his father in particular.

Rewarded for his passivity, Steven would often see his father in his favourite chair in the den looking at nothing, even though the television was on. Steven felt that his father was looking off somewhere, so as to avoid looking at him, his mother, and his sister. Instinctively, he knew that his father set his eyes where he could bear to have them rest, and he wished that his dad could feel joy, or even just relief, looking at him. Steven would have done anything just to make his father smile.

The boy was also afraid. As the first person to see and then react responsibly to his sister's cutting her wrists, he was confused and periodically nauseated with panic. He wondered if it was he who was seeing and feeling too much, or if those around him were blind and unable to understand the danger that he sensed was still hovering over them. And he knew that neither his newly energized mother, nor his tired, unspeaking father could stand his asking. He wanted to love and protect them. So, he did, knowing something was very wrong.

MODERN CHALLENGES

Remarkably typical, this average family held silent sufferers, and ultimately heard at least one loud call for help. While everything was normal on the surface, something came along to interrupt the busy pattern that kept the constellation in suppressed inertia.

The modern family, like the one in the case study in this chapter, is like a well-mechanized hive. Bees with rank and duties come and go, and come and go again without taking or apparently needing the time for touching, sharing, and revealing connections. Humans, we know, regardless of age, need these connections. Yet, we also have to manage, feed, and sustain the "hive." Scrambling with fiscal, material, social, and educational priorities can make well-meaning parents lose track of their children. It is easy to forget why we are doing what we are doing, and inadvertently leave our adolescents to fend for themselves.

A social, cultural, and institutional problem of a revolutionary era, parents need not blame themselves. However, as fatigued and busy as we are, we can learn new ways to connect and remain connected to our children. We have to. Some of these simple ways, such as eating with our children and scheduling time to do things with them, even if it's just grocery shopping, are good beginnings.

Janice, Mark, and Family Revisited

Though therapy was recommended, Janice and Mark were each reluctant to commit to what could be a costly "family healing." Janice was also vocal about not wanting to be told that they had failed just because there had been a problem with Sandi. She proved to be generally much more annoyed and resistant than Mark. Sandi and Steven, however, seemed remarkably open to the idea.

It became clear relatively soon, after several family sessions, and the same number of single sessions with each member, that this family had some deep and, until now, unspeakable problems. It helped that Janice took advantage of her sessions to speak about herself, and discovered a great deal of repressed grief and personal frustration. In his sessions, Mark did virtually the same. Each parent seemed to be prepared to address their open wounds and secret hurts, almost as if they had wanted to talk to someone for years but had not dared.

Janice had courageously, and with incredible persistence, taken responsibility for the organization of the family. Like an air traffic controller, she had kept track of the routes and destinations of the children and ensured that they got to where they needed to be and home again. This was the primary way in which she showed her love and pride, her intense devotion to her children. However, she became aware that she was expecting too much from them.

Steven, the extremely sensitive "helper," would never complain or act out, and Janice now saw that he had been trying to please her and to expedite her organizational efforts. Janice also came to see that Sandi's driving herself had injured her. In fact, though she was initially incredulous, Janice finally accepted that Sandi was figure skating for her, well beyond the point of enjoyment or fun.

Janice and her daughter both realized that Sandi had felt sufficiently locked into the mandate to please and "be" for her mother, that she felt there was no way out, and no way to control her pain and life in general. Starving herself was a way for Sandi to take control of something in a home and world in which she felt she could control nothing—a form of self-destructive acting out distinctly common to middle- and upper-middle-class, success-oriented families. Consciously, Sandi described her disorder as a way to tell those around her that having to be the best was killing her. Sandi admitted that her dangerous call for help—the superficial but very serious act of self-mutilation—was a precursor to something worse. Sandi admitted that she would probably have attempted suicide in a more effective way had her actions not brought the family into a positive crisis.

Janice was appalled by what she felt she had done. She had to be assisted in not adopting a new, self-destructive theme over which to "self-bash," and encouraged to allow herself some latitude for her own imperfections as a mother and person.

It was no surprise that Mark came undone. On some level, he knew, he had absolved himself of the responsibility for running the home and tending to the children, and had long felt guilty for doing so. Contrary to what his children felt for him, especially in the way of a need for intimacy and active intrusion, he felt that his children were disappointed in him, perhaps even held him in contempt. Indeed, they might have later, especially Steven, but they did not. They merely claimed to miss him, to wish he were more present at home, and to long for his affection.

Mark admitted to deferring to his wife the way he had deferred to his mother. He also admitted to backing down the few times he had thought of speaking to Janice about the family and the children—including what he really felt about Sandi's self-destructive actions. He had wondered about Steven's pliable quietude, probably because it reminded him of his own, and he had also worried about the stress endured by his talented but tightly wound daughter. But he had done and said nothing.

During sessions, he further admitted to having felt, since the incident, that he had let his daughter down by not forcing his wife and himself out of denial regarding their problems. He was furious with himself for allowing Sandi to be pushed so hard. It angered him that neither he nor Janice had noticed or wanted to notice that Sandi was in trouble before things came to a crisis.

Janice listened with astonishment to her husband blaming himself for not intervening. He went on to admit that he knew he had much to deal with regarding his passivity and life-long fear of confrontation. He also admitted to being a follower who admired people like his wife. He didn't blame her for being a "take control" and "just do it" woman.

It was evident, admirable, but worrisome to me that Mark was turning himself inside out dealing with massive, historic fears and patterns in his attempt to help the family. Ultimately, however, I was amazed by his remarkable mental resilience.

Mark and Janice discussed Mark's guilt, and he was surprised by how open, even welcoming, his wife was of his desire to express his fears. She was equally open to his need to participate in the running of the home and family. In fact, Janice was relieved. She had actually been angry carrying the load herself. Mark, in turn, was surprised that she hadn't really enjoyed always being the boss.

Sandi and Steven had individual sessions, as well as sessions with their parents. Both children were shocked by their father's periodically leading the sessions, and by what he was saying about his past role and "present-absence" in their lives. Both children wept at seeing him weep. They welcomed what they saw as his struggle to work his way back into a starring role in the family unit.

Janice was equally surprising to her children when, at a point well along in the family sessions, she put her hand on their father's arm as he spoke, and then spoke about how she had accelerated all their lives for what she now realized were the wrong reasons. She stated outright that she had forgotten to just stop periodically, and to listen to them, speak to them, and to tell them that she loved them regardless of figure-skating awards, hockey prowess, or good behaviour. As she escalated in a self-punitive tone, her children became protective, and supported her with great understanding and affection.

Sandi stayed in relatively intensive therapy for a year, and then came every two weeks to talk and to deal with her potential for controlled self-deprivation. She also spoke regularly to her school counsellor and had weigh-in sessions with her doctor and the school nurse. The family restructured their weeks so that there was always talk time. They also made a pact that they would try to be honest, open, and unafraid with one another. Interestingly, as this was being discussed, Janice reverted somewhat and started to take charge, even bringing a flip chart to one of the sessions. Neither I nor the family could help but tease her until she realized what she was doing—and then even she laughed at her seemingly intractable need to run the show. She and dad, at the direct request of their children, reorganized their schedules, and, as much as was possible, slowed down their daily lives.

Old habits die hard. Indeed, Janice had to be reined in almost daily, but Mark took her on with tender firmness. Each child slowly became more talkative, even periodically argumentative, and Steven became less the obedient little soldier, and more the down-and-dirty, periodically sassy kid. The house was noisier in a lively way, and, as an offshoot of the family's healing, Steven and Mark started to do more things together. Janice, having suffered from migraines, started to have fewer, and she and Sandi found themselves talking and giggling together in Sandi's room once or twice a week when the "boys" were out.

Janice periodically telephones me, excited by what she is still learning about her children, especially her daughter. She also has monthly sessions to help her shed her role as controller. She is now aware that her daughter had started to model her well before the crisis, and Janice, herself, learned much from Sandi's reflected behaviour. Janice now wanted to learn how to relax.

Janice and Mark also took what they could in the way of short holidays together, without the children. They were surprised by how close they could be, but even more so by the effect on Sandi and Steven. The children seemed thrilled and secured by the fact that their parents had a strength or life between them. They also noticed that each time their parents returned from a trip they were even more attentive and more interested in them and their activities.

The story is not picture-perfect, nor was the progress quite as easy as this summary would imply. However, what is written here does depict the fundamental steps taken by the family and their overall healing and success. The family, a year later, has not missed a family "Talk Session" held in the comfort of their home, and each member, including Janice, is more relaxed.

As is the case with too many of us, the pace of the middle-class family can be insane. We stop feeling, noticing, touching, asking, even breathing properly until and unless we are among the increasing number of families faced by a crisis, stopped in our tracks by an illness or some other kind of turmoil. Though it seemed impossible to accomplish, this family slowed down just enough to re-acknowledge each other, and then to actively, even routinely, love.

SUMMING UP

As parents doing the best we can outside and inside the home, it is easier to disconnect from our children than to stay connected and attentive to their changes and challenges. Even those of us who do all we can to provide our children with the best opportunities for growth and personal expression can be keeping time with the treadmill while our children are either miserable or in serious crisis.

We must also remember that, even at the point of early adolescence, children emulate one or both parents, taking on the knots in their parents' inner world. Our fear makes our children fearful; our obvious, prolonged depression both frightens and predisposes them to the dangers of adolescent depression and anxiety.

Similarly, an aggressive parent, whether the aggression is aimed at or literally injures the child or not, can predispose a child to aggression. A passive parent can make for a passive, bullied, and then potentially explosive child.

Regardless of the ages of our children, the constellation of the family is primarily defined and affected by our moods, our actions, and our weaknesses and strengths. To learn to manage what we give off or model in the home is part and parcel of the "new parenting" dealt with in chapter 7. For now, what we need to know is that we define and control the family and its components. An extremely heavy load for older, yet still fragile, at times "childlike" souls, we need new, updated lessons in parenthood and personhood.

We also need the assistance of others, in social, academic, and community organizations, to help us guide and attend to our children. As parents, having committed to being responsible for children, we have to avoid the easy out of being busy and over-extended. We have to find a way to be intimately involved with our adolescents and other children, in spite of the reality of high-velocity living and our apparent commitment to cultural and material expectations.

WHAT TO DO

1. Be open with your preteens and adolescents when appropriate. They miss nothing, and secrets in any family are toxic and can affect an adolescent in unpredictable ways. For example, whispers about money

problems can terrify a child and even lead to shoplifting. More seriously, if there is final talk about a divorce, bring the children into the discussion. They know something is going on, and truth is always better than fantasy.

2. Practise the adage "Less is More," with respect to family "busy-ness." We need to focus more on parenting than on producing opportunities and dubious guarantees for success.

3. Find and make the time for mandatory "FTT"—Family Talk Time. Make this time sacred and stick to it even if often there is merely idle chit-chat, or one or more members expresses boredom or criticism of the process. This time can be soothing and life-saving.

4. Find and take the time to observe your preadolescents and adolescents. Behaviours such as preoccupation, nervousness, lassitude, anxiety, changing habits, and so on, indicate that your children have secret problems.

5. Ask your children about their day, their friends, their courses at school, their teachers, and their thoughts. Stop the treadmill and intrusively ask them to speak to you when you sense that something is bothering them.

6. Try not to view your adolescent's behavioural changes as mere quirky stages. Any new twist in behaviour, such as night wandering, loss of appetite, sudden telephone whispering, should be casually inquired about. For example, a drug experience, or a bad sexual episode (especially for a girl) can throw a teenager off track overnight.

7. Respond positively to your children by dropping what you are doing and listening, hugging them, telling them they're loved, when they do come to share with you or in some way try to get your attention.

8. Manage your moods. Children still take emotional cues from us as their salient models.

9. Have a male join in playing a firm, guiding role in the day-to-day life of a boy and a girl adolescent. If there is no available father, enlist the involvement of an uncle, grandparent, or male friend. Arrangements can also be made through most school systems, community services, or organizations like Big Brothers.

10. Allow children to lead where extraordinary talents and accomplishments are concerned. It is too easy for us to confuse our excitement, enthusiasm, and ambition with theirs.

11. If a normal adolescent crisis occurs—such as the teen is caught shoplifting—stay calm, establish how serious stealing is, and set the punishment; but, importantly, use the opportunity to address other issues related to the family, such as how much time you spend together, whether the adolescent feels loved (usually related to stealing), and what mom and dad can do (concurrent with the punishment!) to make aspects of the adolescent's schoolwork or social life easier.

12. If a serious crisis occurs—such as an attempted suicide, threatened suicide, the expression of physical aggression in the home—resist waiting to address it. Get family help. Immediately contact your family physician. Have the boy or girl see the physician on an emergency basis and have the teenager referred to a mental health professional if necessary. Also, notify the school administration and guidance counsellor. Importantly, throughout this process, keep an eye on the teenager. Treat the crisis as you would a serious illness. (See the Action Plan for Parents, page 227, for more information.)

Competing Influences

5

I got lots of ideas from TV and movies—the best ones from movies. We did all kinds of things before we, or I, got caught. It was really cool while it lasted. We didn't really mean to "kill" anyone, just to act out the scene and get all worked up the way we had before. It's hard to remember, but I don't think we were thinking straight when we killed that lady.

—"Jim," 15, imprisoned for 25 years to
life for killing a 52-year-old woman

Children are profoundly influenced by what they see, hear, and passively experience on television and in films. In fact, they are so effectively inculcated with general and specific acts of violence that FBI specialists have determined that virtually all children who have killed did so either as a result of, or in imitation of, something they saw and became fixated on in a movie or on television. Social psychologists are attaching similar, if less direct, influence to video games and "hate rock."

There is not yet enough community and parental concern regarding the effects of the overuse and unsupervised use of the Internet by adolescents. From the young teenager who learned to build weapons and bombs on the Internet, then constructed them in his garage before committing a mass murder, to the child who found a suicide formula on the Net and then consumed it, there is no question that the unboundaried medium is dangerous to children.

Whether our adolescents protest or not, we must limit their time on-line to, say, an hour, three times a week, and only after they have done their homework. Some parents allow their children to watch television only on weekends. We can also make the Internet less accessible by both limiting the amount of time spent on-line and by positioning the computer in a shared area of the household. Any medium viewed or used in secrecy is even more influencial than it would be were it out in the open.

Case Study

Jake

Jake is the son of a single mother who, from the time he was a toddler, was treated as an equal partner, not as a child. Primarily as a result of the power bestowed on him too early in his development, his behaviours became worrisome and he ended up in therapy.

His mother, a nurse, and an articulate but not formally educated woman, showered the little boy with attention and praise. By the age of ten he was as socially poised as an adult, and was lauded by adults for his polite sensitivity and mature ways. His mother was constantly complimented for his social skills with adults. He was, as his mother repeatedly told others, *"such an easy child."* Only a perceptive mental health professional would have seen trouble behind the sheen of social refinement and rehearsed consideration.

By about age 11 or 12, Jake began to commit some of the normal, dishonest acts experimented with by young adolescents. He stole money from his mother's wallet, as well as from his separated father's and his mother's friends. The only differences between his stealing and that of the normal teenager, were the large amounts that he stole, his articulate denials, and his complete lack of fear or shame at being found out. An overweight young man, he had a feeling of entitlement that protected him from the wise and fair, yet admonishing approach taken by the adults in his life. He denied all and any wrongdoing with remarkable agility, especially when he was alone with his easily convinced mother.

However, periodically, certain aspects of his inner world flared up, like a flash fire. This well-mannered boy would, when denied something (which was rare), transform into a profanity-spitting, verbally, and potentially physically, violent creature, completely foreign to the one person who saw him like this—his mother. She did think of seeking professional help, but would soon forget both the scenes and her fear, and proceed as if all was well. Eventually, after a particularly dramatic outburst, she decided to give therapy a try.

Jake was a morass of overlapping identities and a master storyteller. For example, in spite of the stories that he would bring home about students trying to sell him drugs, another student persecuting him, and a teacher treating him badly, his mother eventually got wind of a rumour that he was bullying other children at school.

Jake had had no friends for years, but when he entered junior secondary school he made one friend whom he saw some weekends, and he also attached himself to a group of adolescents who, on the one hand, mocked him, and on the other hand, allowed him to hang out with them when they were in the mood. The four boys and two girls became his backup. He would approach a boy less popular than himself only with the presence of the group, and persecute him until he would not return to school. Again, when questioned by his mother, he denied the accusation and flipped the tables with detailed, convoluted explanations that she accepted.

Regardless of what she heard about her son's behaviour, the mother maintained the role of supportive advocate. Jake was aware of his mother's supportive naiveté and knew he was lucky. He became visibly threatened and threatening when he thought someone might enter his mother's life who would affect their relationship, make him play second fiddle, or reveal his M.O. He therefore did what he could to keep her split off from any potential partnership with a normal, intelligent, and perceptive adult. It was *his* show.

Another aspect of the boy's life that was significant to his behaviour was that he spent hours alone watching television and videos. He developed imaginary girlfriends, choosing from an array of perfectly figured, large-breasted young girls on programs formulated for adolescents, as well as from adult programming and, with his mother often working the night shift as a nurse, he also watched blue movies into the early morning hours.

Along with his solitary, secret, private life, Jake adopted a seemingly rock-solid self-confidence, even a blatant snobbery toward most others. He was open about his belief that he was destined for a financially successful future. Jake did take his homework and other school assignments seriously, but he also took every opportunity to support his image. He went to great lengths to ensure that female adults were in awe of him, that they viewed him as not just special, but superior. He was excessively charming with teachers who let him get away with it, and evoked sighs of admiration from other adults as he spoke of the few sufficiently prestigious Ivy League schools which he felt were equal to his aspirations and abilities. With just above-average marks, he had his constellation of adult friends (mostly older women) convinced that he was not only destined for an extraordinary future, but that he would make history.

Meanwhile, at school, he played the varied roles of the "fat boy" with other boys whom he enviously called "lucky and cool," the bully with boys less attractive and popular than himself, the "articulate therapist" for a girl or two whom he coveted but with whom he was limited to the role of wise adviser and listener, and the attentive, sometimes witty, but exceptionally mature boy with the majority of his female teachers. None of his private or school-related roles included men. He was wary of them all, and kept them at a distance.

It is worth mentioning that while he joked about and discussed his weight problem with the women in his life, he was also self-admittedly vain and was often teased for his fixation with mirrors. He would examine his reflection at every opportunity and, when there were older women around, ask them for commentary regarding his facial features and sex appeal. Flattered by his openness and apparent trust, the women always reminded him of his handsomeness and assured him that he would grow into his exceptional good looks. It was only with his mother that he periodically alluded to what is a common, torturous obsession that eats at the psyches of overweight boys: he was humiliated by and took great pains to hide his femininely large breasts.

After some difficulty with a new relationship, Jake's mother placated her new male friend by seeing a therapist with Jake. The friend had noticed that the boy seemed guilty and distrustful of him. Jake and his mother attended a few sessions, but kept the focus on the issue of weight loss, thus avoiding talking about other problems. After several sessions, the mother was confident that she could end her therapy but encouraged her son to continue to attend on his own. She hoped he would get some ideas about physical and social activities he could pursue outside the home.

I perceived Jake's manipulative approach to others and his world, and was especially interested in his tonally benign, adult-to-adult criticism of his mother and virtually all the other women in his life. Further, when he spoke surprisingly openly about the hours he spent on the Internet, and hinted, in a subtly provocative way, that he regularly visited pornographic Web sites, I sensed additional and more extreme layers of contempt and disrespect for women. I also picked up on his camouflaged anger.

Given that there was an initial understanding with Jake and his mother that I would be discussing his therapy with her if necessary, I asked Jake's mother to check the history or bookmark option on their Internet connection in order to confirm, define, and time his visits to particular pornographic sites. That she had no idea how to get on-line made the exercise impossible, and it also confirmed the boy's propriety in and control over much that went on in the home. The mother's voluntary ignorance of the technology with which she provided her son allowed Jake to have complete explorative freedom with the medium.

I planned a housecall with his mother while Jake was at school to show her how to get on-line and look into his cyberactivities. Prior to my visit, Jake's mother had had to try to "trick" her son into revealing his password so that we could perform the exploration. Jake was sufficiently certain of his mother's ineptitude with the computer that she managed to get it.

From our explorations on-line, it was clear that the boy was visiting violently pornographic sites that fuelled his secret anger and contempt for women. Jake had been spending significant amounts of time at bondage and other sadomasochistic pornographic sites. He had been fixating on video and pictorial representations of women who were hooded, bound, gagged, strangled, forced to have sex at knifepoint, slapped, spanked, punched, penetrated with dangerous objects, and otherwise tortured. The women were regularly referred to by a word that starts with the letter C. They were primarily depicted lying down or contorted, with their legs spread and their full breasts either sweaty or bloodied.

The mother's reaction to how her son had been spending much of his time alone was pertinent to the boy's problems. At first, she watched with surprise and concern. Then she began to make dismissive, qualifying comments about each bookmarked page and image. She insisted that the images were no indication of her son's thinking, and certainly nothing he would ever imagine acting out.

I allowed her some time to think about what we had viewed together, and a week or so later she telephoned and asked me what she should do about her son's habit. She emphasized that her relationship with Jake was harmonious, mutually supportive, and basically nonadversarial, and she wanted to enlist me to "fix" whatever the problem might be. She had also thought about my suggestion that she set mother-son boundaries and reduce the boy's power in the household. She asked me to "fix" this as well while I addressed other issues with her son. Instead, I asked the mother to come to see me herself. The arrangement between mother and son was explosive, and wreaked of cozy but toxic contempt.

EASY FIXES

Adolescents come face-to-face with a void as they realize how suddenly unsafe they are in a complex world with finitely powerful parents. Rather than make the jump right away into the throes of re-formation, a child subconsciously looks for something else to both fill the void and through which to channel fear. With an unconscious sense of having being tricked and abandoned, children search for someone or something to which to assign new loyalties, as well as for a form of rebellious payback. They also, as was the case with Jake, look for new ways to self-identify and self-project, ways usually affected to some degree by family and other influences.

Television

Very few of us could have imagined raising our children without television. Propped in front of the increasingly refined technology, children of all ages, even infants, become quiet, passive, and focused—a state otherwise induced only through hypnosis or chemical tranquilization. Rightly or wrongly, television has been a godsend to parents living busy lives.

We started leaving our children in front of the TV set when they were very young, even leaning them against pillows when they were newborns as we took a minute to put our feet up. It has become a virtual extension of children, as well as a fundamental and powerful sensory learning environment. Once a child is 10 or 11, for example, he, like most adults, turns on the television first thing upon arriving home. Certain of and secure with its presence, it is the first day-to-day relationship or communication we generally count on and access by merely pushing a button. And it is one with which our involvement, and especially that of our children, is distinctly passive and uncritical.

While the relationship with the television is passive, it is also the primary teacher for most children and plays a predominant role in the formation of their beliefs, values, prejudices, and opinions. Moreover, studies have shown, the average teenager watches TV in a state that is virtually hypnotic, and is thus having a learning experience infinitely more profound than a civics class.

The hypnotic and semihypnotic states in which television is watched aside, no individual could compete with the pychological expertise behind prime-time programming. Programmers and advertisers alike position their products and messages with the guidance of the very psychologists who study adolescent needs and dilemmas, thus creating stimuli perfectly aligned with both the shaky identity of the early to mid-adolescent, as well as with the powerful role played by the adolescent in the home. Indeed, programmers and advertisers know how to reach and influence the adolescent (and adult) mind better than most practising psychologists. The only way we can begin to address the negative effects of extensive television viewing is to limit our child's viewing, check on what he or she is watching, and curtail the passive intake of gratuitous violence and characterized amorality.

Television as Teacher

Adolescents and adults interact approximately one-eighth the amount of time they spend watching television (separately) in a week. Furthermore, the average adolescent watches three to four hours of television a day. If the teen graduates from secondary school, more time will have been spent watching television than in the classroom. It is clear therefore, from what source most adolescents choose their models of behaviour. And the source is customized for limited choices.

Adolescents are powerfully encoded with an array of false messages, including the unreality of quick fixes and the benign, even virtuous nature of violence. For example, they learn that killing pays, and is frequently necessary if one is dissatisfied or has been mistreated. Even if only temporarily, children adopt postures and behaviours almost identical to those picked up from unsupervised or unlimited televison viewing.

From early adolescence to as late as their early twenties, the average adolescent addiction to the one-way relationship with television, combined with what is often a lasting impression made by individually pertinent scenes on television, becomes a determining behavioural factor, and is often *the* triggering factor with regard to dangerous or tragic acting out. Barring the more extreme behaviours, "television teaching" is definitely the adolescent's most influential and handy resource for the imagery with which to fuel unpleasant, hostile, and aggressive interactive patterns.

Studies show that fundamental life skills and academic skills are blunted, even arrested, by television viewing because it measurably reduces the amount of time adolescents spend talking, playing, being physically active, interacting with family or friends, and reading. It has also contributed to the boom in teenage consumerism—the "mall syndrome"—more prevalent in the current generation of teenagers than any other. Adolescents are targeted as the demographic group most likely to be influenced by television advertisements related to a variety of products made synonymous with sexual desirability and the appearance of power and success. Our adolescents have picked up the art of stylish posturing, imitative of real individual and social connections. Moreover, they have sexual relations or "non-relations" much earlier than previous generations partially because the ever-present media message connects self-worth with sexuality and sexual marketability.

The television teacher turns our warnings about AIDS and other sexually communicable diseases into the equivalent of dead air. This is why the medium is so powerful. The medium is the message, as communications guru Marshall McLuhan espoused, and the medium penetrates the passive psyche much more convincingly than our words of worry and wisdom. It is little wonder that AIDS is now more prevalent among adolescents from all socioeconomic groups than among any other demographic group, including those hooked on intravenous drugs.

Similarly, adolescents are smoking more than any other group in North America, and their use of tobacco is on the increase. Indeed, cigarettes have become the contemporary adolescent's first drug of choice. Back on television, and especially in rentable videos, is the protagonist who smokes. Adolescents are once again, in a form much more powerful than other generations experienced, prey to the message that smoking makes one "cool," aloofly rebellious, sexy, and a challenged, if consistent, winner. The positioning of cigarettes in made-for-TV and other movies, as well as in some regular programming, is designed to appeal to the adolescent's need for easy rebellion.

Television and Violence

Jack Fleming, professor of criminology at Northeastern University in Boston, has studied the effects of live television coverage of violent events on adolescents. He has also examined the copycatting of specific violent scenes in both real and filmed-to-be real violence. According to Fleming, adolescents who are predisposed to angry acting out are affected, sometimes even triggered, into action by the repetitive, detailed hype of live coverage of acts of individual violence, especially those involving adolescent homicides. They are further affected by such scenes in popular movies. Dr. James Butterworth, of Harvard University, has come to the same conclusion, and the FBI has an entire unit devoted to the profiling of adolescent copycat killers. John Douglas, former head of the FBI general profiling unit, and now a consultant to various anti-crime and police forces, believes that less emphasis should be placed on whether or not television and film can trigger violent activity among adolescents, and more effort should be placed on limiting the violence-inducing nature of television programming and movies.

Now intensely involved in what he calls an "imitative epidemic" of child homicides, Douglas maintains that catching the child-killer after the fact is as easy as catching flies on flypaper. A half-dozen recent murders took place after child adolescents either viewed repeated coverage of a child-homicide, or watched and memorized a detailed scene from a popular, violent movie. In fact, experts in adolescent criminology assert that the numerous adolescent homicides committed in schools in the last three years of the twentieth century have been copycat murders resulting from the coverage of previous tragedies.

While Dylan Klebold and Eric Harris, who perpetrated the mass murder at Columbine High School, in Littleton, Colorado, in 1999, were acting out a combination of specific film imagery, and had been fascinated by at least two previous adolescent attacks, after watching coverage of the crime, another boy in Taber, Alberta, went to school, and killed one boy and wounded another at W.R. Myers High School. The young men who were convicted at the time of this writing for torturing and murdering Matthew Shepard, a young gay boy in Wyoming, also admit that they got the idea for dragging and torturing the victim from a specific movie. Similarly, teen suicide is often signatured in a way that imitates a self-destructive act from a popular movie, or one that is televised or watched repeatedly on video. A related finding shows that drugs, especially the consumption of alcohol, is a common ingredient in imitative child acts of violence, as well as in teen suicide.

Dr. Butterworth, who also studies the overall effects of the media on our lives and the lives of our youth, explains why we and our children are so profoundly affected and directed by the medium. First, he points to the intense and easy purity of the relationships we develop with television or film characters. The frequency with which we watch television, he says, and the unconscious, imaginative, and customized relationships we form with fictitious characters, makes them into real, loved or hated, influential "friends."

Media characters become critical individuals in the adolescent's frequently complex and lonely world. Moreover, adolescents are watching more television at a time in their development when parents are usually playing a lesser role in their lives. Adolescents get their cues regarding fashion, speech, body language, and attitudes from television and movie characters. They also copy their actions, even their apparent world view. It is only logical that if child-adolescents mimic not us, but much more interesting and intensely positioned media characters, they are not practising the values and behaviours we have taught them. They are being passively programmed to model images that pack an infinitely more pertinent punch.

Most adolescents imitate and identify with negative media characters, and privately obsess over specific, violent representations, without getting into serious trouble. However, the intense identification and the illusion of rapport can lead to aberrant behaviours, depression, anxiety, intensified anger, intolerance, and mood swings—all characteristics of the homicide-at-risk and potentially suicidal adolescent.

It is important to mention that it is not only the image or the TV character that is copied and internalized, but also the amorality running through much adolescent-oriented programming and movies. Many adolescents don't understand why they get into trouble for certain behaviours. They earnestly believe that we are wrong or mixed up ourselves if we admonish them for unacceptable behaviours. In addition to developing intense loyalties to media characters, children, beginning before puberty, absorb the medium's underlying messages. And one of the major lessons is related to behavioural consequences.

Evidence that adolescents virtually live and learn in the morally warped world of TV-land and movieland comes straight from the mouths of troubled children. Among the four boys I interviewed who have killed and are currently in jail, none could initially believe that "all was not okay" with respect to their victims. One boy, incarcerated for life without parole for killing his parents, cried out for his mother for over a year before he could fathom that she was really gone, inaccessible to him, and dead. Further, he had to struggle with the reality that he was the one who'd killed her. He thought, even on the day of the shootings, that he would go home as usual that evening and that his mother would be there, preparing a meal. The episode was over, and, on some level, he believed he could just tune back in or switch channels and catch a rerun in which she would still be alive. Shooting was to make a point, to show how angry he was, and to impose temporary power over his mother—not to kill her.

Video Games

The majority of video games are designed to evoke and escalate the anger of the average male adolescent. He who kills the most people or things in the shortest period of time, under increasingly difficult conditions, wins. Adolescents who otherwise appear to "play nice" descend for hours into these consuming games in the privacy of their bedroom, at a friend's house, or in busy arcades.

The games, too, have been linked to attacks and child homicides. Promoting feelings of power and invulnerability, the games speak perfectly to the frustration, helplessness, and anger characteristic of the inner world of the young to mid-adolescent. While a minority argues that video games are a form of release and relief, a majority of experts agree that they are more "revving" of otherwise repressed aggression than they are releasing of it. One-way, inconsequential aggression which takes the place of conversation, physical activity, or social interaction, video games, also deemed to be addictive, remove children from reality and enable them to live in one customized to their demons. As parents who periodically played old versions in corner stores—in which we attempted to, for example, keep an imaginary car on an impossibly winding road, or keep silver balls from falling into corner pockets—few of us have a real sense of what our children are involved in for hours of intensely focused aggression. We have not known to check, nor have we had the time or energy to do so.

Hate Rock

As focusing of adolescent anger as the bestselling video games, the hardest of the hard rock music—"hate rock"—fuses a repetitious, hypnotic beat with screaming racial slurs and social epithets—against police, teachers, parents, and other authority figures. Unlike the music of, for example, the early 1970s, the current target of the pained, antisocial message is not an involvement in a foreign war or lamentable world leadership. Rather, some contemporary hard rock is replete with gratuitous hate.

Studies, partly funded by law enforcement organizations, show that the hate language, edicts to kill police officers, parents, teachers, oneself, as well as to rape, kick, and torture anyone who causes displeasure, increase male adolescent hostility and related acts of aggression. Just as a hymn is calming, screaming ugly threats over a repetitious beat can trigger an act of aggression at worst, and at best, further confirm and deepen anger especially related to authority.

Troubled children have admitted to being egged on by the ugliest of the ugly "Maff Music" or kill music. In fact, a young Canadian boy, deemed at 14 to be suddenly behaviourally challenged, listened repeatedly to a song with a gorily detailed message about shooting at anyone who bugged adolescents. He was listening to the song on his Walkman as he went into a bank with a sawed-off shotgun and threatened to blow everyone away if they did not cooperate. He had also previously shot at the feet of his friends as he pretended to eliminate his parents, teachers, and rich bank executives. He was arrested for armed robbery and sent to a special school for "challenged" boys.

Parents should treat hate rock as violent pornography, and refuse to buy it for their children or permit it in the home. Moreover, parents are well advised to find out if their children have hidden it, and if they listen to this genre of music elsewhere. In that there are no laws banning hate rock, we should. And we should lobby in the community to limit its availability.

The Internet

Among other things, the Internet can be an adolescent's sexual bonanza. They can see, read, and study images that would make most adults cringe. This is what our contemporary adolescents commonly use to explore sex and sexuality. Moreover, teenagers now view the Internet as a way to rebelliously wander to forbidden places. Typically much more adept with the medium than their parents, they can go to, find, watch and, in a way, be anywhere they want without adult supervision. They can also find what they need, when they need it, to hurt others or themselves.

There is little doubt that the nonsexually active adolescent boy is affected by the many pornographic sites on the Net. The adolescent girl, though usually affected indirectly, is also adopting new defences and approaches, depending on her readiness for sexual activity. For the most part, she is responding to the approaches of a superficially sophisticated and imagery-driven young man confused by what he has at his fingertips in the way of cruel and otherwise ugly representations of the female body and its exploitability.

Sexual exploration and self-discovery via the Internet, combined with television advertising, teen-oriented magazine advertising, and the depiction of adolescents in popular films are more than ever providing young adolescents, even preadolescents, with powerful messages and avenues through which to clarify their confusions. Yet, the clarification, coming from live Net-videos and depictions that place boys and girls in suggestive, usually male-dominant roles, do little to assist in the healthy development of their sexuality. The hints and messages about inflicting pain or otherwise bringing (male) anger into the sex act, further confuses the issue for adolescent males and females. Not coincidentally, the imagery ties in perfectly with the separate gender-related anxieties first faced by adolescent girls and boys. Contemporary adolescents in general are learning tough, rather than touching, lessons about sex.

It is essential that we involve ourselves in the process of pre-adolescent sexual discovery. Neither our silence, nor what some see as the controversially progressive sex education in health class, are competition for the more influential lessons our children learn on the Internet. Sex education should begin with *how* sexual and gender-relations are depicted and move on from there.

In the majority of cases where child homicides have reached massacre-like proportions, the boys doing the shooting were merciless, even more tauntingly brutal with girls. Moreover, there has been a significant rise in matricide, when a single parent is killed by a boy, than there has been in patricide. Girls, statistically speaking, tend to kill neither parent, nor to act out with lethal violence against their peers or against boys in general.

When a child becomes pensive, sullen, seemingly embarrassed, or contrite for no apparent reason around the age of 11 or 12, asking them about sex usually pushes a tender button. At this age, both boys and girls are viewing more images more often and are also considering their own sexual viability. Each has reasons to be fearful and each needs our help in diffusing what commercialization has done to the most common representations of sex and gender. As parents we should not only continue to intrude upon what is otherwise a curtain of privacy around our children's sexual nightmares, but encourage schools to establish ways of doing the same. To intrude is to break into minds otherwise full of dark, murky images of sex that are conveniently supportive of anger in boys, and of depression and self-deprecation in girls.

The Internet also affects school performance. A significant number of middle-class children who were once good students are failing at school and missing opportunities to attend university partly because of the infinite seductions and subjects with which they can become engaged while staring at a computer screen. Chat rooms in which strangers talk about everything from peacemaking to penis length are easily accessible both to preteens and to young adolescents. Using code names, our children can form on-line relationships and lead a secret life while living under the same roof as we do.

The thought-inducing adage "Do YOU know where YOUR children are?" has taken on a whole new meaning. And most of us, much of the time, would have to say no. We should ask who our child is talking to on-line, what they are talking about, and why. Even today, parental inquiry into the secret activities of children is distinctly interruptive of the activity, and diffusing of the "kick."

As is the case with television and TAD (Television Addiction Disorder), IAD (Internet Addiction Disorder) has taken its place in the lexicon of modern psychiatric terminology. A repeated activity or behaviour becomes a disorder when it interferes in a destructive way with other important aspects of an individual's life. In addition to distracting teens from their schoolwork, IAD results in a reduction of social interactions and increased alienation from the family.

With the seeds sown during the "Nintendo years," the disorder also discourages participation in outdoor activities and sports. Our children are among the least physically and mentally fit in the western world. This is partly because we have been slow in limiting the use of technologies with which we want our children to be familiar. The effects of "too much" sedentary, purposeless or destructive use of technology should also be something we ask teachers to assist us in conveying to our children.

If the "medium is the message" and the media can so profoundly influence the thinking and behaviour of adolescents, then parents must become the managers of the quantity and quality of the media intake. More easily said than done, it is not, as some parents I have worked with thought, impossible. We are the bosses. In the home we can set strict limits on what is watched on television and for how long, and there are a variety of ways to restrict where our adolescents can wander on the Internet—whether it be with the use of restrictive software or through repeated investigations and punishments of overuse or abuse.

Big business and its media messengers count on our being too busy to take away or limit that which is immeasurably enticing to our adolescents. We can fit these parental responsibilities into the talk time I have suggested throughout this book. Family time together is time not watching television or surfing the Net.

With the media bigger, better, and more seductively influential than ever, teenagers would be inhuman not to gobble it up and be *directed,* not just influenced, by it. However, as parents and teachers, were we not to explain why, and then to set limits on exposure and usage, we would be condoning the intake of the equivalent of both psychological and physical poison. We have to be as creative as possible to ensure that our voice and our messages have meaning and induce direction in our children.

Jake Revisited

The reader will recall Jake, his hours spent on the Internet, especially at heavy, sadomasochistic pornographic sites, and his mother's disbelief and then surprise at her son's activities and preoccupations.

The absence of a firm, admonishing, and respectful-of-women father figure was a contributing factor to the boy's problems. He had a father in the same city, with whom he stayed on weekends, but whom he also treated as a not very respected friend. The father was kind, eager to help others, but socially insecure and ineffectual. He was also without a female partner. The active inclusion of the father into the boy's life had not been an option for the mother, precisely because the father was so insecure and self-deprecating, as well as deferential to his son. If the contempt that Jake felt for his parents had been addressed much earlier, each member of the family triangle would have benefitted.

After a few sessions during which Jake's mother listened to explanations and recommendations related to Jake's Internet-based sex life, she stopped coming. Much less concerned than the therapist about the boy, she came to view his Internet activities as both an isolated problem, as well as one that could be fixed with one of their usual heart-to-heart chats. She reported to the therapist that Jake had assured her that it was a friend who visited the sexually violent sites, and that he would not allow the friend to do so in the future. To the mother, the isolated problem was solved, and the boy was fine.

This parent, though well-meaning and kind, represents an extreme version of the kind of denial many of us fall into when it comes to the questionable activities of our children. We will hear what we want to hear from a calm and responsive child, and breathe a sigh of relief when the child tells us what we want to hear.

Jake has no doubt continued to go to his favourite sites, but he is undoubtedly more careful, even sneaky, about ensuring that he does not leave a trail. More importantly, the boy is able to continue to gather imagery and information that is consistent with his unhealthy view of women, sexuality, power, and manhood. Having extreme problems with his own masculinity, and a dire fear of men in general, he is finding dangerous solace in at least one medium. Since Jake is a periodic moviegoer and avid television viewer, one can only guess at what other impressions he brings to his already heated and angry hunger.

In short, this young boy is floundering in a maze of fears and insecurities. Historically persecuted at school, virtually friendless, and at once conceited and self-hating, he projects his usually tempered hate onto others, including his mother. The absence of boundaries and his control over his mother have both served him and hurt him. It is interesting to note that in most cases of male child homicides there has been an unusual, usually too close, and repressively contemptuous relationship with a mother. This does not mean that in these cases, the boy's actions were the fault of the mother. Nor does Jake's relationship with his mother guarantee that he will become socially violent. However, it does mean that he is among those who are at high risk for violent, destructive behaviour.

Had Jake's mother continued to work on the problem with another, equipped adult, the mother and son could have been guided back to a healthier mother-child relationship. Moreover, limits would have been set for Jake regarding many aspects of his behaviours and activities. His Net time would have been reduced and monitored, and his involvement in intimate aspects of his mother's life would have been terminated. As a result of the latter measure, both would have had to form into attachments with others.

Many of the recommendations listed below would have been suggested to Jake's mother. Most of them involve our knowing more about where our children go in terms of their media involvement and activities, why they go there, how they react, and why they react or get the relief that they do from the experience. This gives us a rich opportunity to find out what our children are thinking and feeling. In Jake's case, however, I would also have recommended that he see a male therapist regularly, and that a strong male authority figure be introduced into his world.

This boy was dangerously young to be running his own show, and entrusted with complex decisions. And while he would have resisted the loss of control over his and his mother's home, Jake would have been given a renewed, if belated, opportunity to stop faking adulthood, and to be real.

SUMMING UP

Both the American and Canadian Psychiatric Associations have published warnings regarding the negative effects of TV viewing.

Too many adolescents are unmoved by violence, and are ultimately unable to separate the real from the imaginary. From childhood, speculates the National Council on Health and Education in the United States, today's adolescents have viewed over 100,000 murders, 500,000 beatings, stabbings or knock-out blows to the head, 70,000 violent car chases, and 300,000 shootouts.

In addition to being unmoved by killing and hurting others, adolescents have also learned that it is okay to problem-solve with aggression, even, according to some movies and popular music, as a form of virtuous payback.

Moreover, children who kill and survive are shocked when they are faced with the consequences of their actions. Television in particular, whether reporting on or programming violent acts, rarely depicts consequences, the horror and human desecration experienced in a maximum-security prison. Our adolescents still copy what they see, and they will take cues and directives from images that communicate with them the loudest and with the most skill. With the thoughtless introduction of the Internet into virtually every home—as if it were a high-tech toaster—adolescents can now find the ways and means for destructive acting out. At the very least, the latter medium, if not restricted, allows impressionable teenagers access to dark places and sick minds. Never before has there existed the perfect mix of media influences and experiences to fuel the anger of adolescence and increase the chances of losing a troubled child.

WHAT TO DO

1. Make TV time minimal during the week, perhaps only allowable on three weeknights (including Friday) and only for one hour each night. This forces children to make choices about what they really want to watch and allows for supervision by parents.

2. Ensure that children be allowed to watch TV only after the completion of all homework. Make this non-negotiable.

3. Regarding the first two recommendations, enforcement will require ingenuity. Adolescents under 16 should not be left alone for hours anyway, so we should try to have one parent home earlier than the other to supervise. Barring this as a possibility, we can establish shared responsibilities with neighbours whereby we can share the monitoring of television time with like-minded parents. If this, too, is impossible, try the honour system. Feel the TV set when you come home (if it's hot, it's been watched), and vary the time you come home. After a few scrambles, slammed doors, and dimming TV screens, revisit the issue and establish punishments. After giving a young adolescent an opportunity to cooperate, there is nothing wrong with locking the sets in a room. Thankfully, one can buy mobile TV stands. If none of the above works, be prepared to sacrifice. You might have to threaten to remove the television from the home altogether.

   Computers can be locked up. One can still buy PC's that require a key and a password. So, if the PC is in a common room, as it should be, the rule would be to get all homework done that does not require the computer (or the Internet) before a parent or other adult arrives. Then unlock the PC for a limited period of time.

4. As much as possible, watch television with your children. Take note of

what they choose to watch and how they react to the programming. Ask them questions about their insights and thoughts. This may be difficult at first. Many children will most likely prefer to do homework than to "co-watch" with a parent.

5. As much as possible, try to watch television as a family. Discuss aspects of the program during commercials, retreat as much as possible from the notion that television is an automatic, filler activity.

6. Watch television coverage of acts of child and/or school violence with your children and make them talk about their reactions, speculations, opinions, and feelings. Children are more frightened by school-related killings than we are.

7. Be aware of what music your children are listening to, either on their Walkmans, or in the privacy of their rooms. "Hate rock" is extremely popular and entrancing. As is the case with what I have referred to throughout as "intrusions," asking your child how the music makes him feel will not be well received. Strongly encourage the teenager to talk with you about the related feelings of anger, hate, and grief, and suggest other outlets such as hitting a punching bag, working out, running, or playing a sport like rugby. I have known parents to confiscate expensive CDs four times until their son could no longer afford to buy one. This is fine in my opinion. If he then steals one, parents know how desperate the boy is to have his "rhythmic drug" and how far he will go to channel already problematic feelings and potential behaviours. This difficult process is as revealing and healing as it is harrowing.

8. Learn about the Internet. Ask your child to teach you what she knows and make it an activity that you can do together, and a way in which your child can both share things with you and experience the pride of teaching you.

9. Check out the sites (and the history) of where your adolescent spends time on the Internet. This says a lot about his thoughts and concerns. Then, of course, regardless of how difficult it might be, discuss the sites, images and his thoughts and feelings about them. If a site is destructive, suggest that he not go there anymore for reasons which are damaging to him, and then check again sometime later, perhaps a month after the

first talk. Likely, the adolescent will have returned, and then measures such as restrictive software (with a password known only by the parent) or a total lockdown of the computer when the adolescent is not being supervised, is in order.

10. Limit non-research time on the Internet to a half hour a night, and demand that one new fact of a useful nature be learned during each visit.

11. Keep the PC in a shared room, if possible. PCs and modems in bedrooms are irresistible to adolescents, and impossible to monitor by adults.

12. Have at least three dinners together as a family each week. Discuss the news, the crisis of child violence, schoolwork, courses, teachers, and relationships with other students. Again, adolescents will be reluctant to share in these areas, but casually encourage them to, and, in that they will usually be reluctant to talk, especially about their feelings, watch their faces and body language. Note when they try to leave the table or the location of a discussion. To the extent that is possible, get them to stay, or ask them to return if the exit is critical for biological reasons. If they are obviously upset—close to tears, red-faced, shaking, sweating, or breathing heavily—you have learned something. Wait a day or so and approach the teenager on her own later.

13. Share your concern over and position regarding TMN (Too Much Net) and IAD (Internet Addiction Disorder) with the parents of your adolescent's friends. Discuss creative solutions such as the "guard-sharing" suggestion in recommendation 3.

14. Discuss your concerns about the Internet with your child's teachers, the school board, and community groups. Open up the secret, infinite medium to the light of examination and control among all adults who have been taking its use for granted. Cooperative community, school board, and parental regulations might seem less unreasonable to teenagers, and arguably, easier to enforce. Suggestions from other parents, teachers, and members of the community regarding restricting Internet and television usage would also be beneficial.

15. Observe how your child deals with anger and frustration. Also, actually discuss the conscious and unconscious effects of the media with your children from about the age of ten.

16. Have the child recall a particularly memorable scene from a movie or program he watched and which has bothered her by causing night-mares or moments of panic. Explain that this is because television and movies can make very dramatic and extreme incidents seem real, and that daily life is usually less dramatic and more routine. At 10 years of age, a child will listen with interest and actually feel better about cer-tain bothersome images. Adolescents fearful of their feelings of anger will remember the talk periodically and will less passively absorb disturbing images.

17. Take note of what magazines your child is reading (and perhaps hiding). If there is anything tellingly extreme in his room, discuss it with him in the ways suggested in previous recommendations. Again, push past your own embarrassment, and keep asking through his resistance. This is a subject to be addressed by parents, but it is the one parents and children like least to talk about. If necessary, regarding sexually oriented maga-zines and Internet sites, father should talk to the son and the mother should talk to the daughter. It is uncommon, but not unheard of, for adolescent girls to find stimulation at sites on the Internet where they are diminished as females. This is something a strong or "strong for the moment" mother should insist on addressing.

18. Disallow time spent at video arcades until the child is at least 15. Remem-ber: the killing games fuel an adolescent's anger; they don't reduce it.

19. Encourage family exercise. Physical activity as a family—even if it is just a snowball fight in a public park—has long been known to be bonding. We have forgotten that we are less "brain" than we are mammal, and mammals not only instinctively exercise, they instinctively know how to play in packs. In modern families where a sport or other physical activity has been a shared family interest, other so-called damaging factors have been virtually moot. This has been evident in families who ski, do mar-tial arts, rock-climb, mountain bike, and off-road bike racing. Families acquire trust, closeness, mutual protectiveness, and mutual considera-tion by participating in and supporting each other in a shared physical challenge. These families instinctively knew, early on, that this was one way to keep the family constellation close and in view.

Secondary School: Today's
Schoolyards, Hallways, and Classrooms

6

I said I didn't like it, and I didn't, but it was more than that. But how d'you tell your doctor-father and your mom who's a judge that you're afraid to go to school, and that you're not learning anything 'cause there's so much shit going down. They thought wanting to do correspondence courses was for failures and that their university investment money would go down the drain. But, they hadn't ever been there. I wanted to learn, but not there. And I sure as hell couldn't say I was scared of school. They'd've sent me to a shrink!

—Barry, 15, left school in grade 9

Many so-called good, suburban schools have become the equivalent of mild to extreme war zones, and more adolescents than we realize go to school in fear. Teachers are fearful as well. As one American teacher recently put it, *"There's nothing you can do with these damn kamikaze kids! They'll just start shooting in class, and we're all dead bodies on the evening news!"* A Canadian colleague who teaches advantaged but "behaviourally challenged" youth sighed as he counted the increasing number of teenagers arriving at his facility after wielding and threatening someone with sawed-off shotguns. Neither teacher displayed fear, just dismay and resignation.

Teaching has become as difficult as learning, and learning in the contemporary secondary school is a challenge for even the most motivated students. So much about education and teaching is now about control, not curriculum, and for students, it is frequently more about a sense of security than about scholastic achievement.

Case Study

Richard

Richard was a self-disciplined child who had taken pride in high marks and repeated accolades from his teachers in elementary school. He entered junior secondary school with well-polished shoes, a fine new jacket bought with money saved from a summer job, and with an excited and glistening mind to match. Within months, he was a broken boy.

Richard's school had been known for three decades as one of the best in a suburb of the city in which he and his family lived. It was a large school, with a population of 2,500 to 3,500 students. Richard worked immediately at adapting to the sheer enormity and complexity of the building and its systems. Having already decided in elementary school to become a chemical engineer, his goal motivated him to spend several evenings mapping out his timetable and the school hallways so as to move more efficiently around the building. He had his timing from class-to-class, and to study hall, down to a science.

The young man also steadied himself to adapt to the initially fascinating, if slightly scary, behaviour of his fellow students. While there were other new, younger students such as himself, there were students as old as 18 in grades only one or two higher than his. At 12, a year ahead of others his age due to the timing of his birthday and his diligent intelligence, he sat beside 16- and 17-year-olds in several classes. However, he tried to appear undaunted. He chose to look fearless, and had the instincts to know that he needed to main tain the act. At 5 feet 2 inches tall, with unstylishly curly hair and thick glasses, he was, he knew even then, fodder for the fighters. Moreover, he noticed within the first week that the rules that had applied in elementary school did not apply here—that teachers did not take on and set boundaries for the more feisty kids, and that one could virtually disappear in the overcrowded hallways and no one would notice.

Within his first two weeks, Richard witnessed three incidents of swarming and "winding," in which several male students descend on another to pulverize the victim's stomach area until he lies on the floor vomiting or gasping for air. No one ever saw the attacks, of course, and they took place in wide, long hallways so packed with bodies to make the unanimous declaration of ignorance sufficiently plausible to be accepted.

Richard learned to look or move, if possible, in another direction, and to get to where he was meant to be. He didn't want to see—and he sure didn't want to be beaten up. And though he wasn't certain about the rules governing who got attacked and why, he knew he could easily become a victim. In fact, he already suspected that, much of the time, there were no rules or concrete reasons for attacks, harassment, bullying, and stealing among a powerful minority within the school.

An only child, treated with respect and affection by his parents, Richard didn't want to tell them about the environment he went to each day. It was, he thought, like going to prison. He was one of very few students, he had found so far, who were intent upon learning, doing well, contributing to the classes, and pleasing the teachers by being attentive, responsive, and respectful. But the teachers didn't seem to expect this behaviour, nor to have the time or interest to encourage it. They were too focused on trying to impose some control, yelling over the cacophony of classroom antics as they tried to teach. His professor parents didn't need to know.

Within two months, Richard had developed his own method of self-directed learning. Even though the actual teaching time in a 45-minute class was limited to about 10 minutes, and often less, it was clear what the students were to review or read for the next class. He worked hard to make sure that he was up-to-date, even ahead in the readings, and kept well-organized binders representing his work, thoughts, and added musings regarding each subject. And Richard was not upset about not getting the kind of praise he had received in elementary school. He felt good enough about having found a way to keep himself on track amid the chaos.

Into his fifth month, Richard was already a commendable nonentity in his various classes. He was a teacher's dream—no trouble, homework done, and as quiet as a mouse. He did not even raise his hand to answer questions the way he used to, because he had learned quickly that this was one way to draw attention to himself and to increase the chances of becoming a victim in the halls. Teachers knew this too, but he had noticed that when someone did answer a question and was hooted at and mocked, the teachers smiled, mildly admonished the troublemakers, and then went on with the class as if there would be no consequences.

Usually, teachers asked three or four times for answers to questions, not really expecting anyone to volunteer, then made some remark about the class being asleep or not having done the home-work, and then provided the answer. There wasn't any great excite-ment when a student did answer a question, and it was almost as if the teacher didn't dare look too pleased for fear of how he himself might be labelled and picked on by the students.

The teachers seemed almost as aloof as the super-aloof trouble-makers. While Richard found this very strange, he felt that he had it figured out. The teachers needed to stay "cool" with the students (each week, several teachers had their tires slashed and worse), and they couldn't appear to be too thrilled with a kid like him. He also came to understand why they wouldn't dare interfere with what hap-pened in the halls. In a way, they set the tone and modelled self-shrinking behaviours for the initially enthusiastic newcomer.

Richard had learned to guard his textbooks and his notes with his life. Textbooks cost money now, which had surprised his parents, and many students borrowed from each other. Moreover, he had chosen and purchased his binders by colour and size, depending on the course, and he had tabs for different subjects, notes, homework, and supplementary questions and readings. Around test time, he walked the halls gripping his work as if it were the Holy Grail.

It was just before Christmas exams. Richard was not Christian, and though there had been remarks thrown his way in this regard, they didn't really bother him. He had had many discussions with his parents and relatives about religious and racial prejudice, and, from what he could discern, there were many others at school who were not Christians, and who received the same degree of tolerance. He didn't feel that this would ever be the reason for his being singled out in a violent way, even though a few fights related to ethnicity and reli-gion had taken place off school grounds. It would be his size and what he accepted and referred to as his "nerdy" demeanour that would get him hurt if he was not careful. In the schoolyard, for instance, where it was mandatory to spend some recesses due to the overcrowding of the library and cafeterias, he kept to himself and read.

One day he was reading when he was slowly approached by six boys, most twice his size, all older, but all taking the same science exam as he was. Four of them he barely knew because they rarely attended classes, and two he recognized as boys who led the class in antics and what even he had found to be the odd moment of levity. Had they not wanted the only thing he cared about—his textbook and his notes—he would gladly have given them what they demanded.

As a scrum basketball game took place beside them, effectively cutting them off from any view from the school, the boys pushed Richard down and repeatedly kicked him. Richard held on to his books and binders, even used them for protection, but eventually four of the boys were doing a victory dance around his battered body. Two boys were still taking the odd kick and mocking the way he squinted without his now-smashed glasses, when the bell rang and dozens of teenagers started to casually make their way around him and back into the building.

Richard tried to get up as quickly as he could to spare himself more embarrassment, but he did not return to class. Instead, with no way out via the schoolyard, he camouflaged himself in the clump of noisy teenagers reentering the building and stayed close to one student who he was certain was heading toward the main door. He was relieved that no one noticed that he was dripping blood and bruising by the moment. He was even more relieved to find no one at the main door when he went to leave. The security guard was on a short break and the door was open. Usually, he would have to be buzzed out, and would need a pass to leave the school early.

After the mugging, Richard went to an emergency-care clinic, was X-rayed, and told that his nose was broken and that he had a mild concussion. He was also in shock. Against his protestations, his parents were called and his mother came to the hospital. Desolate, and in pain, he assured his mother that he did not want to stay overnight for observation. His mother took notes about what symptoms to watch for and obtained the concerned physician's number. Meanwhile, Richard babbled on about trying out for soccer and getting slammed onto the ground a dozen times. His mother nodded as she attended to the details of his care. She didn't know that the school didn't have a soccer team.

Neither on the quiet ride home, nor that night, did Richard mention the loss of his books, binders, or the fact that he wasn't returning to school. He needed to put some thinking into his story, and to formulate a reasoned argument for transferring to a local private school. He knew he would need all the logic and debating skills he could muster to convince his parents that the benefits of the public school were not for him. He had to think it through, but first he had to try to stop the crying jags and panic that had set in soon after he reached his bedroom. His physical pain was the least of his suffering.

A TENSE ENVIRONMENT

Our children receive and enter school with special I.D.'s and, in most North American public secondary schools, a few minimum-wage security personnel attempt to patrol halls, stairwells, cafeterias, and washrooms. Most teens are part of a middle group of students, deemed sufficiently cool by their peers who have learned to remain neutral, deliberately deaf, dumb, and blind to verbal or physical persecution in the hallways.

There is another group, a small minority, that is regularly persecuted and mocked. For this group of students, a day without persecution is a day with at least a ray of sunshine.

Another formidable minority in secondary schools are the persecutors. They set the emotional tone for the school, as well as in many classes. They are mildly to seriously troubled youth, primarily males with supportive female sidekicks, who either regularly hurl verbal abuse at awkward students, or less often, physically hurt them to a degree befitting their mood. They are powerful adolescent underbosses with whom even most teachers must tacitly bargain for both the space to teach and the appearance of respect.

While keen about new privileges and the concept of a driver's licence, most elementary school graduates will tell you that they would almost prefer to be put back a year than to enter the foreign, coded world of the secondary school. Since most preadolescents are keen about getting at least a high school diploma, they proceed with generally unspoken fears about their physical well-being.

Young adolescents are consciously concerned about looking stupid, being different, getting hurt, bullied, even killed at their school. According to a study conducted by the Committee on Education and Security, under the auspices of the Department of Health and Human Services, today's preadolescent and early adolescent child is more afraid of being killed at school than of being killed in any other way or location. This should shake us to our boots!

As parents, though far from indifferent about the proliferation of child homicides, we are able to be more rational, placate ourselves with the law of averages, and at least limit our concern. Children, however, especially at early adolescence, do not and cannot view death, dying, and school massacres with even mildly tempered logic. In addition to their real fears regarding their vulnerability in huge schools with "huge kids," they are unable to dissociate their experience or potential fate from those of other children whom they feel they know as a result of television coverage, and who went to school and never came home. In short, today's child enters secondary school already in a state of mild to medium trauma.

One thing parents can do to help preadolescents get through this frightening stage is to treat this new beginning and educational transition differently than has been the norm. An earlier case study described a young girl who resented her parents for celebrating her leaving elementary school to go to "grown-up" school. This attitude was damaging the child due to her fear of moving forward into the new environment. We must remember that our children start to consider the reality of secondary school about a quarter of the way into their last year in elementary school. If they have an older sibling, they might start thinking about the transition and fearing it earlier. With children who are 11 or 12 years old, however, we have an advantage. They still overtly need us, want us to provide solutions, and are open to communication. An irony of modern life, a chat about birds, bees, and boys and girls should now be accompanied by a serious talk about how the child feels about going to high school. Today's youth are left with a huge gap in their preparation for adolescence and adolescent education if we do not include this, and ongoing discussions, in their development.

As parents with still-attentive children, we have to choose a quiet time—perhaps just before they go to sleep—and ask about their current school experience first. Children usually lead us to where they need to go; in many cases, preadolescent children hint at their fear of moving on and then leap away from the subject. Without jumping on the hint of the moment, we can bring them back gently and tell them that we have heard that many children are afraid to go to a larger, more confusing school, and ask them if they, too, are afraid. Preadolescent children slide into areas that they usually avoid if we go to the touchy area with quiet words and questions.

The initial discussion will begin and flow relatively easily. It is our job to both listen to and not dismiss our children's fears, but to tell them that there are ways to ensure that they are safe. We should reiterate the lesson taught to them at age 4 or 5: they must ask for help, and not be ashamed of or shamed into silence if they are being hurt, threatened, or suffering as a result of someone else's behaviour. By the time they are confronted with the impossible swirl of new and changeable edicts that come with the role of being an "okay" adolescent, the lesson and its saving principle has gone out the window. We must re-assert the lesson about asking for help and the child's right to safety and security (or lack of fear), over the last year before secondary school. However, we must not overdo it. We run the risk of being too intense and by suffusing our message with our own fears, increase theirs.

BECOMING INVOLVED

Once an adolescent has started secondary school there is nothing wrong with first telling our now-reluctant and distancing child to report any threat to his physical or emotional well-being, and second, to express our concerns to the school's administration and teachers. We can also tell these adults that we have instructed our children to notify us of any academic or behavioural problems they experience in the new school. This does make a difference. Generally, parents have not been known to take this approach. However, establishing a relationship with the school often means that the child is observed, even watched out for, more than others.

One of the reasons children become nameless wanderers of labyrinthine hallways is that we do not help the school know who they are. Our child is a "safer" child if the school knows that we are watching both our child, and the school's effects on her. This is not to say that otherwise educators do not care; it merely means that it is easier for them to care if we point out who our children are and who we are as clients in relation to educational services.

We should not let our children know that we have established this rapport with the school, and we should ask for confidentiality from the administration and teachers in this regard. We have not been out of high school so long that we have forgotten what happens to a child whose parents call the school regarding his protection or well-being. If other students know of what is still an unusual role and involvement, we might as well throw our children straight to the wolves!

Unfortunately, to varying degrees, what happened to Richard is commonplace but not often spoken about, and not worthy of coverage on the nightly news. We are usually reluctant to tell others that our child has become a victim, as if it somehow reflects on us and the child, and schools also prefer to handle these incidents with "discretion." It can be a public relations nightmare for a principal to have to answer for the beating a student has taken in a hallway, even in a classroom. The public relations that count, up front, is the school knowing that we are aware of the possibility of children being hurt or persecuted, and that it had better not happen to ours.

A child can have a good half year in school and seem to be fine but still become a victim of a tough minority of students who make a hobby out of victimizing others. Therefore, we should continue to ask our children how they are doing and feeling at school, as well as what they are learning and how, and under what conditions. Again, several meals a week regularly taken together are conducive to this kind of seemingly casual conversation. A silent, reluctant, adolescent, with anxiety evident in muscle tension and body movement, facial expression and eye movement, is experiencing something directly related to our questions. If we see these signs, we can push the point, either get a response or not, and then call the school. We can ask the teacher or principal pertinent questions, and without sounding alarmed, point out that our child is reluctant to discuss what is going on at school, or has admitted to there being some trouble. Indicate that you will call back in a week, and continue, on and off—every second or third day, for example—to ask your adolescent how things are.

If all parents were to call, or arrange monthly meetings at the school to discuss their adolescents' experiences, one can only imagine what kind of changes would be made in a task currently deemed impossible; that is, watching over every child in the school. In fact, a budget would be sought for either extra teachers or for trained, adult school monitors, in, say, their twenties or early thirties, whose job it would be to not only to patrol the halls and schoolyard, but also to keep their eyes open for anxious or solitary students, to discreetly check on them, and to help direct them to the school guidance counsellor or iniate some other action if necessary. They could also develop managed rapports with potential persecutors, and report victimizing, abusive behaviour or threats. School boards, though not directly responsible for the problem, would have to look into the issue of child security more intensely with, and as a result of, actively involved and watchful parents, and governments would have to fork over more money to support such a widespread and public concern.

VICTIMS AND BULLIES

If we remain involved in our adolescent's education in the ways mentioned above, we drastically reduce the chances of our children becoming victims. Whether it is our child who is being persecuted or singled out and victimized in some way, or someone else's, we must impress upon our children that telling *someone* is the right thing to do. And we should be prepared to be the someone our child comes to and to take over from there.

Victimization is no small dimension of an adolescent's learning environment. Children who endure victimization invariably get hurt, or are damaged psychologically for the long term. In each case of child homicide committed in the last five years, the child or children—adolescents but children nonetheless—had been mercilessly persecuted, mocked, and taunted. They told no one, except in one case, just before retaliation and suicide, and another, during his trial before being sentenced to 112 years in prison.

A lonely, emotionally battered contemporary teen is more likely to lash out in retaliative violence, to snap, than so-called normal adolescents of any other era. It is no coincidence that, at the time of this writing, there are at least three new movies out, each aimed at the pent-up anger in adolescents, and each overflowing with violent scenes of payback and revenge. With the powerful reflex toward violence encoded in all our adolescents, a minority are going to fight back with no sense of the consequences.

Victims are usually younger adolescents who do not belong to any unified group in the school. They are always "different," which is an adolescent crime in and of itself, and they are usually quiet, reticent, and passive during their torturous terms as dispossessed teens. They typically find one friend, usually as "different" or more so than they are, and by choice or by default appear to take their schoolwork seriously. Moreover, they usually do not discuss their social problems; they blame themselves and, on some level, feel they deserve the abuse.

I have dedicated a book to a boy named Gary who I will always remember from school. He was persecuted in what were mild ways compared to the more sophisticated and "creative" ways in which teenagers can now inflict pain on each other. I remember him as being potentially very handsome, but with a severe acne problem, and an abnormal shyness. I suspected even then, in grade 8, that something was going on at home and that no one saw that he needed help with his excruciating fear of other people, especially his peers.

What I found most upsetting was that as Gary would clumsily enter a classroom, trip over someone's book bag, or stutter to answer a question deliberately asked of him by a teacher who knew he didn't know the answer, the class would laugh uproariously and snort with contempt, and the teacher would join in. I used to watch him grow beet red, and once or twice saw him holding back tears.

One Monday morning we were all asked to observe a moment of silence. Gary had lain down on a highway in the darkness of a fall Saturday night and allowed himself to be run over like a helpless animal. I wept quietly during the silence, but I wanted to smash everything in the room, and hurl a few imprecations at the teacher and the class. Gary self-victimized rather than tolerate any more of the drawn-out, daily abuse he took in a system that even then was narrowly tolerant. In retrospect, I have no doubt that Gary blamed and hated himself for not being the kind of person who could feel comfortable, liked, or just left alone.

Victims are found by victimizers within three months of the beginning of a school year. Studies show that the victims have as much to do with the initial attraction as the victimizers, with both sending out mutually attracting signals. With at least 85 per cent of communication being nonverbal in so-called civilized adults, one can only imagine the potency of the same nonverbal emissions in culturally unbridled adolescents. Moreover, the signals emitted from all young girls and boys entering secondary school are "lasered" with anxious intensity.

The victimizer, not unlike the sexual predator, unconsciously peruses the new crop of insecure, vulnerable students and picks up on a "matching message." Then, other personal, psychological factors come into play, and the link between victim and victimizer is made. In research I have conducted on adolescent violence for the Southern California University for Professional Studies, I came upon a study that showed that there is a reciprocal relationship between those who need to hurt others and those who allow themselves to be hurt. Otherwise referred to as the "bully," the victimizer is able to quickly find the one or two adolescents in a school of 3,000 who are least likely to defend themselves. Moreover, a victim will also admit to uncanny meetings, initial bumps and jostles in the hallways, bureaucratically relocated lockers to the proximity of the victimizers, finding themselves in the victimizers favourite eating spot, and so on. Thus a mutually charging relationship is created between the two. In 1999, a young boy in Toronto murdered by marauding boys was a shy, recent Russian immigrant, small for his age and serious about the privilege of getting a North American education. He was with two equally as "different" friends who bolted at the sight of the "cool," larger boys swaggering toward them with the intent to at least harass. The attacking adolescents were restless and angry and asked the boy for a cigarette. He didn't have one, so they kicked him to death. They made a beeline for this boy, sensing that he was prey. And he stood still, did not defend himself, and ended up dead.

"Victim-proofing" our children

No child should suffer being victimized. It can be devastating. We must do everything we can to ensure that our child does not become a victim. As early as possible in their development, we should teach our children positive countenance—a way of walking, carrying themselves, speaking and responding to taunts which make them of no interest whatsoever to a victimizer.

Many parents enrol their children in martial arts courses for the mental benefits they will enjoy. Moreover, women who take self-defence classes report that they have a repelling effect on strange men or potential predators after completing their courses. What has happened is that their body language communicates confidence, strength, and pride. We can teach this to our children by explaining how the way we move, speak, use our eyes, hold our heads, even stand in a lineup, affects others, and then we can rehearse movement and countenance with them. Better still, we can enrol a child who we feel might be "attractively" self-deprecating in her posture and body language, in a martial arts or other confidence-building physical activity.

If an otherwise quiet and shy child or adolescent is interested in acting, we should encourage the creative endeavour for a variety of reasons, one of which, ironically, is for protection. A study has shown that of all the counties in the United States, there is the least amount of overt victimization or bullying in secondary schools in and around Hollywood. Actors generally raise adolescents who are least likely to be victimized or to victimize. According to Dr. Steven Drake, a social-psychologist and researcher in southern California, actor parents model emotional postures in such a way so as to have them picked up by their children at a very young age. Children learn to control and consciously direct their body language, their carriage and countenance, and to "self-trigger" or adopt and sometimes accentuate postures of pride and strength patently convincing to other adolescents.

This same ability, or copied behaviour is typical of the children of ballet dancers, police officers, psychotherapists, emergency physicians and paramedics, surgeons, and commercial airline pilots. Each profession requires that the parent adopt the ability to "register" an emotion, or lack of one, and to hold it convincingly for the sake of others. This skill is modelled for children from day one. And while we do not want to teach our children to fake their feelings, it *is* the equivalent of a noninvasive, preventive mental martial art.

There are children who are never bothered, never approached, and who can even make the odd criticism of abusive behaviour and walk away unscathed. This is due to their uncanny ability to communicate confidence and power. As such, they are both unattractive and confusingly intimidating to the victimizer. Countenance counts, and frequently diffuses the scrambled anger of a bully.

Teaching our children the power of nonverbal communication is a protective gift. Added to the necessity of remaining involved in their school days—by asking them about their experiences, friends and teachers and watching for signs of anxiety—and teaching them early on that informing us about incidents of persecution is right, not shameful or cowardly, we are assisting them to both protect themselves from humiliation (or worse) and increasing their ability to learn in an environment tense with fear.

Richard's case was unusual in that he did not freeze in the headlights from his first days. He thought things out, developed strategies, decided not to be a battered hero, and kept his head down and in his books. However, his intelligent strategy did nothing to affect how he was coming across to those who had been watching him and who ultimately hurt him. Further, in spite of his close relationship with his parents, he purported to be protecting them from what he viewed as a dangerous environment. They did not ask, and he did not tell them, that he was working each day to get past his fear, to avoid getting hurt, and to strain to learn. He thought he could handle the tacitly and overtly threatening situation by himself, even when he caught on to the fact that teachers could not.

In spite of his efforts, however, Richard had been targeted early due to his size, his unusual approach to academics, and his disinterest in cool clothes and common adolescent moves and mores. Moreover, his educated, well-meaning, and loving parents had focused solely on intelligence and good manners as the important social skills, not on how their son might handle or position himself in the stressful new environment of high school. In spite of everything he had going for him, Richard sadly, was a perfect victim.

There is another incentive for our remaining as connected to and as interactive as possible with our preadolescent children right through to early and mid-adolescence; and, significantly, to talking with them about persecution and victimization as it occurs in elementary school and beyond. The incentive lies in the fact that most victimizers are recovered, self-re-created victims. This is not to say that our children will be one or the other. However, all adolescents would be more responsibly educated were they to understand the nature and unacceptability of what they see as normal, harmless school shenanigans.

Victimizers (usually boys, but increasingly girls) can be recognized by loud, boisterous behaviour, a short attention span, minimal to no interest in classes, bragging, rudeness, a presumptuously arrogant posture with teachers, little active interest in the opposite sex, and consistently disruptive behaviour. The victimizer craves attention, and victimizing is one way of getting attention by displaying what he perceives as power. Moreover, the victimizer is rarely a new student. He is generally in his mid-teens and presents a sense of propriety regarding the school, teachers, key locations in the cafeteria, and will commonly even control the comings and goings in the washrooms. At home, the victimizing adolescent is commonly much quieter due to the presence of at least one extremely authoritarian parent, but is prone to tantrums that can be borderline dangerous.

The same early lessons about countenance and the virtue of asking for help would have served the victimizer well. Entering the commonly locked door of an adolescent to talk about the consequences of victimizing behaviour is critical to the adolescent's well-being. Just as importantly, parents should inform the school of the possibility of an adolescent acting out in this way. With the consequences of victimization (and victimizing) being as psychologically and physically damaging and dangerous as we know it is, we are serving the best interests of the teenager, the school, and other students by checking in with the administration and having teachers or monitors report victimizing behaviours. Whether a young adolescent is victimized, or a mid-adolescent is victimizing, each is in trouble. Moreover, neither is learning the little that can still be taught in such tense environments.

Depending on the degree of persecution or abuse indulged in by our victimizing adolescent, certain punishments are in order. Both at home and at school there should be zero tolerance for the issuing of threats. Zero tolerance should also be applied to arbitrary meanness and cruelty, the disruption of classes, and the destruction or theft of another's property. Frequently, when a victimizer is found out, she is embarrassed and amenable to a harsh lecture, statements of disappointment, and no TV for a month. However, if the behaviour is more severe—such as beating up a smaller child in the park or schoolyard—the school should be informed and the adolescent sent to counselling in or outside the school. Brief, weekly telephone discussions should be held between the school administration and a parent (ideally the parent with whom the child has the greatest problem), and the adolescent should be made aware that adults have teamed up to observe and respond to his behaviour. This approach will usually be sufficient to drastically reduce the child's persecuting behaviours.

The adolescent should stay in counselling as the reasons for the bullying behaviours become evident, and they are reduced or eliminated. If the behaviours escalate, or if they were dangerously extreme in the first place (for example, violent assault on a student or teacher or even the issuing of a serious threat), it is only reasonable to bring the police and a social worker into the mix as well. With the child in counselling and on file with the police, the school informed and vigilant, and the family supported in its efforts to help the teenager, the likelihood of a positive outcome is infinitely greater than the traditional approach of repeated punishments and serial suspensions.

With normal adolescent anxiety compounded by fear-related anxiety at the top of the list of impediments to learning, all adolescents benefit from our addressing the issue of school security. Danger, trauma, injury, and even the death of students, not to mention an interrupted education, more often than not come from the inside, not from outside our schools. Moreover, the threats from inside originate, and run their course, usually to tragic consequences, partly because of the overall absence of emotional and physical security among students. The maladapted could at any hour be victimized, and the majority look the other way. The silence and the adaptation to the potential for violence is one fundamental reason for the proliferation of persecution and victimization in our schools.

CHAOTIC CLASSROOMS

A mother recently brought her daughter to me due to the teenager's plummeting grades. Her daughter went from solid A's in her last year of elementary school to C's and D's in her first year of secondary school. The woman had asked the school to assess her daughter and, after a six-month wait, the girl was processed through the school district psychologist's office.

The psychologist told the mother over the telephone that her daughter probably did not have a learning disability, but that the young teenager was *"not working to her capacity," "periodically inattentive," "easily distracted and probably suffered from ADD"* [attention deficit disorder]. The girl's mother received a written report in the mail and there was no follow-up. The mother didn't fully understand the psychologist's report and, after reading about ADD, did not think that her daughter had it. However, the child now felt that there was something wrong with her.

In a third session with me, the girl's explanation for her problems, muttered in response to my questions about her scholastic performance, her habits at school, and her relationships with other students and teachers, was also confusing to her worried mother. She said that she could not concentrate in the loud, yelling "craziness" that typified most of her classes. She further admitted that she was afraid to say anything to her teachers, having been told that her statement would not make any difference, and would probably make its way back to the students who caused the turmoil. She was also afraid to offend teachers who *seemed* to accept the situation. She told me about her friend's sister, two years ahead of her in school, who was persecuted for telling students to *"shut up so that [she] could hear."* She had left school three months later with a nervous condition and was now doing correspondence courses.

The young girl could not learn in a state of compounded anxiety *and* nervous apprehension. *No one can.* It took only the few sessions for me to see that this determined, bright girl was, normally, developmentally anxious, but also fearful and nervous every minute she was in a classroom and in school. She was even fearful of the behaviours of some of the teachers who seemed to encourage arguments among students, and who even swore back at them as if they were buddies hanging out at the mall. She could not hear the teacher on some days, and on many days, she felt as if her brain just shut down against her will.

While some children can concentrate sufficiently to manage a decent grade point average, most admit to it being a feat of mental endurance and, in effect, home learning. That is, they re-study at night, what was, they think, taught during the day, and try to stay abreast of both precise course content and potential test questions. The same IICS that looked into adolescents' fear of secondary school found that 60 per cent of students who manage to learn their coursework under their current conditions claim to be exhausted and frustrated by the difficulties of learning in their school environments. All students also admitted to being angry that they should have to strain and strategize to learn.

Real learning takes place when a child feels relaxed, accepted by other students, and liked by their teachers. Private schools for the affluent have been creating just such an atmosphere for hundreds of years, and their students are generally both literate and well-rounded, not to mention advantaged when they enter university and the job market. When a child is fearful or anxious or both, her creative thinking freezes and her logical and analytic thinking revs to compensate and then virtually stalls.

A fearful, young adolescent can try harder and harder, only to find that she cannot think. When the mind is forced into a losing battle, especially when it is pushed in a state of fear, it buckles in primitive self-defence.

Aggravating this primitive, defensive reflex is the recently discovered fact that during the re-formational stage—the early teen years—children revert, for much of their "non-thinking," to an area in the left, temporal lobe of the brain called the amygdala. This part of the brain, sometimes referred to as the "old brain," is, according to neuroscientists, the *only* brain we used when we were at the evolutionary stage of reptiles. And we still have it, and it still plays a role in our lives and experiences, especially in our limited reactivity.

The amygdala is nonreasoning, non-deductive, and solely dedicated to survival. This is a handy explanation for why some of us wonder whether our child has suffered a head injury since we last saw him due to his sudden and apparent dull-wittedness. More seriously, it plays a part in the irrational thinking, the fears, and the various forms of acting out evident during early adolescence. This discovery regarding a kind of mental regression among young adolescents also strongly suggests that schools and classrooms that are chaotic, loud, and open to unpredictable behaviours and incidents are not learning environments for most children. Rather, they are overstimulating, and induce defensive mental and emotional reactivity.

The young girl in the example mentioned above had mental mechanisms that remained open and in fine form in the tidy order or discipline of the elementary school. However, once she reached secondary school, she was among the many students who find it difficult to concentrate. Above and beyond the noise and disorder, primitive mental mechanisms, more poised to take over in early adolescence than at any stage other than infancy, kick in, and reasoning skills and other thinking and learning processes kick out.

When the girl's mother was finally convinced of what the problem was, she was at a loss. In her words, *"Well, I can't change the school system, she'll just have to get used to it!"* Many adolescents *cannot* get used to it. Moreover, this otherwise concerned mother had no idea about the environment her daughter was going to each day. I suggested that she go to the school mid-morning and talk first to a guidance counsellor about her adolescent's fear, and second, to the school administration. The woman went to the school, and was assured that her daughter would be observed, but she was also told that her daughter would ultimately adapt to the unavoidable chaos. We hope. Given what the parent saw in the hallways and heard through closed classroom doors, she doubted it.

I further instructed the mother to urge her daughter to talk about her fears. By first apologizing for not knowing what her daughter had been enduring, and then asking for examples of difficult moments in her daughter's days at school, she induced her child to share her anxieties. The girl was scared of the pushing and shoving of smaller students by students twice their size, and was also nervous about her own physical vulnerability. She did not have attention deficit disorder. Rather, the school itself was in a state of disorder, and students who were so inclined took control of classrooms and hallways to persecute and inadvertently undermine the sense of security of other children. A place of optimal learning the school was not, nor of even moderate developmental comfort.

It is vital that we both check in with our children by asking them about what goes on at school, and viewing their academic progress in light of what they tell us about their experiences. While I repeat that teachers and administrators are not to blame for the ills of our schools, they are also not sufficiently challenged or supported by parents to improve the learning environment.

Furthermore, we cannot expect that modern learning complexes can adequately educate our children. While forcing older elementary and secondary school students to read at home is almost as shocking as asking them to do windows, it is a suggestion I have made to many parents and which has had a positive effect on the adolescents' marks and level of confidence. For example, making it mandatory that a teenager read certain parts of the newspaper, or newsmagazine at least twice a week, and then report over dinner on what she has read, is an excellent way to help the child improve her reading and interpretive skills. It is also conducive to debating and to further understanding the thinking and views of the child.

Taken further, we can place "information boards" in a hallway or in the kitchen, where we post short articles on a variety of subjects, and ask that by the end of each week our children be prepared to discuss them. When this is encouraged in a light, participatory, but mandatory, way, adolescents end up significantly ahead of those who do not read.

In a study done by the National Literacy Coalition (an American group of academics, politicians, teachers, and mental health professionals), which included 300 parents, only .04 per cent (14 parents) said that they "sometimes forced their children to read." All 300 referred to the barriers of time and energy as the reasons for what most felt was remiss on their part as parents. The barriers are valid, and so are the barriers to secure and exciting learning faced by our teenagers.

With teachers and administrators aware of our concerns and our involvement, learning environments that frequently feel unsafe and out of control can improve. Education, no longer what it was even ten years ago, can no longer be just the job of a few educators equipped with sparse learning resources, trying to teach in the environmental equivalent of relatively attractive prisons.

Security and learning come together, as do insecurity and closed minds. First, it is our role as parents to initiate discussions with our adolescents about victimization and safety, and to address our concerns with those who harness our children for much of their day. Second, given the current state of large classes, the limited number of often-exhausted teachers, and the apparent impossibility of establishing order in schools, we also have to supplement our children's learning at home.

Richard Revisited

In spite of Richard's trauma, within a few days he was talking to his parents about going to a private school. He still avoided talking about his feelings, and his parents felt that waiting for him to bring it up was the best approach. He appeared to be casual and philosophical about the switch to a different kind of school, and expressed intense gratitude to a deceased grandmother who had left him some money for education. He didn't know what he would have done could he not have continued his education elsewhere, but he would have "left the earth" before he would ever return to that environment.

What Richard did not know is that after he had insisted on being brought home from the hospital, his mother had telephoned the school and had spoken to the vice-principal about the apparent soccer injury. She wasn't surprised to hear that there was no soccer team, but she was surprised that the administrator was unaware of Richard's beating.

The mother wasted no time and few words in describing her son's injuries. When she finished her story, the befuddled and unprepared man checked the computerized absence list and saw that the unusually punctual and consistently attending boy had not been to school for three days. He told Richard's mother that he did not know that the incident had happened, and that as far as he knew, none of his teachers did either. All he could say was that he was upset and that he would look into the matter. In fact, he was sufficiently upset that he was likely wiping his moistened brow as he tried to find the correct words to manage this potentially litigious situation. He apologized profusely, told Richard's mother that he would look into the matter and get back to her, and asked her to say hello and to pass on his concern and an apology to her son. That was that.

No student had reported the incident and none of the teachers present at the next staff meeting seemed to know anything about it. There was little the vice-principal could do but write a carefully worded letter of apology and suggest that Richard should have come straight to the office and reported the boys who beat him up. He was not unaware of how the bright young boy would react to this unrealistic suggestion. But it was all he could recommend.

Richard asked his parents if he could talk to someone professionally. They were surprised but glad that he could take such a step without feeling that there was something wrong with him. Later, I would suggest to his parents that they should have asked him at that point, if not earlier, what his real feelings were about being grabbed, pushed to the ground, beaten until he bled, and robbed of his most cherished possessions. I further suggested that they might have asked him immediately upon arriving home, or when he felt well enough to talk.

Even in the first session with Richard, he attempted to manage the session in such a way as to be as little trouble as possible. He downplayed the incident and his injuries and said that he was merely concerned that he kept having nightmares and sudden anxiety attacks during the day. We talked about this aspect of his fear, and about his nightmares, and eventually got to the incident itself.

Richard was bulging with contained rage and grief. He felt violated. He even went as far as to say, *"The way a girl might feel if she were..."* and he stopped. He did feel a part of himself had been taken from him and that his strategic exterior had been penetrated. He now had to find a new way to be in the world, and with other adolescents, even with his parents, because he felt so horribly exposed.

He was also experiencing a classic loss of innocence. His formative beliefs about other people, about learning, knowledge, school and education had been challenged. He wasn't even sure that he could handle the private school.

With Richard's reluctant permission, his parents came to a session and he told them much of what he'd told me. They were saddened that he hadn't come to them, and angry at themselves for taking their boy's social competency for granted. Their son was protecting them, and they were being considerate of his right to privacy. But it had been too early to allow him so much freedom and responsibility. He had been such a good kid that the sophisticated parents had treated him as if he were another adult and friend. Their approach to Richard changed, especially as he entered the new, tamer school. They were glad that, though private, it was a day school that allowed them to spend time with Richard in the evenings, and work on problems with their son.

After explaining the circumstances to the headmaster, they arranged for Richard to check in with the excellent school counselling service whenever he wanted to, and he and his parents had a chat at least once a week. Richard began to change. He had never been a very affectionate child, nor had his parents been openly affectionate, and they found him receptive to the odd hug and good-night chats with one or the other parent sitting on the side of his bed. They asked him so often how and what he was feeling that he would make a joke out of reporting before being asked each morning at breakfast. However, they all knew that the joke was a kind of relief, a statement of gratitude that things had changed and that so much inner tension in the young boy had been released as a result of the crisis. And while no private school is a perfect learning or living environment, the elements of order and discipline worked fine for Richard.

Richard continued to see me in private sessions once a month for almost a year. His panic attacks and nightmares tapered off as he spoke more and more about his feelings related to the incident, as well as about earlier fears he had never voiced.

His parents came three or four more times to ensure that they were addressing this bright boy in the right ways and to the right degrees. I urged them not to be overly cautious, but, to remain open to Richard and to be directly inquisitive if he seemed closed or quiet.

Though they were concerned, they were also heart-warmingly excited. They were experiencing their child growing younger in order to grow up, and they were having fun with him. They realized that there had not been enough play, silliness, and roughhousing for this exceptionally bright only child. They knew they were lucky to have a second chance to know and be intimate with their child.

Little explanation is required where Richard's parents are concerned. They just did not see any reason to ask their son about school, his teachers, his classes, or his feelings. They thought he was fine because he behaved as if he were. However, they had never seen him behave in any other way. With all our children, regardless of whether or not they exhibit strange behaviours or seem emotional, we have to ask about their social and educational experiences. With their going into an insecure environment already uncertain and anxious, how could there not be challenges, worries, new anxieties, and problems? As Richard's parents found out, the onus was on them to ask, not for Richard to tell them. Moreover, they learned, appearances with a young adolescent are about as much of a reflection of reality as tea leaves.

SUMMING UP

Secondary school is a frightening prospect to the preadolescent, and should be discussed with the child before the end of elementary school. The child should know, even before entering this next level in her social life and education, that we are aware, involved, and supportive, even if they are pushing away from us.

Young adolescents are fearful of these large, comparatively chaotic schools. They fear being harmed due to the prevalence of victimization; they are also fearful as a result of the media coverage at school shootings and other attacks.

Parents should regularly inquire about their children's classes, relationships, teachers, and their feelings about going to school. In this way, we are equipped to watch for physical signs of anxiety or fear in our children.

Furthermore, parents are wise to establish a rapport with administration and teachers at the beginning of the school year to show that they are concerned about student security, but also to indicate a degree of support for and understanding of educators' impossible mandate.

Parents should immediately address any statement or sign from their child regarding persecution or abuse, whether it be of their child or someone else's.

Parents should also address the issue of victimization by having children learn the art of non-aggressive self-protection, something they will carry with them well into an empowered adulthood.

In that adolescents experience compounded insecurity in secondary schools, an impediment to learning in environments already too crowded and usually chaotic to fully prepare them in key areas such as reading and mathematics, we should provide children with exercises to do at least twice a week, and then discuss them with them. Education is no longer just a school experience; it requires parents linked with teachers in complementing and mutually assisting activities beneficial to and protective of all adolescent youth.

WHAT TO DO

1. Bring up the subject of secondary school while your children are still in elementary school. They are concerned about the transition to the new school, and we can assist them in dealing with their anxiety. It is best to broach the subject by asking how they feel about the change during a meal, while taking a walk with them, or during a shared activity such as washing the dishes or the family car.

2. Before a child starts secondary school, contact the vice-principal and communicate any concerns expressed by your child, as well as your own.

3. Regularly ask your teenagers about their experiences with other students, in classes, in the hallways, cafeteria, and so on. Generally, they will not tell us if they are having problems. We have to ask.

4. If your child shows any indication of being victimized, contact and meet with school officials immediately. At the very least, there are long-term effects of adolescent victimization or persecution.

5. Contact the school and report the victimization of other children if you hear about it.

6. Know all your children's teachers by name—ideally by their first name—as if they are our associates or partners in caring for our teens. This makes a significant difference when we want to work with them on a problem.

7. If your child's academic progress falters, first ask him direct questions about the nature of his classes, the teaching style of specific teachers, and how the other students are doing and behaving. If a child's grades fall suddenly, there is invariably an emotional factor involved.

8. Give your children the opportunity to learn a martial art, or introduce them to acting or some other activity that teaches them about how body language and level of confidence affects victimizers. This is an enormous, lifelong gift and certain protection against persecution.

9. If your child is victimizing others, notify the school, arrange a counselling session at the school, as well as one outside the school for the child and family. If the child is even moderately physically aggressive, ensure that he is on file with the police and tell him so. This kind of parental intervention has recently resulted in the halting of serious plans to attack fellow students in large suburban schools.

10. Encourage your child to read and do other mental exercises. Discuss these exercises with the child in an enjoyable way over a meal or when you find him sitting alone in his room. Mandatory home learning is a necessary weekly supplement to the current inadequacies of the secondary school system.

The New Parenting

7

What are we supposed to do? Go to school with our 13-year-olds? My child is frightened and what can I tell her? She's suddenly older and cynical, and she doesn't see any point in even going to school, or in growing up. A few days after it happened, after she found out we were separating, she told me that she knew her father and I were scared all the time too, and that we hated our lives. I didn't know what to say, so I lied to her because she was scarily right on the mark. We are scared, but she's terrified. And what can I possibly do to change her view of life, and of her own damn parents?

—*unhappy mother of a fearful adolescent girl*

Parenting is never easy. It is more than having a baby. It is the art, science, patience, applied common sense, and sheer grit required to raise a human being. At the supposedly easiest of times, it is the hardest of tasks.

Generally, those of us who are parents to contemporary adolescents are a unique breed. High- and low-end baby boomers, studies show, claim to have attempted to adopt a parenting style both less punitive and more dialogue-oriented than any generation of parents before them. However, the same group decided to have children and brought infants into the world in a completely different social, political, and economic context than the one in which they now, as parents, face.

Today's parents speak of their fearful inability to cope. This includes their feeling inadequate and insecure in their jobs, being financially behind where they thought they would be by this time in their lives, and attempting to manage adolescent children who push them to the end of their short emotional ropes. In spite of our being a generation that has attempted to talk more openly with our children, we are not faring that much better or, in some cases, as well as our parents did with us. Our children are alienated from us, they act out, and both children and parents face unforseen influences and challenges in what is a periodically overwhelming world. We did not see certain lifestyle-changing circumstances coming, nor did we ever plan to parent under contemporary social and global conditions. There is so much to explain to our children that, were they to ask us, we would have to admit that we haven't got a clue.

We are also the generation that was to transform the word "parent" from a noun to a verb. We have always felt strongly about involving ourselves in our children's lives, as opposed to merely putting food on the table, making sure they go to school, and providing efficient discipline when necessary. We had planned to do so much more, and many of us are quietly frustrated by the circumstances that have removed us from our children.

We have also been described as "kids raising kids," due to what has been referred to as our relatively unchallenging childhoods and our reluctance to mature. Children of children of the Depression, and, for the most part, children who escaped the direct effects of war, baby boomers have been described as regressed and sophomoric, narcissistic and fearful of adulthood and aging. We are also more consumption-oriented (a reaction to the Depression mentality of our parents) and more inclined to use credit and to live beyond our means than any previous generation. Moreover, we apparently displayed these characteristics before we were hit with the social and economic changes that knocked our socks off. We were also exhibiting these characteristics before we had children and became parents.

We know that there is episodic danger in our organizations and workplaces. We see and sometimes know those who drop out, either violently or in quiet illness. However, we were never prepared to think of our children going to unsafe places to learn arithmetic, or to keep tabs on their bedroom nightlife in their preteens due to the easy access to danger provided by information technology. Nor, when we propped them in front of the television set, did we realize that we were sowing the seeds for both an addiction and the inculcation of ideas, beliefs, and behaviours foreign to any we would have taught or even thought of in relation to our children.

A "young" breed of parents, we still attempt to hold to ideals as we sense our children moving further and further away from us as a result of the pull of influences much greater than our will to talk or our proclamations of love. And while we are apparently not fearful that it will be *our* child who is killed in a schoolyard (or, at least, not as fearful as our children), our sense of helplessness and frustration is proportionate with our early enthusiasm to actively love and sacrifice for our children.

However, our lifestyles have made this difficult. As much as some of us have remained devoted to early promises related to the raising of our children, many of us lack the time or energy to do so, especially if we are also intent on providing as much as possible for our children and ourselves in the way of material comforts. As studies show, we are fatigued, frightened, and often as frustrated with respect to our identity as are our preadolescent and adolescent children. More than previous generations, we have had to change our perspectives on the spot. We have either given up on our dreams, left stressful careers voluntarily or involuntarily, or been the victims of organizational change. We were unprepared for what confronted us as adults, just as we find ourselves unprepared to parent adolescents in these revolutionary times. In all fairness to the panicked parent, we could not have known.

Case Study

Peter

Peter is the only son of a father who is a successful architect and a mother who is a financial planner. School bored him even at the elementary level, and after a few years in high school his parents gave him a chance to apply himself in the real world. They were personally embarrassed by their boy's "failure," but hoped that he would be one of a rare breed that finds prosperity and satisfaction without the benefits of education. Peter was articulate and had the air of the educated upper-middle class, and his parents hoped that this would serve him well.

Peter asked his father for a start-up loan. He had an older partner, necessary because Peter was only 15, and they needed computer equipment on which to input customer names, job details, invoices, and schedules in what was to be a growing landscaping business focusing on high-income neighbourhoods. Impressed with the idea, his father lent him the money with the understanding that it would be paid back when Peter and his partner were solvent. They shook on the agreement.

Both Peter's parents were astounded. Within months their son was driving a new ATV and barely had time to visit them. He was also travelling, which his parents found strange but interesting. They assumed that he or his partner had contacts in other parts of the continent where landscaping was needed. The father pictured his son having to find labour and write contracts. He kidded that his boy, who used to be a source of worry and a bit of an embarrassment, was soon going to be able to support him! He didn't care that his son hadn't paid back the start-up loan.

Then, one evening when Peter's parents returned late from work, they found a card in their mailbox from the U.S. Postal Inspection Service and the RCMP. The card had a note scribbled on the back asking that one of them call a specific number and ask for a specific agent the next day. They wondered if something they had mailed to a relative had been mistaken for something else, or if something was on the way to them.

The next day, the doorbell rang as they were eating breakfast. The husband went to the door. Slightly perturbed, and very curious, he backed up as two men showed him their official badges. He thought he saw "FBI" at the top of the postal inspector's badge. His wife joined the men as they settled in the living room. She offered coffee and left to prepare it.

By the time she came back, her husband had admitted to recognizing the name of his son, but insisted that Peter had done nothing wrong, nor was involved in criminal activity.

The investigators told the parents that their son had been dealing in illicit drugs and child pornography via the Internet for a little over three years. The men asked if the parents knew that their son had offices, with an associate, in three major cities, and that he had acquired, before he was of legal age, both a fake driver's licence and a Mercedes.

The parents were aghast. The father, having done the math, realized that his son had started these apparent activities in his own room, on his home computer. Visibly upset, and desperate to hear his son's side of the story, the father left the room. More stoic, and apparently less shocked, his wife asked the officials what they wanted them to do. The parents, she found out, would be solicited to trap their own son. Already thinking ahead, the sensible woman was hoping that at now 16 years of age, some leniency would be shown her son.

The men couldn't help but notice the fury beneath her tempered worry and calm request for more information regarding her son's activities. When they left, the wife and mother went to help her husband cope with what was for him a final heartbreak.

PARENTING CHALLENGES

Misguided Protection

One of the hardest lessons for parents to learn is when to stop protecting a child. There had been signs with respect to Peter, but they had been ignored and forgotten by his father, and merely noted by his mother. It is in the fibre of our being to protect our children at all cost, but given what they now have access to in the way of technology, imagery, weapons, drugs and so on, we need to protect them from tough social consequences by imposing the same in the home.

Although we all speak about limits and boundaries, and about not letting things go too far or allowing our children to cross the line, we are often the ones who push the limits of acceptability in order to keep the peace or to give our child another chance. I have done it, and our children know we are inclined to do it. I can remember, after too many months of coping with an "out of control" adolescent boy, having to make the decision to let him spend a night in jail. It was a heartbreaking decision, especially when the police allowed him to speak to me by telephone. He wept, begged, moaned with fear, and swore himself to perfect behaviour for eternity. He didn't know that I was weeping on the other end of the phone. But I could not back down. Not again. He spent the night in jail.

However, when he awoke from finally collapsing with exhaustion into a deep, three-hour slumber, he found me asleep on a metal chair in the corner of the cell. I noted the terror in his eyes as he opened them. In that split second between sleep and consciousness, he remembered where he was, and he was about to weep, when he saw me. The relief spread through his entire body. He hated me for making him stay there, but he was glad I was there, having watched over him. It was the epitome of both compromise and paradox. He did experience the terror, the consequence of his actions—a night in jail—but I joined him in his incarceration. The paradox was that I had had to abandon him, and protect him with assurance. He found himself hating me for letting him stay in a cell overnight, and loving me for being there when he woke up. While his behaviour continued to be trying, and no doubt knocked a few years off my life, he never spent another night in jail.

When we find it difficult to make the hard decisions related to the hard lessons our children have to learn, we tend to show little creativity in our dealings with them. When it comes down to it, the individual adolescent psyche is too full of unidentifiable themes and schemes for us to treat each child in either the same way, or even in the same time frame.

Contemporary adolescents have had the equivalent of postdoctoral studies in trickiness, and we are unprepared for their antics, particularly their hurtful, dishonest ones. We also have to recognize that there is less homogeny among adolescent youth due to the fact that each child has access to information that supports their particular confusions or preoccupations.

An important principle of modern parenting is to ensure that we address and reach the child in good time and in a way pertinent to the child's actions and personality. To do nothing, or as many of us do, to merely ask the child to stop what she is doing, is to give her permission to continue and to further hone her skills at avoiding irritating flack.

We have to act even when our child is in only moderate trouble. For example, in chapter 6, I referred to our taking relatively harsh and courageous action if we find out that our child is victimizing others. The easiest thing to do is to deny that our boy would do this. The hardest solution is to directly talk to him, involve other adults, and put him on a kind of "adult watch." This approach is creative and definitive, and it means something to the recalcitrant child in the way of consequences.

As maturity-resisting adults ourselves, we can be inclined to martyr ourselves to the persuasive powers of our children, rather than to make hard decisions where they are concerned. The children lose if we hesitate, and we all lose amid the danger of unaddressed problems, fears, secrets, and lies.

Guilt

When we are not making the quick, off-the-cuff move related to our child's latest misbehaviour, we may be bloated with guilt over our own imperfect responses, actions or inactions, lack of time for our children, or some other aspect of what we feel is our inadequate parenting. Moreover, with no social recognition of the related needs of today's youth and parents, we parent alone and with our ideals regarding best practices out the window. Ironically, given the urgent, speedy proliferation of new templates for everything from corporate affairs to growing vegetables, no one has suggested new guidelines for parenting. These factors combined—the context in which we are trying to apply "new-old" models of parenting, and the isolation in which we are struggling—is hurting us and hindering our ability to be resourceful parents.

We need to look at how we approach every aspect of our day-to-day lives in order to address and change our overall *modus operandi*. As we cope, spinning in a harried world, feeling we can never complete anything, and that we are eminently dispensable, we push the same untended buttons related to our success as parents.

Furthermore, we live at such a high level of tension that we rarely assess our own emotional needs, let alone attune to those of our spouses and children. Our sense of inadequacy is epidemic, and is an unnecessary impediment to the level of parenting we can manage without handicapping ourselves with expectations pertinent to another, kinder era.

PARENTING SOLUTIONS: THE "9 C's" OF EFFECTIVE PARENTING

We have to take steps to change our thinking so that it is pertinent to the task and the times. We have to take steps to eliminate and replace thinking that is no longer useful or relevant to our effectiveness as parents. In that our preadolescents and adolescents are already examining our viability as protectors, mentors, and exemplars of successful living, our frantic postures and approaches to the day-to-day decrease our ability to be accessible, as well as our resilience.

Furthermore, our busyness exacerbates what is already a child's reluctance to bother us, lean on us, or to enter the world of adulthood. While they may watch an episode of "ER" and decide on the spot to become a doctor, they sublimate their real sense, their fear of what they see every day in us, as the reality of adulthood. Child-adolescents hear, usually *ad nauseam*, how there is always too little money, no security, how ruthless associates are at work, and how they had better apply themselves because of how much less there is out there in the way of opportunity, and how much more in the way of danger and malevolence. This is precisely the kind of thinking that we have to change in order to stop projecting it at our children.

On a very basic level, we have to watch how we act and what we say to and around our children. Expressing fears about our own futures and constantly referring to theirs in the same way makes them more fearful and despondent. Further, finding ways to manage our stress so that we are not constantly sending our children nonverbal messages about hardship and struggle is also wise, as long as it is done with sustained commitment.

A significant dimension of "the new parenting" involves:

1. making a commitment to apply basic principles to our daily interactions with and around our children and others;
2. changing ourselves from the inside-out, by examining our thinking and feelings, particularly as they affect our children and our ability to parent with energy and positive attentiveness; and
3. forming alliances and supportive links with others in the community.

The second step is an ongoing one on which much of the success of the others depend. Otherwise, the steps and other key points about resourceful parenting are nice in theory but eminently forgettable over breakfast. The mental framework for modern parenting comprises these three recommendations, and the recommendations are components of what I have tried to simplify here as the "9 C's".

The 9 principles represent the foundation of effective, agile, and responsive communication. They are principles which are practised, in one form or another, by successful organizational and corporate leaders, successful and still-enthusiastic parents, and global peacemakers. Internalized, they make us aware, keep us attuned, allow for investigation, and keep us on track in an increasingly challenging world. They also allow us to consistently model behaviours that we would be proud and relieved to see adopted by our easily influenced youth.

The "C's" which, as mentioned, encompass the three fundamental dimensions of the new parenting, are not quick fixes. Principles are just words unless we are willing to encode them in our psyches. Therefore, the principles presented here, while fundamental to increasing our chances of raising healthy adolescents, should not just be read or memorized. We have to take the second step to create a shift in our psyches so that we can incorporate the 9 C's into our resistant minds. If we ignore the final step of taking a look at old thinking that still propels old behaviours and parental models, we can easily miss the boat.

Principle One: Creativity

The creativity (agility, flexibility, intuitiveness) required to parent is more critical than ever at a point in time where nothing stays the same and during which there are few promises we can make to our children about their futures. We were taught the "old way" of conducting ourselves and of parenting, that is, in logical, linear ways that discourage creativity, and so we are understandably inclined to be rigid in our approaches to our children. And it is this rigid, left-brain approach that prevents us from being creative parents.

Why is creativity so important to the new parenting? We have to be creative to compete with both what our children's minds are exposed to, and with our children's very different minds. While our creativity is at an all-time low, adolescents are exposed to more, stimulated by more, have more free time, and are more inclined to express new ideas and to try new things. Overworked and worried, we inadvertently revert to old models of defensive and limiting thinking. And, on the defensive, we are less likely to be innovatively effective in guiding confused adolescents who still look to us for a model of behaviour, as well as for permission to take risks and to grow.

One way to become more creative is to put aside our fears of the future so that we can enjoy the present. When we relax and put away our concerns about an uncertain future, we become more attuned to and accessible to our children—a truly creative activity in and of itself.

When we are not relaxed, we cannot ask questions and show empathy in ways that make sense to our adolescents. Parenting is not a static, repetitive activity. It is a highly innovative dance to the vagaries of someone else's drummer and beat. And with contemporary youth, it requires a dance with ever-changing twists, steps and movements. Revising our old thinking gives us access to our innate creativity, and allows us to meet the distinctive needs of our children.

A small example of creative—that is, flexible and innovative—parenting was the "bad guy, good guy" approach I chose to take when I had to make the responsible but difficult decision to have a troubled boy spend a night in jail. He got his just deserts and smartened up, and I lost a night's sleep, but the child benefitted. Another example mentioned in this book is to show the effects of negative or dangerous behaviours, such as smoking, rather than just telling one's teen "not to" until the admonishments become screaming matches. A cancer ward speaks louder than our anger and perceived contempt.

Principle Two: Courage

It takes more courage than ever to raise a child, and to stick with the child through adolescence. We are fearful parents because we are fearful adults, and this state is communicated to our children. As a result, their fears, to which many of us are ill-attuned, are blocked from our understanding by our own defensive mental postures. Adolescents not only pick up on and incorporate our fears with theirs, they model our fearful postures toward others and the world.

Working at examining and diminishing our fear is critical to becoming a more effective parent. However, we need not be in a place of "no fear" before we can experiment with, for example, creativity. One component will affect the other, either way. Courage is not waiting until there is *no* fear—it proceeds with the hard lessons even as one is shaking in one's boots. This is the particular kind of courage necessary to raise a child in a scary world. If we were not sensibly, *responsibly* fearful, we would be unable to assess where and when to apply and manifest courage in raising our children. And if we wait until we aren't afraid to make a mistake, we might never intervene.

I have advised more parents than I can remember to remove PC's and the Internet, as well as televisions, from their adolescents' rooms. The parents balked at the notion, and almost every one said something like *"But he's always had a TV [computer] in his room!"* My response, akin to *"And your point is?"* was meant to indicate to the parent that I am not unaware that it requires courage to take away or to discipline, especially where habitual perks and patterns are concerned. Out of approximately 50 cases, perhaps three removed the television set and computer, and only after a month-long fight and emotional lockout. It takes courage to say no, to initially inconvenience or anger our children as we break their negative patterns. It takes even more courage to explain why we are doing so, and that we were wrong to have established the situation in the first place.

Principle Three: Clarity

We have to be courageously, creatively clear about what we expect, and unequivocally, demand from our children in the way of respect and behaviours. The shift from moral relativism (the theory that there is an "excuse" for all social ills and behaviours) to moral responsibility, a much clearer, more comforting posture for our children, must start with us, at home.

We should show no reluctance in making our rules and expectations clear to our children, nor should we obscure or back down on consequences. Clarifying to children the relationship between cause and effect provides them with a healthy, limiting sense of boundaries. However, this major dimension of modern parenting requires both our moral courage and our adaptability. What works in the way of applied values and behaviours for one child might not work for another. So, in our behaviours, applications, and initial assessments, we have to be sufficiently insightful and creative to present and model values, and to provide clear consequences in ways customized to the personalities, needs, and dilemmas of the individual child.

Finally, to be clear and truthful in a family environment provides a basic framework for sanity. Clarity in what we say means a great deal to the child when most everything else, except the meaning of the school bell, is obscure and changeable. Clarity in any relationship also tends to induce more discussion and more work, but it is the labour of real bonds, lasting trust, and a powerful, unconscious sense of security.

If we think back to the case of Jake, the boy who visited violent sex sites on the Internet, we will recall that he told his mother that it was not he who was going to the sites on his computer, but his friend. This explanation satisfied his mother. It should not have. She did not make her point clear. The point was, the boy was going to the sites, whether on his own, or with a friend. It didn't matter. If she had taken the opportunity to clarify her message, she would have said, *"So? You're still going to the sites! Stop!"* The boy not only stumped the mother by lying, he also managed to obscure her message and concern. If I do not allow a child to smoke, but there is clearly cigarette smoke in her room, is it acceptable if she tells me a friend was smoking, not her? Certainly not. While these are the kinds of situations that can wear us down, we have to maintain our ground, stay clear in our own heads, and communicate clearly to our children.

Principle 4: Concern

If you talk to adolescents, approximately one in four will say unequivocally that his parents care. This should be surprising, but it is a fact. While a younger child starts to spurn our open attentiveness and affection, the adolescent has virtually forgotten it. Moreover, when we try demonstrating our affection, our adolescents are often uncomfortable and suspicious.

Adolescents are also, we must remember, going through the "push off" stage, trying to prove to themselves that they both do not and should not need us. Again, therefore, we have to find ways to convey our love and support. Whatever works, including asking if they need help with a school assignment, listening attentively to an otherwise free-associative story, or going to bat for them with a neighbour, the form doesn't matter, just the effect. Every day we should show our love and concern for our children in ways in which they see and feel it. It is the child who feels "no one cares" who ends up either in serious trouble or lost.

One way in which many of us have fallen short in this regard is in giving up the constant struggle to know where our child is, at what time and with whom. And though such a discussion usually turns into a one-way interrogation, it does not have to. There is a way to ask our children, in a firm and nonconfrontational way that implies that we are merely asking because we love them and just need to know that they are safe.

I recall a mother and her teenage daughter coming to see me over something that had been bothering the girl. The child had wanted her mother to come to her first session. They were healthily, extremely close, and it was the same as asking a friend to join her. As they were giving me some history, the mother and daughter enjoyed a private joke about an earlier display of the mother's concern. I asked them to share what was clearly a memorable event.

About four years before their visit, the young girl had gone to her mother in tears explaining how she was continuously taunted and mocked at school. The child of a racially mixed marriage, and a girl of extreme beauty, sensitivity, and talent, she was being victimized by her peers, who were calling her names (including the "N" word) and berating her for being a "mongrel." It took some time to tell her mother, and it was only when she was ill one day that she did.

The girl's mother, a formidable, stubborn, and self-made woman, was beyond rage. She wanted to go to the school immediately and speak her mind to the teachers, the principal, and the tormentors. Her daughter begged and cried and made her mother promise not to contact the school. Reluctantly, the mother relented and they decided that the girl would tell her if the verbal assaults continued. The next day, the child left for school, and her mother, still shaking with anger, tried to calm herself. But over the next hour her resolve weakened significantly.

As the young girl looked out the window in history class, she was certain that she saw her mother peering out from among the branches of a huge maple tree on the school grounds. At first she wasn't sure, but, as the woman's head appeared slowly between the branches, the child paled with embarrassment. At the same time, however, she was both moved and amazed. She realized that her mother had been unable to do nothing, and that she had left the house, headed to the school, then thought better of what she was doing, and tried to watch over her child from afar—and on high. The mother had to allow the child to learn to take care of herself, but her instinctive need to protect her child drove her to watch over her. The women and her daughter would joke for years, wondering what would have happened if the mother had fallen out of the tree. But the girl never forgot her mother's driving need to protect her and to seek assurance that her daughter was not being humiliated. It was this crazy scene that, from then on, gave them both much laughter, and further grounded the child in their relationship as she grew in confidence to deal with other issues. The bond would be significant in the resolution of future challenges.

Principle Five: Consistency

Inconsistency in behaviour leaves any person confused and angry, but especially adolescents in relation to parents. It is also, to early adolescents, as painful as a lie. Discipline has to be consistent, regardless of whether we are tired or depressed, as does our show of affection. Children of unaffectionate parents speak openly of hating their parents for putting on a show for other adults, when in fact the child is never touched when the family is not "on stage." Consistency also plays a role in the area of activities between parents and their children. We cannot make a commitment to hike every Saturday, and then allow the activity to dwindle after the third time because we are too tired or have become bored with it. Our children remember these hurtful inconsistencies, as broken promises, and adolescents can be launched into estrangement by them.

We must also be consistent in our treatment of our spouses, friends, and people in general. Adolescents watch like hawks; they see everything and miss nothing. Consistency is one of the powerful influences we have as parents as we struggle to maintain an effective role in our child's development.

Principle Six: Congruency

Congruency, critical to a relationship between any two human beings, means that what we say is what we do, and what we do does not vary according to who is watching or listening. When child-adolescents mention parents, which is rare, they generally do so in a critical manner. One of the recurring themes is parental incongruity. They call it our "bull. . .ting." Incongruity is different from inconsistency, but has the same emotional effect. Our children too often hear us say one thing, and then watch us do another. Or, they observe us treating a neighbour in a respectful, helpful manner outside, and then the same neighbour becomes the object of our wrath inside the home.

Incongruity can show up in the different treatment of siblings. If the adolescent boy, out of say, four children, the rest of whom are girls, is treated roughly and insensitively by his parents, while the girls are coddled and adored, this constitutes damaging incongruity. Equal damage occurs if the boy is treated like a prince, and the girl child like Cinderella. A virtue encouraged but rarely lived up to, congruency is a critical element of trust, stability, love, and sanity.

Principle Seven: Communicating with Our Children

Communication can make or break our relationships with our adolescents. It is our responsibility to change the way we communicate with our children as they enter adolescence. By then we are already losing out to the competition, but we can change with our children in order to stay with them during the worst of the re-formational years. We do this by maintaining close ties with them and keeping a close eye on them during their last year of elementary school, and then participating as much as possible in their preparation and initiation into secondary school.

As our children enter this same period, we have to set times for "sit-downs," for meals together, for input hours during which we share information about our lives, worries, and interests. And while we limit ours so as not to add to the adolescent's fear of our diminishing strength and presence in their lives, we find creative ways to get our children to talk.

Furthermore, *we talk back*, and pick up the hints and symbols and subtleties of their language and movements. We respond in a way that is attuned, supportive, and memorable of earlier times. We can reformat and upgrade the tender talk we had with our toddlers at bedtime. We have to be smart enough and, again, creative enough, to make the discussion relevant and interesting to them. The onus is on us as parents, not on them as children, to create ways and manage themes and approaches to remind them of and maintain their attachment to "home."

A daughter of a patient became suddenly truant and estranged from her home upon her thirteenth birthday. She avoided meals, missed curfews, and was sullen when she was at home. Her parents chose to give her some space and to wait for her to come to them. However, this common practice is rarely the most effective one, and is often destructive. The longer the child is left, the harder it is to get the child to talk. More than a month passed before the child's mother decided to confront her, or, as I encourage parents, to "just ask." Within an hour of asking, the mother knew what was troubling here daughter. The child had been suffering with unbearable feelings of self-disgust due to extreme menstrual flooding. She would pack herself, even wearing an adult diaper at times, and wander the streets so as not to have her brothers or her parents experience what she felt was her smell, or in her words, her "grossness."

The child's mother was heartbroken and worried. They saw a doctor the next day, and an X-ray uncovered what the doctor suspected. The girl had a massive cyst that was tearing the wall of her uterus. The confused, non-communicative child had also been in excruciating pain. If left to her own devices, or readiness to communicate, she might have become sicker or worse from a loss of blood. When it comes to communicating, the adage of the *new* parenting is "parents first."

Principle Eight: Communicating with Ourselves

The second way in which communication plays a major role in our remaining effective parents to adolescents is the way in which we use our internal communication to affect external change in ourselves.

We can change the way we think, perceive, and communicate, especially as related to our parenting, by becoming aware of our thinking, beliefs, and related perceptions. In fact, often, simple awareness of our thinking allows for effortless change. Once we realize that our thinking is either inappropriate or outdated, we begin to make different choices in our responses. Figuring out where we got our ideas and beliefs also helps. By doing so, we pull out the roots of old thinking to replace it with thoughts and beliefs related to new, more effective behaviours. Practising the new behaviours reinforces the new thinking. We can release much heavy mental baggage in this way, and also more easily open up to and access the inner world of the adolescent.

An executive sent to me by a large corporation had been asked to change his ways or leave the company. He was dismayed and demoralized. He had been, a decade before, "the best and the brightest," and now he was told that he lacked leadership, people skills, and creativity. He disagreed, and only worked with me because he had to.

Among other things, we went through the process described above. He went away and returned in ten days with his "homework" done. He made a very long list of the ways in which he was self-bashing in his inner world. And, already, to my surprise, he was getting insights into the ways in which he affected others, including his family. He realized that he was constantly on his own back about performance, about not being good enough, doing enough, and producing enough. He realized that he dumped the same message on everyone he came in contact with, either verbally or nonverbally. Moreover, he saw that his constant inner war kept him from being creative. He was too wound up and angry to be creative. He had been taught that creative people were the "fluffy-puffy" failures in society. The little boy in him, the dreamer who had once imagined owning planets populated with zebras and unicorns, had been beaten up to the point of mental paralysis, and he had done the beating.

The executive changed his ways sufficiently at work to keep his job. More importantly, he changed his behaviours at home. In fact, he changed so drastically that his teenage son telephoned my office to ask if his father was *"dying or something"* having bought into the made-for-TV theme that only terminally ill people show their affection and love. The son worried when he saw his father become more attentive with his mother and with him, and when he teased and played with his younger sister. In fact, the whole family wondered what had happened to him. Nothing had happened, of course, but something had been removed, a weight lifted after years of self-punitive, self-harassing stress. Moreover, the executive stopped demanding the impossible from himself and was, in the end, a better father and manager.

Principle Nine: Cooperation

Teachers can no longer be expected to teach without community support and parents cannot be expected to parent in isolation. However, accepting this idea requires a change in our thinking and our beliefs about family and parenthood.

Cooperation is one aspect of the new parenting that will require the kind of rethinking discussed in the last principle. Most of us were brought up with strict, tacit, or not-so-tacit rules about the privacy of the family. Our parents could not have fathomed asking other parents, social organizations, even teachers, for help. Similarly, we place an unnecessary burden on ourselves by expecting that we can always understand, guide, and problem-solve with our adolescents on our own. Even before adolescence kicks in, we frequently find ourselves feeling helpless and isolated, primarily because we are determined to keep our problems related to parenting to ourselves. We have to change our thinking and learn to reach out, especially given that there are now more single-parent homes than there are two-parent homes. The modern mandate of child-raising is just too much for one person, even for two.

As previously mentioned, we have to re-create communities responsible for the care and guidance of our children. Various models have already been created in a handful of states, including Mississippi, Oregon, Colorado, Ohio, Wyoming, and Washington. However, in each case the strategic alliances related to adolescent care had their roots in tragedy or near tragedy. The alliances include regular meetings and emergency links among educators, parents, police forces, municipal representatives and mental health professionals. We can take the initiative, if we are among those lucky enough to do so prior to a crisis, to establish links and alliances which are both preventive and effectively enriching of family life. Ideally, such alliances should be established in every community to monitor the behaviour of adolescents, and to act immediately and effectively should there be signs of a crisis.

Peter Revisited

Peter was called home to account for his illegal activities. Peter's father had prepared a legal team even before he contacted his son, in spite of the advice to the contrary provided by Peter's mother. Ignoring his wife's argument for making the boy pay the piper, the boy's father was irrationally determined to protect him from a criminal sentence and record.

Within an hour of the boy flying to his parents' home, Peter's father was instructing him as to what to say and not say, and what to do and not do. While his mother looked at her son with a mixture of sadness and disgust, his father became a partner in crime.

Now just 17 years old, the boy was sent to me for an assessment. Sessions revealed the reason for the boy's apparent lack of fear and sense of consequences. Ever since Peter was born, his father had had a soft spot for him. The boy's father had always had great plans for him and had been very vocal about them, in spite of Peter's disinterest in things academic. After the boy left school and seemed to be an overnight success at his landscaping business, his father was so relieved and proud that he went into denial regarding how he could really be earning so much money. The boy's mother, however, was suspicious all along. As she would say to me much later, *"He looked dirty, but not in the right way."* She had never been able to see her son down on his knees in dirt, lifting rocks and planting trees. And though she loved her boy, she had always been concerned about his ability to talk his way out of or into anything.

I assessed Peter as being mentally healthy but without a developed conscience or sense of cause and effect. He was not sociopathic, but he was sadly spoiled. He had a very high I.Q. and had been treated like a prince by his father during his childhood and with intensified adulation in his preadolescent and adolescent years. He was a "papa's boy," not a "mama's boy," the distinction being that he felt he could do anything and the omnipotent father would take care of it. A mama's boy dares little and seeks the regressive comfort of mother. Peter had tacit permission from his father to do anything.

Peter's mother played a significant role by remaining quiet as Peter was "damaged" by his father. A strong, professional woman, passive acceptance was completely out of character. She admitted that she knew very early to stay out of their way, that there was nothing she could do when her husband set his sights on anything, let alone on their son.

The dream team of lawyers hired to defend Peter could do very little but drag things out. In fact, the father was charged because he had provided Peter with an apartment, and the apartment had been used for the illegal enterprise. This charge was manageable. However, the boy was charged with multiple crimes and sentenced to at least five years at an adult facility. The verdict is being appealed. And will continue to be, thanks to the boy's father.

Denial in one parent and passive acceptance in the other might as well be "double denial." The mother did not dare ask, though she suspected, and the father had to have suspected on some level but did not want to know. Peter, who will not do well in prison if he loses his appeal, would have fared much better if his illegal activities had been interrupted, had faced a charge or two, had the wits scared out of him, and had to start again.

SUMMING UP

There are steps that we can take to parent more effectively in a techno-driven culture more concerned with productivity, "new and improved," and "billing and person hours" than with the mental health of youth and parents. Contemporary adults are too fatigued and overwhelmed to simply "do more." Fortunately, there now exist tested ways in which we can refurbish our thinking, and therefore our approaches to parenting and to other aspects of our lives as well.

The 9 C's or steps of effective parenting is a manageable framework from which to improve our communication and relationships with our children, and to create cooperative, supportive connections outside the home. The principles or "C's" include the concepts and application of *creativity, courage, clarity, concern, consistency, congruency, communication with our children, communication with ourselves,* and community *cooperation.* Were we to diligently learn, practise, and reflect these principles in our parenting, our adolescents would be significantly less likely to become lost to us, and us to them.

By daring to "go forward to the past" and to create cooperative bodies in our communities, we are both increasing the number of adults involved in the welfare of our children and widening our own support system. Establishing these cooperative bodies or committees would also be one more way in which we communicate to all children that they are not alone, and that they are vitally close to our hearts and the heart of what can otherwise seem like a hostile and uncaring community.

WHAT TO DO

1. We have to make changes in the way we perceive our roles as parents (and breadwinners). By reviewing our thinking and behaviours, and adopting new thinking, we will be more responsive to the specific needs of our adolescents.

2. There is no virtue in parenting in isolation. Seek help, and nip any moderate or serious damage in the bud. Though modern parents hesitate to do so, we can go to relatives, other parents, the school, the board of education psychologist, the family physician, a police social worker, a child or teen mental health professional, or, depending on the urgency of the situation, to an emergency facility for a psychiatric consultation. Most importantly, we must not make the mistake many parents of disturbed teens have made by trying to hide or keep the problem a family secret.

3. Ascertain in what ways you add to the already enormous challenge of guiding adolescents toward adulthood. In what ways are you holding yourself back by holding on to ideas and beliefs from the past.

4. Be truthful, clear, and consistent in your behaviours around your children. Children model us well into their teens and they are looking for reasons to push off from us. Inconsistency in what we say feels like lying to a teenager. For example, to promise a child that we will attend her hockey games and to show up at just one out of ten games might feel fine to us, but is damaging to an adolescent.

5. Be congruous in what you say and do—with your children, spouse, and strangers. Again, our child-adolescents are on the edge of distrust and must be reconvinced of our trustworthiness and their security with us. For example, we should not make speeches about fairness and then overreact and unfairly punish a child, or lie to our child's teachers about why we cannot attend parent-teacher interviews.

6. Do not protect your child from consequences. On the contrary, have her face them, and see her through them, assuring her throughout that your love is immutable. If your child is caught shoplifting, severe sanctions are in order. However, tell your daughter that her having stolen this one time has not affected your love for her.

7. Take one hour every two months to meet with your child's teachers. Compare notes. Parenting and teaching should overlap.

8. Have at least two or three "sit-downs" a week with the family. Share and ask and ask some more. Our children need to be reminded in blunt, active ways that we are concerned about them, love them, and have not left them to their own devices. Tuck your child in at night or enter the room with permission to say goodnight, for as long as your child will let you, or until you cannot stay up as late as he can. Sitting and talking with a teenager before he falls asleep is something he or she will probably resist, but we should contrive to at least show them that we are available.

9. Meet with other parents. Decide on and assign action steps related to speaking to other members of the community, including, of course, teachers and school board members, toward establishing community groups to guide our children.

10. Make this period of parenting a re-formational one for you, as it is for your child. Dump old habits and beliefs and prepare yourself for easier parenting and easier living. Otherwise, we are stressing out more than necessary, and not dealing as resourcefully as we could with our children.

11. Take care of your own mental and physical health by taking "quiet times" for yourself at least twice a day. These moments are balancing, and enable us to be more responsive to as opposed to reactive with, our adolescents.

12. Don't overprotect your child or be afraid to say an unequivocal "No!" regarding a pleading request for something which is either of little use or destructive to the child. "No" should be the response to excessive requests for money, for an increased allowance without increased duties, and for, among other things, permission to be alone in the house with a member of the opposite sex.

Common Problems and Advice

8

Where do you go for answers, and who has time? My son has every so-called "questionable" behaviour ever mentioned, and my daughter can't speak English anymore! I have a preteen who's watching all this, and I want to blindfold him and plug his ears so that he doesn't follow in their stomping footsteps! I'll go mad!"

—*Allison, mother of two adolescents and one preadolescent*

Generally, the most challenging time for adolescent children is the period between early to mid-adolescence from approximately 13 to 15 years of age. This is also the time when they are more likely to experience the anxiety related to the re-formational period and to be searching for new, transitional identities. Much of their problems during this period are related to either the need to substitute some form of identity, or to act out in anger over the loss of their childhood identity. But take heart—the vast majority of their problems are soluble, if challenging to and demanding of parents and teachers.

It is important to remember that *any* of our children can get into serious trouble during the critical adolescent years. I hear again and again from parents who have four children, three of whom have been fine, and one of whom ended up on the street, drug-addicted, even as a suicide statistic. In the long, futile attempt to figure out what they did differently or "wrong," parents add to their pain. The factors discussed in this book which have a negative or questionable effect on our children do so randomly and to varying degrees. The vast majority of parents of children who have become "celebrity killers" did nothing overtly wrong—certainly not anything evident before the luxury of hindsight. Moreover, a number and combination of factors can affect one child in one way, and a hundred in another. The "one child" can be any of ours, regardless of acceptable parenting. In the following pages we will look at various challenges common to adolescents and address them from the perspective of providing solutions.

ANXIETY AND THE UNKNOWN

Anxiety is the predominant emotion of children from early to mid-adolescence and sometimes beyond. Most adolescent problems and teenage acting out show up in behaviours related to safety, security (and trust), sexuality, social relations and peer pressure, drug and alcohol abuse and smoking, school performance, and issues related to re-forming and asserting a new identity, power and will. Further related to these issues are challenges such as loneliness, anger, and an intensified need for active parental guidance. Today, teenagers also experience the tangible fear for their physical safety at school and in neighbourhood playgrounds.

Case Study

Karen

The story of Karen, a young adolescent, and her family's trials with her, is among the many so-called normal cases I have been involved in as a psychotherapist.

Karen was a sweet, lovely middle child, with a brother two years older and another three years younger. As is the case with most middle children, she was a helper around the house, pleasingly affectionate with her parents, enjoyed by her teachers in elementary school, praised and adored by neighbours. As her mother once put it, she was "the perfect child."

Karen had gone to an expensive camp during the summers, ever since she was ten years old, and she did the same the summer after her celebrated graduation from elementary school. Her parents were thrilled with her good marks, superlative reports from teachers, and the numerous awards she'd received for her contribution to the small school she was now leaving. Neither parent noticed anything different about their daughter's behaviour prior to her leaving for camp.

Into the third week, however, the girl's parents received a letter from the camp director—a woman they had known for years and who had watched Karen grow into her preteens. The note was casual in tone, but alluded to some problems the counsellors were having regarding Karen's "unusual" behaviour. Karen had been uncharacteristically aggressive with other campers and recalcitrant with counsellors to whom, during previous summers, she had always shown deference and affection. The director ended the letter by noting that she and her staff were "on top" of the situation, but she wondered if the parents could offer any insight into the girl's behaviour. Perplexed, Karen's parents decided to make sure that they went to the parents' day coming up the next week.

When they arrived at the camp, the director immediately brought the parents into her office. As gently as possible she told them that they would have to take Karen home. The parents were stunned. As they heard stories about their daughter hitting other children, swearing at counsellors, throwing food and deliberately wetting her bed, they slumped in their chairs. They were staring straight ahead in silence when Karen arrived with her sleeping bag and duffle bag, accompanied by a senior counsellor.

The parents eventually looked at their daughter with a mixture of shock and curiosity. Karen kept her eyes to the floor. They could all see that the child was humiliated, even contrite, but it was also clear that the director's decision was irrevocable. There had been complaints from parents who had received letters from their children in which they complained about being hit or bullied. The sympathetic and concerned director had no choice but to send the child home.

After the long, silent drive home, things were quiet for a few days as Karen's parents considered this inconceivable change in Karen. They were meant to go away the following week and were anxious to address the problem before they left. Karen spent most of her time in her room, only forcibly joining the family for meals. She didn't telephone her friends, nor did she go out to practise her favourite sports. It was as if she were suspended in some kind of shocked confusion of her own.

Finally, there was communication, but primarily one-way; Karen's parents did most of the talking. In all fairness, they repeatedly asked Karen about several incidents, as well as about how she was feeling, what was on her mind, and how they could help. They would have accepted almost any explanation for their child's change in character. But she was quiet and appeared to be unwilling or unable to articulate what had motivated her to behave so uncharacteristically.

Several such attempts at communication failed, and her parents concluded that she would soon snap out of whatever it was that had been bothering her. She would return to normal after a couple of weeks of rest and reflection. They left for their week-long trip hoping that Karen and her brothers would be fine while they were away.

Immediately upon their return, the parents were faced with more problems. Karen had been arrested for shoplifting from a drugstore. In that her parents were away and she carried no I.D. and was determined not to call any relatives or other adults, she had spent two and a half days in jail. Mortified, her parents went to pick her up and brought her home.

Again, for another two weeks, Karen remained silent. As registration for secondary school loomed on the horizon her parents sought out several referrals. Though they didn't state it, to themselves or to each other, they felt that their daughter was getting worse, not better.

Karen's parents were more comfortable exploring medical options first. They spent a great deal of money expediting a neurological workup to establish that she did not have a brain tumour, and made sure that Karen had every test in the book related to anything that might affect her behaviour or personality. They were determined that her problem was neurological or biochemical, or related to blood sugar, or whatever. But all the medical examinations and workups came up negative.

ATTENDING A NEW SCHOOL

Insecurity

It is normal for a child to question everything in his world and to experience extreme anxiety when he is suddenly no longer in a "school for children," sharing a yard at recess with six-year-olds and a few adults, and finds himself thrust, ready or not, into a school promoted as a launching pad to adulthood. It is interesting that while most parents celebrate a child's graduation from elementary school to enter secondary school, virtually all children go through a period of panic during the transition.

During their last year in elementary school, throughout the summer, and near and into the first days and weeks of secondary school, children are in anxiety states. We were anxious when we made the transition, and now, with most parents being less available, and given influences that push our children to premature independence and gender mandates, they are extremely anxious and loath to show or discuss it.

As mentioned in chapter 6, the transition warrants increased attention from the beginning of the last year of elementary school, all the way through the first year of secondary school. The meaning, feelings related to, and plans attached to the change should be discussed with the child as often as possible, especially through the "last summer." However, a necessary caveat: we must not go overboard and let our intense attentiveness increase our child's anxiety. Many, as I have hastened to say, muddle through in spite of the turmoil in their inner worlds.

Regardless of the issue, children will respond when they are ready, and our asking and periodically indicating that we are aware of what they might be feeling is sufficient for most children. By so doing, we are communicating that *they can communicate* and are de-isolating them and an issue so that they do not have to isolate themselves with it. Our children brood, especially from early to mid-adolescence; they take in an array of issues and worries. Our positive intrusions regarding their school experiences and feelings should be calm, unrushed, and firmly implanted in our child's heart and mind. I often recommend that parents touch their child's arm when talking to him, both to induce eye contact and to enable him to fully experience our presence and warmth. Positive intrusions, with as much physical contact as possible, are one way in which we can assist our children to remain as grounded or balanced as possible during the dizzying flight from childhood into adolescence. It is also a critical form of ongoing support as they face the trauma of entering a new social environment.

Given that the transition from elementary to secondary school is also the period when the child is questioning everything, including his viability in and worth to the world, and his as-yet-undefined new role with us as parents, the child is feeling insecure and distrustful. The once-unconditional sense of safety and security in the family home crumbles for many children, even for those who do not get into serious trouble. The child now sees us as separate individuals, familiar strangers who still make an attempt to control him, but who, he believes, no longer love him in the way and to the degree that we once did. Further, the child irrationally blames us for his feeling of separation or exile, as well as for pushing him into new roles and situations. So, in addition to the anxiety related to the transition from elementary school to secondary school, the child also copes with feelings of abandonment and the fear that comes with a loss of trust.

While varying degrees of the insecurity and anxiety described above are normal, obvious signs should not be ignored. For a significantly large number of children, behaviours which are strong indicators that the anxiety is endangering, damaging, or in some other way an obstacle to the child's development can appear out of nowhere.

Behaviours such as shoplifting, lying, experimental smoking and drinking, and hostility toward siblings are common symptoms of adolescent anxiety related to transition.

School: Non-Attendance

One classic sign of transitional anxiety, as well as adolescent anxiety in general, has its roots in the adolescent's attitude toward attendance and performance at school. If a child suddenly refuses to go to school, she is likely suffering from what is known as "non-specific anxiety"—that is, an ever-present fear that is unrelated to anything specific. Alternatively, she is dealing with fears and nervousness related to security in the new environment. However, at the foundation of non-specific anxiety is the fear of separation. The child unconsciously fears, even in her early teens, that if she goes off to this chaotic, strange place, either her parents will disappear, or she will. Interestingly, this anxiety can beset children in their mid-teens, even into the later adolescent years. It can also come and go. Parents should inquire about any rise in anxiety during the child's secondary school years; they should be especially concerned about changes in the child's school attendance. If a teenager who otherwise has a good attendance record is suddenly resistant about going to school, parents are well advised to investigate the cause, and assess its severity.

At the same time as a child fears separation from her parents, she is also becoming increasingly aware of her own mortality. Those strikes of white-hot terror we may remember when we were children hit hardest between the ages of 11 and 15. Whether we remember or not, we, too, were often afflicted with signs of anxiety such as precipitous stomach aches (often used as a *real* ploy to stay home from school), and either repressed or let go temper tantrums of the singularly early adolescent variety. Such outbursts remain a sign, and a serious warning if they are regular and drawn-out.

Parents enduring a child's temper tantrums more than twice a month should seek professional help for the child. Repeated tantrums might also be related to other fears or experiences the child feels that she cannot share with her parents. In this case, speak to a school official to ascertain what kind of behaviour preceded her absence, and then make an appointment with a counsellor. The same goes for a teenager with whom the problem persists. If symptoms recur which make it impossible for an adolescent to go to school, a professional should be seen and parents and school officials should conduct an investigation.

Other signs of adolescent anxiety which are also related to school attendance are sleeplessness, an obsession with the safety of the child herself or her parents, regressively clingy behaviour, and debilitating anxiety attacks.

Ironically, while an adolescent is straining to get on with the process of growing up, he can be pushing his parents away by, on the one hand, adopting annoying and alienating behaviours, and, on the other, clinging in odd and sporadic ways. On a weekend or holiday, for example, it is not unusual for a once-gregarious child to suddenly refuse to make social visits or to travel to see relatives with the family. In early secondary school, the child does not want to leave the familiarity of home when she does not have to. Moreover, she feels disillusioned with all adults, including those who were once favourite adult relatives as they, too, have abandoned the child to maturation and to attendance at what feels like a threatening environment.

Increasingly, adolescents adopt a bunker mentality, both not wanting to leave the home, and making their bedrooms into a cavelike sanctuary. Retreating to her room provides a child with a sense of control, safety, and self-containment, and intrusions can be met with hysteria, and an increased tendency toward absenteeism. It is from their bunker that young adolescents gather the wherewithal to push themselves to go to the mandatory new learning environment. It is also from this now private space that our children contemplate their physical safety at school—a fear fuelled by tangible realities that exacerbate their already sordid view of the secondary school environment.

Two high achieving young adolescents I have dealt with in the last year have suddenly refused to go to school, and neither set of parents could figure out what was going on. One mother asked about physical safety, but not directly enough, and not seated next to the child so as to assist the child to state the unspeakable. In each case, however, the children had gone into a kind of overnight paralysis, a fear state based on the belief that they would be killed at school.

As mentioned in chapter 6, children are much more afraid of what might happen to them at school than their parents are, and they are overwhelmed by the media coverage and notion of child homicides. Their realistic and exaggerated fear must be carefully and firmly addressed. It is every child's nightmare to kill—and a new, modern nightmare, in North America, to be killed at school. In addition to their sense that we have sent them to a dangerous place, they are getting evidence of it too often and in a powerful way. This gruesome confirmation of what are normal fears is already having an effect on overall school attendance, and the old and new ways in which children are revising and devising to get out of having to go.

The fundamental rule is simple. If a child exhibits behaviour that is first, out of character; second, continuous; third, damaging to either her education or her relationships; fourth, destructive in the family environment; or fifth, extreme and sudden, she should be firmly, supportively attended to by her parents. If certain behaviours continue or escalate, professional help should be sought. Where a child's fear of safety at school is concerned, the issue should be addressed whether or not the child exhibits anxiety, and whether or not we want to talk about it. Our children are thinking about it, do not dare to talk about it among themselves, and need us to gently lead them into an area of discussion they fear more than most of us can imagine.

School: Poor Performance

Both boys and girls experience various forms of performance anxiety just before their mid-teens and for a time after. One variant is related to how they are forced to take on an imitation or version of gender identity and behaviours, and the other is related to how they fear they will do in the new social environment. Only a minority worry as much about marks as they do about coping and fitting in. Each form or variant can be addressed by parents in the same observant and then, if necessary, active way.

As mentioned, a child's performance at school can give us hints about his anxieties. A child who has traditionally done well at school and who suddenly fails or gets poor marks is either suffering in some extreme way, is involved in something which we should know about, or is seriously depressed.

Unlike Richard, in chapter 6, who merely left school after being beaten up, most children do not have, and should not be expected to have, the strength of character to address serious social problems on their own. Like Richard, however, young adolescents will try to keep their problems from their parents, thus falling deeper into the morass of adolescent confusion.

Embarrassed that they might appear to be unpopular, early secondary school students to mid-level students will either continue to take harassment, humiliation, or abuse, or they will submit to behaviours that lift the pressure of persecution or loneliness. One bright girl I treated graduated from elementary school at the head of the class, entered a Canadian secondary school, and within two years was dead. She deemed her strict parents, as well as the seemingly less concerned teachers, to be unapproachable. She was a distinctly plump child and, though she would have grown out of her baby fat, she was, from day one at the huge, new school, called "Piggy Patty" by a few students, and very soon after by virtually the entire school.

The girl's marks plummeted, she became truant, she had secret anxiety attacks and bouts of bedwetting which she kept from her parents by washing her sheets in the middle of the night, and eventually bonded with a small group of heavy drug users. When she would not appear at school and her parents were notified, she was severely punished and eventually stopped going home. By the end of her first year in high school, she was on the street; halfway through what would have been her second year, she overdosed and died. This gut-wrenching story is a reminder that we have to observe, ask, and be gutsy enough to march into our children's lives, or schools, and demand that they not be damaged.

Our early adolescent children are not equipped emotionally or intellectually to cope with the confusion of re-formation and the dress code, sex code, language code, and other requisites for social acceptance or tolerance. Beyond what we used to call peer pressure, there is now institutionalized peer abuse, harassment, even a kind of school-gang violence. And we are seeing the increasing signs and actions of youth who decide that they are *"angrier than hell, and are not going to take it anymore!"* Before our children's experience becomes extreme and their reaction the same, we must intervene. The closer rapport between parents and teachers mentioned earlier would help in this regard, but the initial onus to notice that our child is in trouble is on us.

Where academic performance in secondary school is concerned, there are two major factors to be aware of, and around which we must be supportive and encouraging. First is the social factor mentioned above, which frequently limits what even the brightest of secondary school beginners would otherwise accomplish were schools smaller and certain pressures more controlled.

The second factor is the fear and doubt on the part of the new student as to whether she can cut it in what she perceives as a much more difficult academic process. This initial wariness wears off after about a year and a half, but it can affect grade point averages in the early stages of high school. After this point, peer pressure and related personal and social problems are frequently the cause of decreasing performance. For all students, the death of a family member, a family separation, and drug and alcohol abuse invariably affect school performance. Another reason for us to be attentive to our children, we can influence them at these critical turning points in their lives, and assist them in staying on track.

Sex, Aggression, and Fitting In

Too much stock has been put in the notion that young adolescent boys, in particular, are pressured to be sexually active. As mentioned in chapter 1, sexual anxiety, though slightly different for boys and girls, is less related to prowess than to appropriate gender behaviours and appearance. Moreover, when children enter secondary school, gender behaviours are more strictly defined and enforced than they had ever imagined. Initially, therefore, children see their mandate to be appropriately "cool" as a male, and similarly cool but also potentially "hot," as a female. A difficult and daunting enough task, actual sexual viability rarely comes into play before mid- to late-adolescence.

However, when sex itself does become a factor in a teenager's life, it is a major one, but not necessarily based on performance. It is, first, far more likely to be an extension of the need to fit in and to demonstrate another gender-related behavioural requirement. And second, sex has become the drug of choice for a large percentage of today's teenagers.

As mentioned, for girls, sex is soothing of the need to re-belong, to be cared for and held, and for this reason among others, it is often a repeated experience with sad consequences for the searching girl. For boys, sex is a deflecting relaxant, a momentary flight from insecurities related to the incomprehensibility of manhood and the ill-perceived world of adulthood. And sexual activity with multiple partners is so prevalent among adolescents that we do have to address it as a serious threat to our children.

The best we can do for our child in this regard is to stay as open to casual conversation about the subject of sex as we can; and keep a close eye on where our child is, with whom, and under what circumstances. We must also face the point when we find evidence or suspect that our teenager is engaging in sex, and ensure that the adolescent is taking the proper precautions. Asking an adolescent to stop having sex is like asking the sun not to rise. We might as well move to the level of protection that we *can* provide as parents of independently sexually active individuals. However, we can also try to discuss the nature of their activities.

Each parent, and then a relative or a close family friend—anyone who is admired and trusted by the boy or girl—can assist us in ascertaining why our adolescent is having sex. For many, it is for a feeling of closeness, and for others, to escape from other feelings or troubles. If we can figure out why, we can learn a lot about the problems facing our still-vulnerable youth. New studies about sexual addiction show that the disorder has its roots in adolescence, is more often an addictive problem with males, and can ruin lives. Regardless, we have to be willing to get beyond what is still a generational discomfort to discuss sex and its consequences with our children.

In general, young adolescent boys are less likely to initiate sexual encounters than confused young girls are receptive to seduction. In fact, young boys fear and avoid the encounter until the high-pressure years between 16 to 18 and, not surprisingly, often have their first encounters with girls significantly younger than they are. The girl is more needy than willing, and the boy can feign greater confidence due to the age difference.

Young girls typically attach themselves to, have sex with, and even participate in dubious or criminal behaviours with older boys, just to be able to be with them. In fact, if parents notice that their female adolescent is, particularly in her early teens, spending a great deal of time with an unknown group of children, there is cause for concern and investigation. To have sex too early can derail an adolescent's development, especially if an adolescent is faced with pregnancy. But this goes for boys, as well as girls. Staying out all night and experimenting with other lost and confused teenagers does not only put the child at sexual risk, but also at risk for a multitude of illnesses, as well as for the use of momentarily comforting, calming, or confidence-inducing drugs.

Cigarette smoking commonly comes with the territory as well. Sexual energy in a child-adolescent can trigger a variety of other aberrant or unacceptable behaviours, the use of illegal and legal drugs being just the tip of the iceberg.

There are indicators common to both male and female adolescents regarding their experimentation with sex. The more common signs are: increased secrecy, moodiness, whispered telephone conversations, extreme sensitivity around appearance, especially with siblings, increased spending, and, of course, the usually well-hidden possession of contraceptives. However, there are behaviours that are also unique to boys and girls which are usually linked to their being involved in sexual activity.

Boys manifest distinct and confusing changes in how they relate to female members of the family. A boy who is prematurely sexually active often adopts a strained and angry relationship with his mother and sisters. He can be reticent one moment, avoiding eye contact and conversation, and the next, hostile and insulting. This erratic behaviour is frequently a sign of the child's feeling guilty and confused about his sexual approaches or activities. On one level, angry that he has to "perform" this last part of the sexual mandate, he can most easily take out this anger on females in his life. Moreover, the anger is compounded by his discomfiting sense of their sexuality and sexiness. Not having fully separated from his mother and siblings, a boy can feel guilty about his actions with any female body reminiscent of those he attaches to the women he loves.

When a boy is irritable, short-tempered, and seems particularly averse to physical contact with female family members, some gentle inquiry and guidance is called for—ideally, by a father or uncle, or close, male adult friend. This latter form of intervention is usually better performed by a male. However, it is even then somewhat complicated by the fact that boys are, though aggressive with younger male siblings when testing their sexual wings, strangely reticent and embarrassed with older males. The boy feels that he has discovered a secret that he is not yet sure he can speak about or share with more powerful and experienced males.

Generally, when girls start having sex, they are also moody, often sullen, prone to fits of temper, fearful, and periodically regressively affectionate. They are confused, and at times angry about having sex or about issues surrounding what to them is usually an important new relationship. They, too, must be creatively approached during this period by an older female. Mother is ideal, but an older admired friend is even better. A young, sexually active girl is confused about both her mother's overall role in the family, and her need for her mother's unconditional, protective affection. The girl can feel competitive with the former, and fearful of losing the latter. If there is an urgency to get the facts, better to call in a friend.

In summary, early adolescent sexual discoveries, awareness, and explorations can be distracting, potentially devastating, and conducive to the introduction of new behaviours or indulgences. The overlapping layers of guilt and confusion, the pressures related to sexual self-image, and the child's experimentation itself can induce moodiness, result in long periods of absence from the home, and affect how the adolescent interacts with members of the family. When it becomes a salient dimension of the child's tentative new identity, sex can take both boys and girls, especially girls, far from home. It can also be lethal. We should be talking about sex with our children from about the age of 11 on—unless they ask earlier—and we should be at least as frank as are the media and their friends. Moreover, we should be aware of the increasing incidence of the seduction of young girls on the Internet.

Extreme gender-identity behaviours are almost as worrisome as sexual activity. These imitative behaviours are also usually stepped up once the child enters secondary school. We must ensure that our child's acting out is not sufficiently extreme to either put him in harm's way, or on a dangerous course toward more serious problems. For example, sudden seductive and manipulative coyness on the part of a girl, or acts of experimental physical aggression, or more than the average adolescent use of sexual profanity, should be immediately and seriously addressed. The adolescent should be asked in a direct but nonpunitive way what it is that he is doing, or trying to get across with the use of imagery, language, or gestures. Then, the issue of gender distinction and inequity should be discussed, and guidance provided to offset the powerful, ugly imagery related to gender behavioural and sexual roles.

While boys find themselves under extreme pressure to act, talk, and generally ape extremes of stereotypical male behaviour, girls are predominantly tormented in a more tangible way. Most girls become obsessive about their bodies, trying to live up to an impossible feminine image. This self-hating compulsion can have consequences just as serious as those resulting from male aggression, and significantly more common. This behaviour should be curtailed, possibly counselled, and parents and teachers should remain vigilant regarding further expressions of gender superiority (or inferiority) or contempt.

On December 6, 1989, Marc Lepine, a young man who told all the men in an engineering class at Montreal's L'Ecole Polytechnique to leave because he "only want[ed] to kill the bitches" had been overacting stereotypical masculinity and misogyny, and speaking openly and hatefully about women since his preteens. He was echoing the views of adults in his life, as well as those voiced by his friends. Lepine had collected the added backup of newspaper editorials and other media regarding what is still refered to as the white-male-destroying role of affirmative action for women and minorities. He could have been stopped well before he acted out with an automatic rifle, killing 14 female students and a professor, and wounding 13 before killing himself. Sexually inactive, and with no previous record of active aggression, Marc Lepine's incessant verbal profanity related to women was ignored. Such is the case with profane and contemptuous behaviour among a large number of adolescent boys, and naively dangerous, seductive behaviours among some young girls. These behaviours must be interrupted and brought into both the light of discussion and, if necessary, the arena of creative and cautious admonishment *and* punishment. If these behaviours are not appropriately addressed, damage is done either to the child, or to both the child and someone else pays dearly for snow-balling expressions of hate.

As for a young girl, a clumsy, innocent attempt to adopt the appearance of female sexual viability can take on a life of its own and become the girl's primary sense of and expression of self. As such, she can become inadvertent prey to confused and angry predators. And, again, such predators have proliferated with the unboundaried breadth of and access to the Internet.

Drugs, Alcohol, and Cigarettes

Drug use is frequently a way for overwhelmed children to protect themselves from harassment or feelings of exile in the new social environment of the secondary school. This being said, most parents would be surprised to hear that more students are using illegal and legal drugs than was the case five years ago, and that younger adolescents are currently more likely to seek substance relief than ever before.

In Ontario, studies indicate that more than 55 per cent of all grade 9 students use alcohol, 26 per cent use tobacco, and 24 per cent smoke marijuana. There has also been a dramatic increase in the number of grade 7 students using drugs, with 32 per cent admitting to using alcohol, 10.5 per cent to smoking cigarettes, and almost 4 per cent to using cannabis. Moreover, these and similar U.S. statistics are not based on inner-city users. Over 60 per cent of adolescent drug use takes place in middle-class, suburban neighbourhoods.

Drug use, especially cigarette smoking, is a way to fit in. While smoking was cool and sophisticated for previous generations, it is now perceived by adolescents as virtuously "tough" or "bad." The further use of illicit drugs requires and allows teens to align themselves with a specific group, with one or two members counted on to acquire the drug, and given power and status accordingly. This is a powerful inducement for children to form unhealthy alliances outside the home.

The affiliations allow children to keep the secret of their prior social rejection and unpopularity from their families, and allows them to form tight, secret bonds to temporarily replace those they feel are lost to them at home.

Children who have not been sufficiently prepared in their preteen years to avoid drugs, or who are left overwhelmed by the new, wild world of adolescent and secondary school culture, are at great risk for drug use. To our children who have used or use drugs, the "Just Say No" adage that was well known, and ineffective, during the Reagan administration in the United States, is laughable. Most communities, including several in Canada, and many in the United States, have formed community groups to both address and police the increasing problem. However, there are signs that we can look for to find out whether our children are taking drugs, and we must act if they are.

The signs of adolescent alcohol consumption are frequently right in our faces, across the breakfast table. Glassy eyes, volatility, moodiness, excessive headaches, an inability to get up in the morning, dry mouth, facial, hand and feet swelling, and the classic, red facial sheen are among the signs we pinpoint immediately in adults, and they also apply to adolescents. We may be too quick to accept our child's explanation of late parties or all-night study sessions, and it is little wonder that adolescents are amazed that they can say almost anything, and our need to believe them makes their explanations credible.

A drunk adolescent is easy to pick out, but a hungover one can slip by us due to our preoccupation and lack of energy. A girl or boy stoned on grass, hash, mushrooms, cocaine, or, alternatively, Dramamine, aspirin, Tylenol with codeine, or cough syrup with codeine, is frequently completely beyond our limited scope of recognition. Adolescents who use these and other drugs tell therapists like myself how amazed they are at what they are able to get away with in the family room, and later, when they light up in their own bedrooms. They do not express their amazement in a jocular way, but in a bewildered, almost sad way. They wonder why we do not see what even *they* know are obvious signs of drug or alcohol use. There is a distinct sadness in adolescents who once were ambivalent about being caught and stopped. One thing is certain. When we don't notice the more obvious signs of drug use, their faith in and sense of security around us is drastically diminished.

Adolescents stoned on downers (all except the cocaine mentioned above) are desultory, passive, forgetful, constantly sleepy, glassy-eyed, eventually unkempt, indifferent to school, family and other relationships, adopt strange or blurred speech patterns, miss school, frequently lose things, often suffer from stomach problems and other digestive disorders, and are prone to colds, flus, and anemia.

Children who smoke take on attitudes and behavioural changes, as well as a new odour, as they associate themselves with the weed- and nicotine-smoking adolescents. The most prevalent signs that our children are smoking are familiar to adult smokers: adolescent smokers cannot sit still for long periods of time, they take breaks during meals, they develop a sudden affinity for fresh air by leaving their windows wide open in the dead of winter, and they are rarely seen not chewing gum. "Attitude" also comes with adolescent smoking and is distinct to this particularly noxious habit.

The signs of drug use are rarely hard to see if we really look for and are willing to see them. And looking is the strongest remedial recommendation of all. We should be checking biweekly for physical signs, and daily for emotional signs that something is amiss with our children. And if we are certain that they are using drugs, it is not sufficient to just tell them to stop. This is telling them to drop their new support system and transitional identity. However, we can increase or refurbish their old support system. First, we can go into therapy or counselling with them to discuss their drug use. Second, we can keep them in counselling while we monitor their daily activities, and continued or discontinued usage, from the home. And, third, we can insist that the school monitor our children's behaviour. In addition, we should both punish children for drug use and reward them for either never using drugs or discontinuing their use.

I have a child in my life to whom I gave repeated and consistent warnings about drug use because she was almost always stoned on something. In addition to describing the perils and consequences of drug use, I took her on a journey. First, I took the 14-year-old to a "bad drug" intervention, and then to an emergency ward where a young girl was having her stomach pumped in an attempt to rid her system of a lethal dose of Tylenol. My adolescent guest was sick to her stomach as she watched the girl vomit, choke, and spew forth a black, tarlike substance and then go into seizures.

In the car, shaken and sweaty, the otherwise silent girl asked me if the child in the hospital would be okay. I told her, in a casual monotone, that, no, she'd most probably be dead within a week unless she was exceedingly lucky. When my passenger twisted abruptly, grabbed my shoulder in panic and asked why, I explained the torturous after-effects of a Tylenol overdose. The patient gets better, and then suddenly dies of kidney or some other organic failure. My passenger fell silent again. I could see out of the corner of my eye that she was sweating profusely. I could only imagine what she was calculating.

The next stop was a psychiatric ward for adolescent drug users who had overdosed and been "saved." My adolescent ward protested dramatically before we entered, and the poor girl's knees buckled as I left her side for a moment to speak to a nurse. She couldn't help but stare at the catatonic teenagers before her. Some good-looking, some just fair, but all just like the kids she sees and hangs out with every day.

Two of the children had visitors. One, a well-dressed, attractive, and articulate woman, sat by her son and spoke to him about the weather, the family, and her work. Meanwhile, he pushed the knuckle of his forefinger into the center of his forehead as if he could somehow plow through and relieve some mysterious inner tension. He was so severely brain damaged that he couldn't hear a word she said. And he never would.

The journey had a powerful, positively disturbing effect on an otherwise bright and confident young teenage girl and drug abuser. But it wasn't enough. Just as a surgeon colleague's taking his son to a terminal cancer ward where adults of all ages breathed and spoke through holes in their throats was not sufficient for his smoking 13-year-old son.

I further arranged that the girl see the school guidance counsellor once a day, another counsellor once a week, and I personally drove her to distraction by doing daily pupil and pulse tests. When I was travelling, I had someone else, someone more intimidating, as well as unfamiliar to the girl, do the checkups. The beset teenager received no allowance until a blood and urine test (to be performed at a time unbeknownst to her and randomly thereafter for two years) showed that she was clean. Then, she would receive an allowance contingent upon her taking on responsibilities regarding her room, her schoolwork, community involvement with the elderly (her choice) twice a month, and some healthy work on her ignored intellect. She was to read about current events daily, especially as they related to adolescents, and discuss what she read and how she felt about what she had read at least twice a week.

Once she was drug free for six months, her allowance was nominally increased with the understanding that it would be rescinded with the recurrence of any drug usage for nonmedical purposes. At one point, the poor thing asked permission to take an aspirin for a no doubt well-earned headache.

The girl made it through the period during which drugs helped to fill the parts of her inner world that had been left unattended as she reached adolescence. Her new, compulsory activities, as well as the renewed and intensified attention she was getting, and was ambivalent about, re-filled her. And the re-filling process left her little time to meet up with the gang and risk a return to the hospital, to "poverty," to the absence of various freedoms, and to fear. The girl, now a young woman, has done well.

Tougher laws in both Canada and the United States are not solving the problem of adolescent drug use. As is the case with the overall education of our children, communities have to create environments in which our children are noticed, limited in their behaviours, and supported. If over 43 per cent of Canadian and 47 per cent of American parents claim to be distressed but unable to control the behaviours of their adolescent children, we have to face two facts. First, we have to change how, when, and in what way to make the time to approach our children, and actually schedule *intimate* time or encounters. We have to become more influential in our children's lives, more filling of their empty spaces and psychic gaps, as well as supportive of their transitional period. Second, as already mentioned, we have to realize and enforce the fact that parenting can no longer be a private affair if it is to work with contemporary adolescents.

AT HOME

The Battle of Wills

More parents come to psychotherapists and counsellors because of problems related to fighting with their children than for any other reason attached to parenting, including drug use and scholastic performance. And more calls are made to the police related to adolescents physically acting out than for vandalism, shoplifting, or other criminal activity. Adolescents, for reasons which should be understandable, are prone to fight, argue, stand their ground even when they know they are off the wall, and to pick fights for no apparent reason. They are particularly inclined to do so with adults— parents and teachers—and with siblings. But, as we know, they also, and usually as an outlet for their anger at adults, pick fights and act out aggressively with other, weaker or resented children.

When we look at the notion of conflicting wills, or head-to-head wilfulness, we are really looking at two or more people trying to protect themselves from the shame of admitting that they have done something wrong, or have failed, or have disappointed the other. When we, for example, go at our child over her low marks, the child can do little but defend herself, either vocally or with inattentive, eye-rolling silence. The child knows she has "failed," knows she has disappointed her parents and is dealing with the same kind of looks and admonishments from adults at school.

We are being particularly dull-witted if we think that our child will immediately agree with us, and then skip up to her room to study. As is the case with all our adolescents' challenges, we have to be the ones to take a managed, strategic approach to issues in order to get the optimal response from the child. It is up to us, as *adults*, to manage our communication with our child so that it is resourceful and encouraging, even when there is a problem to be solved. For example, bad marks do not make for a bad child, and we all know the dangers of implying this, at least in theory.

Part of the creative and consistent parenting discussed in chapter 7 is ensuring that we put such theory into practice. So, again, time is required for us to address the child's scholastic and other problems. A lengthy, parent-child talk to get to the root of the problem, as well as a meeting with teachers, set homework times, no TV on weeknights until marks are brought up, and a positive incentive for all involved to contribute to a balanced solution, can save a child not far along in bad or self-destructive habits. With this, or more serious problems, such as aggressive acting out, in addition to a multifaceted, parent-directed approach to solving the problem, we must ensure that the child still knows that she is loved and supported. It is no coincidence that preteens or young teenagers who get in trouble tend to stay in trouble. They are condemned and usually inadvertently shamed, while at the same time they lose vestiges of their old identity and sense of parental love. If a child feels condemned early on by ill-thought-out reactivity, he takes on the identity of bad and holds to it. "Mis-punishment" can provide a child with a questionable identity and eliminate his need to explore a new one. "Bad" sticks.

The bottom-line rule related to parent-child interaction is for parents to put our egos aside, so the child can hear us without the deafening effects of shame and humiliation. Even lying and stealing should be discussed in a way that does not imply the child is going to become a sociopath or an international jewel thief!

A child lies in an attempt to exert control, create new realities and identities, protect herself from shame, punish parents and adults, or to get away with something that, if found out, would induce more shame and more punishment. Lying is expected, if highly disturbing, in young adolescents. However, appropriately addressed through repeated discussion over time, the behaviour should stop or taper off.

Stealing is related to assertion, as well as to a sense of loss. Stealing for the sake of stealing, whether it be from parents, siblings, or in the form of shoplifting, is an attempt to retake something from the world and to manage feelings of powerlessness. Again, then, regarding stealing, we decide on a punitive process with a general and specific understanding of why a child is stealing, and then proceed with a punishment process that includes giving the child new powers or responsibilities appropriate to the age and character of the child.

Normal, irritating, even worrisome behaviours call for appropriate and responsible communication and punishment. But there has to be more than admonishments and assigned "time for the crime" during which a child is waiting for the punishment phase to end. There has to be active understanding, involvement, individualized overlapping efforts, and expressed love.

Butting heads does not work. A child always wins a battle of wills, but should not even be allowed to enter the contest. Fair, firm, and tangibly helpful processes of redress do more than improve unacceptable behaviours. They also show the child that he is still loved, supported, and is a solid member of a family with rules and consequences.

An example of a courageous and creative action taken by a parent of a young adolescent girl who suddenly began to ignore curfews falls into this category of redress. Over a period of just a few weeks, the daughter of good, and busy, parents started to stay out all night and frequently reeked of alcohol when she tried to sneak into the house in the early morning. After two weeks of each parent talking to the girl, asking her where she went, who she was with, and demanding that she at least respect her curfew, the mother threw her hands in the air in frustration. The father, as stubborn as the girl, but getting nowhere by issuing orders, didn't want the conflict to escalate to the point of their losing their child. But he was also terrified about her being out drinking, and then being driven home by some stranger also under the influence of alcohol.

The father did the unthinkable. He would pretend to go to his study, or to doze off in front of the TV, or to go to bed, but would remain dressed, alert, and with his car keys in his pocket for a quick takeoff. When his daughter would wander off, he'd watch as long as he could from a window and then from a bush beside the driveway to see where she went to be picked up. He announced that he had to go out, when he knew his daughter was going out soon herself, and would park in a concealed spot near her pick-up point. Sometimes, he would wait a while at home and then go in pursuit. Either way, he stayed a safe distance behind in the darkness, and followed his child to what became one of three destinations.

Initially, he'd park a block and a half away and keep an eye on the house she was partying in. He'd sit for hours until he saw her emerge, a few times within two hours of when he'd have to be at work, look for any signs that the person driving her home was under the influence, and follow her home. Again, he'd have to fall back, wait, park on a back street, and come in the back way as she was falling asleep. After the fifth surveillance, he moved the car closer to his daughter's destination, knowing that if she looked out a window, she would be able to see his car under a street lamp.

The girl's behaviour the next evening over supper was strange, as if she suspected her father of following her but wasn't sure. She asked her mother whether her father was tracking her; her mother told her to go ask him. The daughter and father had always been close, and the mother believed that whatever antics they were up to, the two of them should discuss together. The daughter didn't ask him.

However, two nights later, during what her father could hear from the street was a raucous party, his daughter suddenly emerged from the house alone, and an older boy followed, yelling and swearing at her. It took all the father's willpower to stay put. He watched as his daughter turned on the boy, hurled an angry remark at him, and hand-signaled him in a way that indicated a definite good-night. Then she shocked her father. She walked straight toward the car, knocked on the passenger door, was let in, and announced, *"Tonight you can actually drive me home instead of just following me, okay, Dad? And you can come in the front door!"*

Flabbergasted, he did as he was told. When they got into the house, his daughter told him he looked exhausted and that he should go to bed and stop roaming the streets at night. In the same tone, she thanked him for being there on this specific night. The boy had been drinking heavily, had tried to force her to have sex, and had been determined to drive her home when he was so drunk he could barely walk.

The father accomplished several things by tailing his own daughter. He put himself in a position to keep an eye on her, something he had to do to deal with his worry, and he also deliberately, if subtly, let her know that he was doing it. If she was not willing to comply to very reasonable curfews, then he was willing to stay up and sit in the streets into the morning hours until she was ready to come home. That he was there for her when she ran into the very kind of trouble he had spoken to her about was a bonus.

The teenager wasn't angry with him. None of her friends had seen him, and she was *"freaked,"* to use her word, by the crazy, self-sacrificing lengths her father went to, to both protect her and make his point. It was especially meaningful to her after the near miss with the drunk, older boy. She pondered what her father had done, but she felt a renewed, different love and appreciation for the dad she had always been able to be silly with and whom she had always adored. She loved him for what he had done, even though she called him "nutso" for doing so, and was in awe of how much he obviously still loved and cherished her.

The girl's parents talked some more with her about curfews and telephoning to say where she was and if she'd be late. Generally, her wandering decreased significantly. And while she never quite met a curfew, she came home at increasingly decent hours.

Making Threats

Commonly, adolescent children will induce a situation, with an adult or other children, to strengthen the most recent version of their transitional identity. They will further create such a scene to channel otherwise unrelated anger. A boy, for example, may have no reason to fight other than to feel dominant instead of weak and ineffectual. And it is common for adolescent children, especially boys, to extend this kind of destructive, self-stimulating, and cathartic verbal sparring into the issuing of physical threats.

Adolescent threats against adults are common. We have all heard them, been subjected to them, and we have commonly put little stock in them. Similarly, but for some different reasons, our adolescents do not come to us when they have been threatened by another child. Adolescent threats have traditionally been part of the verbal one-upmanship often seen at this developmental stage, and, until recently, most threats have been largely ignored by the so-called middle group of reasonably coping, generally untaunted teenagers.

Furthermore, it's always been bad form to go to a parent or teacher because one has been threatened by a peer. Better to take a pummeling than to stoop to calling in the grown-ups. But things have changed.

It is now the case in virtually all schools, at all levels, that there be a zero tolerance approach to personal or school-related threats, and that all such threats be reported to parents and school officials. As understandably skittish adolescents try to adapt to what would, ideally, be a process of weeding out serious from non-serious threats, we have to take almost a black-and-white an approach to threats from our own children.

If an adolescent threatens us, we have to respond in a flash, with both fury and strength reflected in our body language and facial expression. This alone will shock the teenager. The point is not to brush off the threat, but to shock the child into submission. Otherwise, as has become the case, threats are issued with increasing ease and with escalating violence at the heart of the verbal attack. Once the adolescent has submitted, she should immediately be sent to her room, and she should be left alone for a few hours. This period of solitude is critical to the adolescent's intellectual processing of his threat. In effect, the fury directed at the parent bounces right back at the child, and she is almost bowled over by the force. After a period of solitude the adolescent will probably appear meek and want to talk about the incident.

Where this kind of an episode is concerned, we should remain relatively aloof, not yet have eye contact, and make the child wait a nominal period of time until *we* are ready to address his actions. The process is both memorably frightening and humbling for the child, and very revealing for us as parents. A child will want to tell us why he attacked in order to "have us back" and to shake off the kind of primitive fear we can induce by reminding him of a time when we were, in his eyes, omnipotent. We can then establish what additional consequences or punishments will result should any further threats and insults to our authority occur.

A child I treated who was adopted into an extremely unloving home entered the kitchen, picked up a carving knife, and told the mother that she was going to stab her. This was after years of attempting to get the mother just to talk with her. When the woman reacted the same old way, without even acknowledging the child's presence, the basically gentle child threw the knife, hitting but not wounding the woman in the back.

The child left the room, and the house, and never returned. She current-ly lives in a group home and is taking night courses. The child needed her mother to react with anger and recriminations. The threat, in this case, was issued to communicate the need to be cared for and contained, even if in the form of punishment. The girl knew that, in other ways, she was sliding out of control. She could have acquired the illusion of safety were the mother to have exerted her authority.

Up until the recent implementation of zero tolerance policies at most schools, students would threaten other students, and isolated reigns of terror and the accompanying tension would pervade classrooms and schoolyards for months. Now the threats occur via the Internet, in the park across from the school, or whispered in hallways—and being the victim *or* the perpetrator is no small glitch in the adolescent's experience.

If our child is the victim, and is taking the threat seriously, we then need to practise attentive, responsive parenting to find out what is bothering her. It is perfectly acceptable to ask your child if she is being threatened. We will know if we have struck a chord. A child will typically look up, meet our eyes, even go red in the face, and then look down again, issuing a nonverbal or muttered denial. Then we can ask again, say that we will investigate on our own if the child cannot tell us, and by so doing, induce her to tell us what is going on. A child will act the same way if she is worried about a threat she overheard being made against others, and this too can be brought into the open by noting the first signs of quiet anxiety, asking about it, and going from there.

Importantly, we have to keep an eye on, even take notes regarding, our adolescents' behaviours, and address any signs of increased anxiety reflected in quietude, angry outbursts, extended absences from home, or the issuing of threats. Continued, habitual stealing, lying, or threatening behaviour should be addressed in a formal setting involving either a therapist, school administrator, police official, or, ideally, all of the above. A child who is threatening incessantly and who is unaffected by the sanctions discussed in this chapter should become the object of intense observation on the part of the school, the police, parents, relatives, and neighbours.

Karen Revisited

Karen, the bright young girl who, as her father put it, *"went to camp and came back a liar, a crook, and a deaf mute!"* was put on medication by the family doctor at her father's request. However, her behaviour did not change other than her staying in her room for longer periods of time and missing more school. The medication made her sleepy.

Karen's parents reluctantly brought her to therapy. When I spoke with Karen alone she was not forthcoming. However, her body language went from very tense, to somewhat more relaxed. I asked her questions about what I suspected was bothering her and arranged for her to come back and talk in a few days, making it clear that she was only to do so if she felt that she would like to talk. Her father left a message that evening asking why I was giving his daughter choices at a time when her future lay in the balance. But the young girl had telephoned earlier, meekly indicating that she would be at the next appointment.

When, after a series of gentle inquiries, I asked Karen why she had shoplifted, the question brought her to tears. First, she told me, she felt she had "nothing left" of who she was, and second, that who she had been no longer mattered. She felt that her "reward" for being such a "good girl" in elementary school was to be sent off to a school about which she had heard terrible stories, and she wasn't ready. She didn't have a clue as to what to do, or what to be, or how to act.

When I asked her what had happened at camp, she wept again. She told me that the director and the counsellors she had known over several summers were all congratulating her, teasing her about starting to date, and generally excited about her new life as a "teen gal." She hated them for not knowing how she felt, just as she had come to hate her parents for not knowing and apparently not caring about how frightened she was. She explained her closing down as an attempt to lower her parents expectations in order to prepare them for her failure at the high school. She stole and lied in an attempt to get out of going to school altogether. She thought she would be sent to jail—and she considered this a lesser challenge than going to the *"huge school with older kids where younger kids get beaten up for being stupid, getting lost, and where girls have to do what boys want."* She said that she also got quieter and angrier at her parents as they sent her to doctor after doctor to find out what was wrong with her. For the first time in her life she felt *"like an alien or something, when I thought they knew me."*

Karen was going through an exaggerated form of transitional anxiety, a preliminary and usually overlapping stage of re-formational anxiety. And hers, having been dealt with quickly and intensely, but misguidedly, only increased with each action taken by the parents she had always adored and trusted. Her anxiety included general fears, such as the feeling that she would *"lose her family and everything would change,"* to worries about sex, drugs, and her academic performance. Since age six, she had wanted to be a doctor, and had been lauded for her ambition. Now she felt as if her dream, and that of her parents, would be made impossible by virtue of her having to go *"into the 'Pit,'"* the term used to describe the local secondary school.

Karen was sick with terror and experienced bouts of severe anxiety, but she was not mentally disordered. Her well-meaning parents did as much as they knew how to get her ready for the very thing she dreaded. But they did not understand the deep and complex nature of her fear, or that of any child, having her last summer as a child, and then entering the enormous, chaotic environment of the average secondary school.

While her parents remained angry with her acting out, even when Karen and I explained her actions to them, they made a sincere effort to understand *"what all the fuss was about."* I gave Karen's parents a list of recommended activities and methods of communication to use with their daughter, including more active listening, open displays of affection, verbal declarations of love, and a stated openness to her need to talk. Karen was permitted to continue her sessions as long as she felt she needed them. In her second year of secondary school, she is still coming to therapy, and I still have to push to get her to share her experiences with me. Her parents still get periodically annoyed by the loss of their "little girl," and Karen feels this, and then feels worse about her own wish to regress. Her parents have not yet fully grasped that, on the surface anyway, the "little girl" has had to retreat and to adopt a protective image in order to reluctantly fulfill her female mandate in a social environment which is also, unavoidably, a boy-run school.

Karen's story is a common one. Her parents, though busy with their careers, had always been supportive, proud, and affectionate. But when their child changed, and in Karen's case, acted out in negative, worrisome, and embarrassing ways, they went into "punish and fix" mode, as opposed to slowing down, sitting down, and listening to or discerning what was going on with their daughter. At her last session, she spoke about the improved relationship with her parents, but of their continued confusion as to the exact nature of her anxiety. This was all the more reason for Karen to stay in therapy; to gain further understanding, encouragement, and confirmation of her sanity. Slowly, her parents are learning to play this role in the home.

SUMMING UP

When looking at even a limited variety of common challenges faced by adolescents, we need to examine the process or period of suspension between childhood and adulthood differently. We need to be more aware, vigilant, and involved in the day-to-day behaviours and activities of our adolescent children,

Adolescent anxiety—particularly the anxiety associated with insecurity and trust—pervades each step they take toward facing both intangible and tangible challenges. They can adopt habits, such as smoking or shoplifting, as part of a transitional or "filler" identity, and they need parents and teachers to assist them in finding more resourceful ways to make the shift unique to adolescence.

While not reducing the time secondary school students spend studying, parents, teachers, and community representatives should encourage them to become involved in an activity that benefits the community. This could be, among other things, visiting the elderly, working at a food bank, or helping out at a shelter for the homeless.

An obvious way to assist adolescents to re-form in healthy ways is to increase their extra-curricular activities. The benefits of team sports and group physical activity have been lauded since the days of Aristotle, yet the opportunities for these crucial experiences decrease by the semester in today's public schools.

We have to be prepared to actively admonish or protect our children from adolescent behaviours, such as making threats and harassing weaker children. Whether our children are having sex, threatening teachers, or lying and stealing, we have to act swiftly, intelligently and armed with intimate knowledge of our children to establish courses of action or processes through which they can be kept from harm. These actions and processes must increasingly involve more than one or two parents and a visiting grandparent. Teachers, parents, law enforcement representatives, mental health professionals, and community volunteers should come together to establish support systems and noncriminal processes of restricted activities and restitution.

WHAT TO DO

1. Observe your child in his last year of elementary school. In particular, watch for signs of anxiety and self-sabotage. It is not uncommon for a child to consciously study less and lower his marks in an attempt to stay where he is. Delinquent behaviours are also sometimes adopted in an attempt to slow down the process of forced maturation.

2. If your child asks what seem to be either jesting or overly dramatic questions about going to high school, don't make light of them. Determine how serious the child is and, regardless, answer the questions seriously

and in such a way as to reassure him. Bring the issue up regularly and emphasize your ongoing support.

3. Even if your child expresses excitement about going to secondary school, observe her and ask her about other feelings. Children think that there is something wrong with them if they are reluctant or fearful about moving forward into adolescence and into the next phase of their personal and academic development.

4. Do not assume that an "easy" child will be an "easy" adolescent. Change with the child, especially in the ways in which you are supportive to him, in the last year of elementary school. Also, if one adolescent is out of control, keep in mind that the next so-called "easy" child will probably be more frightened than most by the prospect of moving on to high school.

5. Remember the principle regarding adolescent anxiety: any sudden change in behaviour, including excessive sleeping, altered eating patterns, sickness and extreme quietude call for a dialogue with the child.

6. Do not get into battles of will with your adolescent. Ask the child to make her point, indicate that you are listening and have heard the point, and then make your case. Also, remember that "punishment" is still "in." But it must be preceded with attentiveness and explanation, an ongoing process of remediation, and include follow-up and ongoing support.

7. Understand that lying and stealing are common to early adolescence, but, of course, must be addressed. Make the child return any stolen items to a store manager or make retribution, but only after an informative discussion about why the child has stolen has been initiated. Go with the child as support (not defense) when the child returns the item. If the police do not become involved, the child should "do the time that fits the crime": work around the house, no TV privileges, no videos, and so on, for a month for a typical adolescent theft (eg. a pair of jeans).

8. Do not make light of lying, even the innocuous white lie. If the adolescent is lying to conceal truancy or a more serious problem, choose a time to sit with the child and to firmly and supportively address the lie, as well as the concealed truth. Keep at it in daily half-hour sessions until your child fesses up.

9. Watch for signs of drinking, but do not overreact to an adolescent's first bender. Make it clear that drinking under age is illegal and that even you will have to take action, perhaps even report the incident to the police, if you sense that she has been drinking again. Remind your child that if she is ever around alcohol and others who are drinking and is in need of a ride home, she should call home. Cover all bases regarding drinking and driving.

10. A preadolescent or adolescent child is less likely to ask questions about sex than a younger child. At the latest, in the last year of elementary school and into the first year of secondary school, bring up the subject in an appropriate way, in a casual, family atmosphere. Continue, even when the adolescent rolls her eyes and expresses embarrassment. Adolescents are both curious and anxious about their sexuality. Be prepared to answer reasonable questions about your own.

11. Ideally, in a child's preadolescent years, he should be discouraged from issuing threats of an aggressive nature. However, during preadolescence and adolescence, there must be zero tolerance. If your child seems to be "fuming" and threatening frequently, ask what is bothering him. If you get nowhere, contact the school and the school guidance counsellor to ask them to help you find out what is bothering your child, and to ensure that the child is observed. Do not assume the worst. Assume that your child is in pain and is threatening to inflict pain due to an irrational need to even the score.

12. Ask, ask, ask...about your adolescent's days, relationships, and feelings about school, especially in the first and second years of secondary school. These are the critical years in the lives of teenagers who have become "lost" to us.

13. Watch for signs of depression in your adolescent. Quietude, excessive solitude, oversleeping, undersleeping, drinking, *any* kind of substance abuse (including aspirin), temper tantrums, a lack of tonal inflection (*when* she or he speaks), over- or undereating, and so on, in any combination, should be taken seriously. The child should be approached tenderly and regularly over a period of a week to ten days. If you are getting nowhere as a parent, see a counsellor with your child.

14. *Always* take a child's self-destructive remarks seriously, especially those related to his life. Talk with, spend more time with, and step up the support of your child when you see signs of plummeting self-esteem or self-hatred. If, in addition, your child actually talks about death, or gives his things away, organizes his possessions (when it is out of character for him to do so, or is not focused on another agenda), leaves violent quotes on pieces of paper around his room or around the house, or repeatedly says *"What's the point?"* when talking about school, friendship, or other aspects of his life, make an appointment to see a counsellor even before you speak to your child. Even if all is well, the appointment cannot hurt. The self-anger at the core of an adolescent's troubling behaviour should be investigated and understood.

15. Sex among teenagers is one of the realities most difficult for parents to discuss and manage. Again, as much discussion as possible about the why's, when's, and how's (as in protection) of sexual activity when the child becomes or is soon to become a teenager is of critical emotional and practical importance. Do everything possible to convey the benefits of not having sex as an adolescent but, in the end, make sure your child is sufficiently fearful of AIDS and sexually transmitted diseases (STDs), to be super-savvy about protection. Disease may be the most hyped concern around adolescent sexual activity. But teen pregnancy, a fundamental concern, is on the rise.

16. If you have sufficient reason to believe that your child is doing drugs, approach her yourself and, first, ask her why she "needs" the drugs (whether she admits to taking them or not); second, remind her of the dangers involved; third, remind her of the illegality and your shared liability as a parent for the presence or use of drugs in the home; fourth, arrange for some schedule of drug testing; and fifth, elicit support from the child's school in observing the child and in ascertaining the source of the drugs.

17. Do not ban *any* of your child's friends from the home, except for some inappropriate or dubious activity or behaviour. Anything you can do to keep your child at home, even with "unusual" acquaintances, serves both the child and the parents in the short, medium and long term.

18. If your child brings up the fact of school violence, even if there has not

been a major incident at his school, do not tell him that these things happen "elsewhere." Listen. Then assure the child that something terrible will *probably never happen* at his school. Go further, and discuss what he *would*, and then what he *should*, do in the highly unlikely event that something violent occurs at his school.

19. Remember that adolescents are not adults. In spite of their demands that they be given the freedoms of adults, they cannot, as yet, handle the space and responsibility which would be easy to give them and allow them. They still need us, our active, communicated love, and our willful setting of limits and boundaries with respect to their behaviours and activities.

Shaping the Future

9

"My parents had one. You had one. We're not stupid or blind, y' know! We know there's nothing left, and that even you—all adults—know there's no point in our counting on a future."

—*Claude, 15, in theapy*

The video tapes made by Dylan Klebold and Eric Harris as they planned the massacre at Columbine High School in Littleton, Colorado, were released to the media. Adults and parents watched with the muted shock and the easily dismissible horror that comes with distance and the unconscious ability to twin what is real with what is not. Knowing much about these boys, I, too, watched their videoed preparation, their frenzied celebration of what they knew would change the face of their community from one reflective of comfortable innocence, to one turned downward and inward in infinite darkness.

In the videos, seen too late, the boys alternated between their blissful anticipation of the relief that would come with the *"kick of killing,"* and primitive dances of rage, revenge, and spitting hatred. They laughed hysterically, screamed, threatened, and swore at us, the camera, with an anger and contempt so intense that it could have been the condensed searing strike of an entire generation. Still looking into our eyes, knowing that we would be watching passively and dumbly, unafraid due to the illusory layers of separating lenses, they recited personal trials of persecution and humiliation at the hands of those they planned to kill, including, in a way unknown to us, the viewer.

They explained how they already thrilled at images of their once-cocky predators turned pathetic—begging for basic mercies they once wished for themselves—and how they would deny it, slowly, face-to-face, with the banal ecstasy of revenge. They'd make a tomb of a once spit-clean building where perfectly rowed desks would be replaced with the chaos of overlapping bodies; and polished, disinfected hallways would become slippery avenues of blood, forever echoing with screams. And they'd have fame, they told us—the only identity that counts—a celebrity status, a perverse acceptance and place in history bestowed upon them for killing for the cameras, and then standing out, memorable among the massacred, by taking their own lives in the line of retaliation.

Dylan and Eric were determined to have the camera show us their sanity, and in their plan they included a posthumous opportunity to explain what they were doing, why, and what we had done to them. Even this shocked us—that they would want us to know, and to understand. Right up to 20 minutes before they entered their school and started to kill with the automatic efficiency brought to the task by high-tech weaponry and light-less souls, they spoke of cause and effect, of the inevitable logic of destroy-ing that from which they had been cruelly dispossessed. And then, reveal-ingly, the last thing said by one of the boys was, *"Mom and Dad? I'm sorry. I love you."*

One of the reasons I wrote this book is to help parents, teachers, and other adults understand that adolescents who become violent have general-ly displayed many of the so-called normal or accepted behaviours and signs of disturbance discussed in the preceding chapters; conversely, many adoles-cents who do not act out aggressively, let alone kill, feel similarly lost. The distinction lies in the fact that killing children turn their grief and anger on others, as well as on themselves, in ways in which most children would not dare. Those who do not act out, suffer quietly, even angrily, and try to hide and live with their pain. And perhaps the obstacle, the thin line between the daring madness required to shift from thinking about and wanting to kill, to actually killing, lies in a few strands of connection and hope.

The encapsulation of the contemporary adolescent dilemma, of the trauma of re-formation shared in detail by Dylan Klebold and Eric Harris only when they knew they would die, is what we must address in various forms and to varying degrees in our own children. Dylan and Eric, as well as their victims, both dead and living, are martyrs for the dispossessed. They, the incident, and the incidents that have followed, have left many of us at least more curious about the adolescent condition, but not necessarily more actively concerned or informed. However, many good families, uni-formly represented in the media as families with high incomes, residing in upscale neighbourhoods, and owning two or more expensive cars, would, were they able and willing to address us, urge us to change how we deal with our teenage youth. Barring the impossibility of subverting influentially destructive forces in a culture defined by acquisition and power, they would advise us to parent more actively and intelligently, and to take almost nothing about our adolescents' behaviour for granted.

Adolescents need to remain connected to us as they attempt to meet the premature and increasingly complex mandate of maturation. Girls and boys tread softly into the world of secondary school, an environment both chaotic and potentially cruel, and strictly enforcing of gender and other forms of conforming behaviours. Children fear entering this place, part of the transition from simpler realities, and, as a result, they come to view us differently, for urging them along, and for being unable or unwilling to protect them.

We have to support our children before and during the transition from childhood to the suspended, identity-less state of adolescence. In spite of the cultural and often familial imperatives for adolescents to push off and grow up and away, it is the job of adults to remain involved, alert, and to intrude into the eventually guarded lives of our youth. They also need us to ground them in active love, explained and personified values, and within behavioural parameters necessary for their well-being, and for their journey to and successful arrival at adulthood. We have misunderstood their resistance, and taken it as permission to distance ourselves, when it is actually a tension, a false conflict they create to assist them to leave us.

Adolescent children need more love and guidance than ever, not less, as they reach a stage when everything and anyone can be accessed, and everything influences them more powerfully than we do. They need us to assist them with identity issues, and they need us to serve as their unwavering advocates in the complex and initially cold world of modern adolescence. Even if they will not talk to us right away, they need to experience us *trying* to talk to them. And trying and trying again.

As parents, we must also become involved with our children's school environment, with teachers and those who run it. We need to take action when our children are being persecuted, taking drugs, threatening others, having sex, or failing in schools with teachers too overwhelmed to attend to their troubles. Our children would further benefit from our forming formal alliances with other adults in renewed communities, including school officials, teachers, other parents, law enforcement agencies, and adolescent psychologists. We all need to observe, listen, and ask, and we need the resources to act as soon as there is an indication of suffering turning to aggression.

We can do this, in spite of our own schedules and problems. To do so, however, we have to streamline our activities and ways of coping. In fact, we have to grow with our children—to change to be able to understand them, and to become creative communicators to stay with them. Our children need us, and we need them, even though as they enter adolescence they anxiously assume that their protective lessons with us are over. Far from it. However, we have to learn to communicate this, to keep them firmly grounded in the home, remind them when to come home, and to bring them home if we believe that they could be potentially lost to us.

The hardest lessons actually begin with us—parents, teachers, and entire communities. We have to be willing to look deeper and respond more creatively and courageously to the challenge of adolescence in today's more complicated than brave new world.

May our shared lessons begin.

There is no backwards,
But no forward, either.
Just speed, and a pressure
in my chest and head
I can't stop.

Is there only living
or dying?
Can't someone find me
an in-between?

—*Hart, 14*

ACTION PLAN FOR PARENTS

Parents who have experienced challenging or seriously troubled youth, have, by necessity, established strategies and alliances which can be established in all communities. The following outlines these basic strategies.

If a teenager exhibits worrisome or delinquent behaviour (i.e., shoplifting, other stealing, lying, missing school, making threats, speaking or behaving self-destructively, hitting friends, siblings or parents, exhibiting prolonged signs of depression or anxiety, and so on), parents should contact any or all of the following for help:

1. a family practitioner, that is, an M.D. who specializes in family matters;
2. a specialist, if the physician deems this necessary and provides a referral;
3. depending on the nature of the behaviour, a police representative from the youth division of the local police force;
4. the administration and key teachers at the teenager's school; explain the problem and elicit their support;
5. the school board psychologist, from whom you can seek advice regularly;
6. a friend of the teenager;
7. your neighbours; let them know that there is a problem and ask that they let you know if they see or hear anything relevant to your concern.

If the situation becomes urgent and you fear that the teenager may commit a crime, may hurt himself or someone else, or is seriously out of touch with reality (and you need help immediately):

8. take your teenager to an emergency ward and see the psychiatric resident on duty;
9. notify the family physician, police officer, school board psychologist, and school administrators of the details and nature of the emergency and keep them informed;
10. stay in touch with this support group during and after the escalation of the problem;
11. ask for weekly reports on the teenager's behaviour, and provide the same.

INTERNET RESOURCES

There are two particularly comprehensive search engines that provide a wide spectrum of information regarding the behaviour of teenagers.

GO.com has a family section, which is broken down into a variety of issues. There are statistics, advice, and a great deal of information on and analysis of adolescent behaviour.

SNAP.com also has a family section and provides information on teenage behaviour and related responses.

The IICS (International Institute for Child Security) page has ongoing discussions regarding adolescent care and behaviour (www.iics-quest.com).

The American Academy of Child and Adolescent Psychiatry site also provides a variety of articles on adolescent issues (www.aacap.org).

SOME USEFUL BOOKS

Bradshaw. *Family Secrets: What You Don't Know Can Hurt You*, New York: Bantam Books, 1995.

Clemmer, J. *Growing the Distance*. Toronto: Stoddart Publishing, 1999.

Glennon, Will. *Fathering*. Berkeley: Conari Press, 1995.

Goleman, Daniel. *Vital Lies, Simple Truths*. New York: Simon and Schuster, 1985.

Greenfield, P. *Mind and Media*. Cambridge: Harvard University Press, 1986.

Healy, Jane M. *Endangered Minds*. New York: Simon and Schuster, 1991.

Katz, L. *Engaging Children's Minds*. New Jersey: Ablex, 1989.

Kindlon, Dan and Michael Thompson. *Raising Cain: Protecting the Emotional Life of Boys*. New York: Ballantine Books, 1999.

Lerner, H. *The Dance of Anger*. New York: Harper and Row, 1985.

Lickman, Thomas. *Educating for Character*. New York: Bantam Books, 1995.

Mammen, Maggie. *Who's in Charge?* Carp, Ontario: Creative Bound Inc., 1998.

Pipher, Mary. *Reviving Ophelia: Saving the Selves of Adolescent Girls*. New York: Ballantine Books, 1995.

Pollack, W. *Real Boys, Real Men*. New York: Henry Holt, 1998.

Shengold, Leonard, M.D. *Soul Murder*. New York: Fawcett Columbine, 1989.

Waller Krueger, Caryl. *1001 Things You Can Do With Your Kids*. New York: Gallahad Books, 1985.

Witkin, G. *KidStress: What It Is, How It Feels, How to Help*. New York: Viking Penguin, 1999.

SELECTED BIBLIOGRAPHY

Alter, J. "Time for Re-Thinking." *Newsweek Magazine*, September 1999.

Anderson, D., and P. Collins. *The Impact on Children's Education: Television's Influence on Cognitive Development*. Office of Educational Research and Improvement, U.S. Deptartment of Education (April 1988): 34.

Anderson, E. "The Code of the Streets." *Hope Magazine*, March-April 1996.

Allen, G. "Why We Need to Improve Youth Fitness." *PTA Today*, February 1987.

Aster, L. "Kid Killers." *Boca Raton News*, June 14, 1998.

Barry, Vincent. *The Dog Ate My Homework: Personal Responsibility: How We Avoid it and What To Do About It*. Kansas: Andrews and McNeel, 1997.

Beaty, L.A. "Effects of Parental Absence on Male Adolescents' Peer Relationships and Self-Image." *Adolescence*, 30(120) (1995): 873–80.

Beentjies, J., and T. Van der Voort. "Television's Impact on Children's Reading Skills: A Review of Research." *Reading Research Quarterly*, 23(4) (1988): 389–413.

Bernadett-Shapiro, S., Ehrensaft, D., and Shapiro, J. L. "Father Participation in Childcare and the Development of Empathy in Sons: An Emprical Study." *Family Therapy*, 23(2) (1996): 77–93.

Bly, Robert. *Iron John: A Book About Men*. Massachusetts: Addison-Wesley, 1990.

Bornstein, M. H., ed. *Sensitive Periods in Development*. New Jersey: Laurence Erlbaum and Associates, 1987.

Bradshaw, John. *Family Secrets: What You Don't Know Can Hurt You*, New York: Bantam Books, 1995.

Brody, L.R. "Emotional Expression and the Family." Ed. R. Kavanaugh, B. Zimmerman-Glick, and S. Fein. *Emotion: Interdisciplinary Perspectives*. New Jersey: Lawrence Erlbaum, 1996.

Brooks, A. *Children of Fast-track Parents*. New York: Viking, 1989.

Brooks-Gunn, J., and A. C. Peterson. "Studying the Emergence of Depression and Depressive Symptoms During Adolescence." *Journal of Youth and Adolescence*, 20(2) (1991): 115–19.

Bruner, J. *Actual Minds, Possible Worlds*. Cambridge: Harvard University Press, 1986.

Burns, J., and D. Anderson. "Cognition and Watching Television." Ed D. Tupper and K. Cicerone. *Neuropsychology of Everyday Life*. Boston: Kluwer Press, 1992.

———. *Healing the Shame That Binds You*. Deerfield Beach: Health Communications, 1988.

Campbell, A. *Men, Women and Aggression*. New York: HarperCollins, 1993.

Canada, G. *Fist Stick Knife Gun: A Personal History of Violence in America*. Boston: Beacon Press, 1995.

Carcarterra. "Why Carding Kids is a Bad Idea." *Time Magazine*, June 14, 1999.

Chau-Eoan, Howard. "In the Image of Our Heroes." *Time Magazine*, June 14, 1999.

Clemmer, J. *Growing the Distance*. Toronto: Stoddart Publishing, 1999.

Cloud, John. "Taking Aim at Show Biz." *Time Magazine*, June 1999.

Coles, R. "The Moral Life of Children." *Atlantic Monthly Press*, 1986.

Crossen, C. "Mind Field." *The Wall Street Journal*, June 5, 1997.

DeLuccie, M. F. "Mothers as Gatekeepers: A Model of Maternal Mediators of Father Involvement." *Journal of Generic Psychology*, 156: 115–31.

Duckworth, E. "Understanding Childrens' Understanding." Paper presented to the Ontario Institute for Studies in Education. Toronto, 1981: 51–52.

Easterbrook, M. "Taking Aim at Violence." *Psychology Today* (32)4: 52.

Edelman, G.M. *Neural Darwinism*. New York: Basic Books, 1988.

Eisner, E. "The Ecology of School Improvement." *Educational Leadership*, February 1988: 24–29.

Elias, M. "Fathers Focus Increased Care on Boys." 6D, *USA Today*, June 14, 1999.

Epstein, H. "Growth Spurts During Brain Development: Implications for Educational Policy and Practice." Ed. J. Chall and M. Mirsky. *Education and the Brain*. Chicago: NSSE, 1979.

Friedlander, K. *The Psychoanalytic Approach to Juvenile Delinquency*. New York: International Universities Press, 1961.

Freidman, S. et al. *The Brain, Cognition and Education*. New York: Academic Press, 1988.

Gallagher, J. and C. Ramey, eds. *The Malleability of Children*. Baltimore: Paul H. Brooks, 1990.

Geeleerd, E.R. "Some Aspects of Ego Vicissitudes in Adolescence." *Journal of the American Psychoanalytic Association*, 9: 394–405.

———. "Re-evaluation of the Process of Working Through." *Emotional Growth*. New York: International Universities Press, 1971.

Gibbs, Nancy and Timothy Roche. "Killers Reveal Their Hatred and Their Lust for Fame." *Time Magazine,* December 20, 1999.

Gilligan, J. *Violence: Our Deadly Epidemic and Its Causes.* New York: Putnam, 1996.

Glennon, Will. *Fathering.* Berkeley: Conari Press, 1995.

Golden, Frederic. "Making Over Mom and Dad." *Psychology Today,* May-June 1999, (32)3.

Goleman, D. "Infants under Two Seem to Learn from TV." *The New York Times*, November 22, 1990.

Goleman, Daniel. *Vital Lies, Simple Truths*. New York: Simon and Schuster, 1985.

Googins, B. *Work-family Stress—Private Lives, Public Responses.* Connecticut: Greenwood Press, 1991.

Greenacre, P. "General Problems of Acting Out." *Trauma, Growth and Personality*. New York: International Universities Press, 1969.

Greenfield, P. *Mind and Media*. Cambridge: Harvard University Press, 1986.

Healy, Jane M. *Endangered Minds*. New York: Simon and Schuster, 1991.

Hechinger, F. "About Education." *New York Times*, March 16, 1988.

Henry, T. "Nation's Report Card Flunks Student Scribes." *USA Today*, September 29, 1999.

Herbert, W. and M. Daniel. "The Moral Child." *U.S. News and World Report*, (June 3): 52–59.

Holland, P. and L. Salero. "Contributing Factors in Contemporary Teenage Dating Patterns and Deviant Sexual Behaviors." Paper presented at the annual APA meeting, Toronto, 1998.

Hulse, D. J. *Brad and Cory: A Study of Middle School Boys*. Huntington Valley: Ohio University Press, 1997.

Inhelder, B. and J. Piaget. *The Growth of Logical Thinking from Childhood to Adolescence*. New York: Basic Books, 1960.

Jackson, A. and D. Hornbeck. "Educating Young Adolescents." *American Psychologist*, 44(5), 1988.

Jones, D. C. and S. E. Costin. "Friendships Quality During Pre-adolescence and Adolescence: The Contributions of Relationships Orientations, Instrumentality and Expressivity." *Merrill-Palmer Quarterly*, 41(4), October 1995.

———. "Relational Development: Therapeutic Implications of Empathy and Shame." *Stone Paper Working Studies Series* (Wellesley College, Massachusetts) No. 39.

Kals, C. and C. Rogers. "Stress and Kids." *Newsweek*, June 14, 1999.

Kantrowitz, Barbara. "A New Age of Anxiety." *Newsweek*, June 14, 1999.

Katz, L. *Engaging Children's Minds*. New Jersey: Ablex, 1989.

Kaufman, I. and E.A. Makkay. "Treatment of the Adolescent Delinquent." *Case Studies in Childhood Emotional Disabilities*, 56, Vol. 2, 1958.

Kellerman, J. *Savage Spawn—Reflections on Violent Children*. New York: Ballantine, 1999.

Kindlon, Dan and Michael Thompson. *Raising Cain: Protecting the Emotional Life of Boys*. New York: Ballantine Books, 1999

Kozol, J. *Illiterate America*. New York: NAL, 1986.

Krugman, H. "Brain Wave Measures of Media Involvement." *Journal of Advertising Research*, 2(1) (1971): 3–9

Kutner, L. "Heroes Offer Ways to Explore Feelings and Situations." *The New York Times*, December 23, 1993.

Lerner, H. *The Dance of Anger*. New York: Harper and Row, 1985.

———. *The Dance of Intimacy*. Harper and Row: New York, 1989.

Leonard, Andrew. "We've Got Mail—Always." *Newsweek Magazine*, September 20, 1999.

Lewis, M. and J.M.Haviland, eds. *Handbook of Emotions*, Hartford, Connecticut: Guilford Press, 1993.

Lickman, Thomas. *Educating for Character*. New York: Bantam Books, 1995.

Lifton, Robert Jay. "The Psyche of a Gunocracy." *Newsweek Magazine*, August 1999.

Lopez, J. "System Failure." *Wall Street Journal*, March 31, 1989.

Mammen, Maggie. *Who's in Charge?* Carp, Ontario: Creative Bound Inc., 1998.

Manning, A. "Teens Starting Substance Abuse at Younger Ages."*USA Today*, August 14, 1997.

McIntosh, H. "Research on Teenage Friendships Dispels Old Myths." *American Psychological Association Monitor* (Washington, D.C.) June 1996.

Moody, K. *Growing up on Television*. New York: Times Books, 1980.

Morrison, A. *Shame: The Underside of Narcissism*. New Jersey: Analytic Press, 1989.

Odier, C. *Anxiety and Magic Thinking*. New York: International Universities Press, 1956.

Okrent, D. "Raising Kids Online." *Time Magazine,* May 10, 1999.

Palmer, E. *Television and American Children: A Crisis of Neglect*. New York: Oxford University Press, 1988.

Peritiz, Ingrid. "Crown Wants 3 Murder Suspects Tried As Adults." *The Globe and Mail*, September 29, 1999.

Peterson, K. S. "Teens Unlikely to Talk About Depression." *USA Today*, August 7, 1996.

Picard, Andre. "Teenagers and Reckless Stereotype." *The Globe and Mail*, September 28, 1999.

Pipher, Mary. *Reviving Ophelia: Saving the Selves of Adolescent Girls*. New York: Ballantine Books, 1995.

Pollack, W. *Real Boys, Real Men*. New York: Henry Holt, 1998.

Postman, N. *Amusing Ourselves to Death*. New York: Viking Press, 1988.

Reeves, B. et al. "Attention to Television: Intra Stimulus Effects of Movement and Scene Changes on Alpha Variations Over Time." *International Journal of Neuro-science* 27 (1985): 242–55.

Ritvo, S. "Late Adolescence: Developmental and Clinical Considerations." *The Psychoanalytic Study of the Child*. 26 (1971) : 241–263.

Rutkowsa, J. and C. Crook. *Computers, Cognition, and Development*. New York: John Wiley, 1987.

Santez, P. And Martin, L. "Television and an Array of Explanations for Whatever Ails or Frightens Us." *UCLA Psychological Abstract*, 1999.

Schwartz, J. "Closing the Gap Between Education and the Schools." Ed M.A. White. *What Education for the Information Age*. Lawrence Erlbaum, 1987.

Scott, J.P. "Critical Periods in Behavioral Development." *Science* (1972): 957.

Seppa, N. "Keeping Schoolyards Safe from Bullies." *American Psychological Association Monitor*, 1996.

Shapiro, L. "The Myth of Quality Time." *Newsweek Magazine*, May 12, 1997.

Shaw, James. "Violence and Education." Doctoral thesis, UCLA, 1996.

Shellenbarger, S. "Losing Today's Rewards." *The Globe and Mail*, December 24, 1999.

Shengold, Leonard, M.D. *Soul Murder*. New York: Fawcett Columbine, 1989.

Shrof, J. M. and S. Schultz. "Social Anxiety." *U.S. News and World Report*, 126(24), June 21, 1999.

Staff editorial. "Tougher Penalties for Youthful Offenders." *The Ottawa Citizen*, March 13, 1999.

Tanouve, E. "Antidepressant Makers Study Kids' Market." *The Wall Street Journal*, April 4, 1999.

Tollen, G. "Teachers Complain of Lack of Parental Support." *New York Times*, December 12, 1988.

Toman, Walter. *Family Constellation*. New York: Springer Publishing Co., 1976.

Turkle, S. *The Second Self: Computers and the Human Spirit*. New York: Simon and Schuster, 1984.

Tyler, S. *The Said and the Unsaid*. Toronto: Academic Press, 1987.

USA Today Poll. "Children's Time Spent with Family." *USA Today*, 1999.

Vaillant, G. E. *Adaptation to Life*. Boston: Little, Brown, 1977.

Walberg, H.and T. Shanahan. "High School Effects on Individual Students." *Educational Researcher*, 12(7) (1983): 4–9.

Waller Krueger, Caryl. *1001 Things You Can Do with Your Kids*. New York: Gallahad Books, 1985.

Wells, G. *Language, Learning and Education*. Berkshire: NFER-NELSON, 1985.

Winn, M. *Unplugging the Plug-In Drug*. New York: Penguin Books, 1987.

Winnicott, D. W. *The Maturation Process and the Facilitating Environment*. New York: International University Press, 1974.

Witkin, G. *KidStress: What It Is, How It Feels, How to Help.* New York: Viking Penguin, 1999.

Wong Briggs, T. "Exercise Lifts Spirits at a Bargain Price." *USA Today,* June 14, 1999.

Woodhouse, L.J., A. Tate, L. Morse, and Anderson et al. "A Comparison of Parental, Adolescent and Teacher Perceptions of the Potential Dangers Faced by Teachers and Students in Secondary Schools." International Institute for Child Security, 1999.

———."A Comparison of Parental versus Adolescent Perceptions of Adolescents' Sense of Being Loved." International Institute for Child Security, 1999.

Woodward, K.L. "The Making of a Martyr." *Newsweek Magazine,* June 14, 1999.

INDEX